Mediations: The Silent Workshops of Democracy

Studies in Restorative Justice

VOLUME 10

This Series is divided in the following four sub-series:

Studies in Restorative Justice – Monographs and Edited Volumes

This subseries publishes theoretical and empirical work on restorative justice. It features studies on principles, practices, and impacts of restorative approaches in response to crime and social conflict, including victim recovery, desistance and community rebuilding. Contributors include both established and emerging scholars.

Studies in Restorative Justice – Anthology

This subseries covers 'anthologies' of work by selected authors, who choose a number of their own publications that have shaped the discourse and debates on restorative justice. They will, within the anthology, be able to reflect on their impact on the field, on the controversies and debates that they have contributed to and how they have responded. They will also reflect on the future of restorative justice.

Studies in Restorative Justice – Translations

This subseries covers translations of seminal books in the field of restorative justice having originally been published in other languages than English.

The International Encyclopaedia of Restorative Justice – edited by Ivo Aertsen & Jennifer Llewellyn

This subseries presents a comprehensive overview of restorative justice worldwide. It examinesorigins, development, legislation, and practice across regions including Africa, Northern America, Asia, Europe, Latin America, and Oceania, while comparing key challenges and developments. Spread over six volumes, it deepens and broadens understanding of this evolving field.

The titles published in this series are listed at *brill.com/sirj*

Mediations: The Silent Workshops of Democracy

By

Jacques Faget

Translated by

Audrey Tweed

BRILL | NIJHOFF

LEIDEN | BOSTON

This book was originally published in French by ÉRÈS ÉDITIONS & FORMATION in 2015 under the title, *Médiations : les ateliers silencieux de la démocratie.*

Cover illustration: Island's Edge, taken from an original mixed-media drawing by Kittie Jones, www.kittie jones.com.

Library of Congress Control Number: 2026931455

Typeface for the Latin, Greek, and Cyrillic scripts: "Brill". See and download: brill.com/brill-typeface.

ISSN 3050-7839
ISBN 978-90-04-73405-0 (hardback)
ISBN 978-90-04-73406-7 (e-book)
DOI 10.1163/9789004734067

This book is printed on acid-free paper and produced in a sustainable manner.

Contents

Acknowledgments

Je voudrais témoigner ma reconnaissance aux éditions Erès (Toulouse, France) et à leur directrice Marie Françoise Sacrispeyre pour avoir cédé gratuitement les droits de mon livre et ainsi permis sa traduction en anglais.

Je voudrais aussi exprimer ma profonde gratitude à Estelle Zinsstag et Tinneke Van Camp sans lesquelles cet ouvrage n'aurait pas vu le jour. Elles m'ont fait l'honneur de l'intégrer dans leur belle collection et en ont suivi, pas à pas, la réalisation.

Enfin je remercie ma traductrice Audrey Tweed pour s'être confrontée avec doigté au style parfois complexe d'un universitaire français et Marlies Talay pour sa méticuleuse et avisée supervision finale.

I would like to express my gratitude to Editions Erès (Toulouse, France) and their director Marie Françoise Sacrispeyre for having ceded the rights to my book free of charge and thus enabling it to be translated into English.

I would also like to express my deep gratitude to Estelle Zinsstag and Tinneke Van Camp, without whom this book would not have seen the light of day. They did me the honour of including it in their fine collection and followed its production step by step.

Finally, I would like to thank my translator Audrey Tweed for her skilful handling of the sometimes complex style of a French academic, and Marlies Talay for her meticulous and wise final supervision.

Foreword for *Mediations: The Silent Workshops of Democracy*

With the book series, we seek not only to highlight new and original research through the publication of monographs and edited collections, as well as anthologies offering an overview of the work by pioneers in the field, but also to make seminal contributions on restorative justice, not previously published in English, accessible to more readers.

This is the second translated volume for the book series *Studies in Restorative Justice*. It was initially published in French in 2010. Jacques Faget kindly accepted our invitation to work with us on an English translation of the book. Audrey Tweed agreed to join us on this endeavour and translated Jacques' original French manuscript. This was done the old-school way, with a lot of back and forth between Jacques and Audrey, and in later stages with the both of us and with Marlies Talay to fine-tune the translation. Since our aim was to make sure Jacques' ideas and unique style would not be lost in translation, this was quite an intense and time-consuming process. A lot of wordsmithing took place to ensure that we respected the original text and sentiment as much as possible without diminishing the accessibility of the text. And it was well worth the effort. We are very pleased that now a greater number of readers are able to delve into Jacques' important theoretical reflections on the many different forms of mediation and their impact on society and diverse communities. Though originally published in the 2010s, they still resonate so much today and are certainly more needed than ever.

We owe immense gratitude to Audrey Tweed, for having undertaken with energy and enthusiasm this quite substantial amount of work. *Mille mercis* also to Jacques for working with us and allowing us to play around with your sense of prose! Last but not least, thank you to Marlies Talay, whose sensitivity for and proficiency in language is invaluable.

A few final notes: We decided to keep most of the original formatting from the French book in the translation (such as footnotes, title formatting, use of pronouns), even though this is not necessarily compliant with the book series' house style. There are a few differences between the French book and the translation to ensure clarity (*e.g.*, some French expressions were impossible to translate, so they were either taken out or replaced with new phrasing, and in some cases additional explanations were added to provide context).

Jacques' writings have inspired the both of us in our own work in this field, and we hope this translation will inspire many others. *Bonne lecture*! Happy reading!

Tinneke and Estelle
Fresno and Glasgow, 9 January 2026

List of Figures

List of Tables

Introduction

Linguistics, neurobiology, psychology, philosophy, sociology, political sciences, law, mathematics, as well as our daily language, all use the word mediation to refer to a connection, a dialogue, an intermediation, an exchange, a type of communication between grammatical groups, lines, cells, psyches, norms, ideas, and people. However, the objective of this work is not to get into the different meanings this term holds, this work is specifically targeted. The objective here is to analyse the purpose, the terms, the consequences and the stakes of institutionalised and social practices known as mediation. These practices started to develop in the 70s and 80s, and became widely implemented thereafter.

The global analysis of this practice has not yet been undertaken, neither in France nor abroad. However, we may notice De Briand and Palau's input,[1] and the work of the team of researchers that I mobilised for the conference organised in Bordeaux[2] in 2003. Its multidimensional aspect probably rendered it invisible. The growth of mediations has developed on a large scale in different areas; it is both a tool for political conflict management and a tool for national policies in the context of the decreasing role of the welfare state. It has also been a tool for local politics, helping the management of social and geographical fragmentation, and finally a tool for pacifying relationships between individuals. Mediation has also been an interdisciplinary practice that transcends the traditional academic disciplinary barriers. It is a domain that interests politicians, but also sociologists, psychologists, lawyers and specialists of communication. The partitioning of scientific points of view certainly did preclude a wider approach to it.

Although it started as a marginalised social practice that emerged from the imagination of idealistic pioneers, mediation has become both commodified by and the product of public policy from the moment public authorities decided to institutionalise its implementation.[3] All institutions from international organisations to the European Union, public administrations and local communities, have progressively created their mediators.

1 V. De Briand, Y. Palau, *La médiation. Définition, pratiques et perspectives*, Paris, Nathan, 2000.

2 J. Faget (sous la direction de), *Médiation et action publique. La dynamique du fluide*, Presses Universitaires de Bordeaux, 2005.

3 J. Faget, 'Gouverner par la médiation' dans T. Berthet, O. Costa, R. Gouin, X. Itçaina et A. Smith (sous la direction de), *Les nouveaux espaces de la régulation politique*, Paris, L'Harmattan, coll. 'Logiques politiques', 2007, 231–255.

DOI:10.1163/9789004734067_002

Table 0.1 below seeks to shed light on the diversity of the public and private processes that are more or less institutionalised and qualified as mediation. An exhaustive inventory of all mediators (here focusing on the French mediators, from general practitioner to specialists) is difficult to establish, not only at an international level as the institutional designations are diverse, but also at a national scale, as the momentum of creation of the new programs seems to increase exponentially.

For now, I will leave aside the debate on the use of the term mediators. I wish to include all mediations to demonstrate that the dynamic they create deserves an in-depth analysis. However, it is necessary to clear an ambiguity beforehand. It is common practice to use a simple classification in order to distinguish conflict mediations from relationship mediations, or as Michèle Guillaume-Hoffnung phrases it, dispute mediations and differences mediations.[4] The former have the purpose of regulating or solving obvious conflict, and the latter to prevent these problems from arising by triggering communication between institutions or citizens. Far from being opposed, these two categories merge together when the creation or restoration of a relationship is considered the most efficient way to prevent conflict or to resolve it. In mediation, the concept of conflict is therefore always central, which justifies a brief anthropological explanation of it.

1 Conflicts

We all have been children tormented by parental conflict, teenagers wounded by injustice, adults with broken ideals of peace and harmony. These conflicts have impacted us profoundly. However, the meaning we give to them is changeable. Some experiences are felt as unbearable by some, and manageable by others, because the nature of conflict is ambivalent. It can be analysed as a tragedy, a pathology foreshadowing a disorder, an omen of chaos for a system or an institution. Conversely or simultaneously, it may be understood as a driver for the creation of an individual or collective identity, or for the clarification of social rules, or as a way to challenge a group's cohesion, and as the seed of political and social change.

Conflict exists in innumerable forms. The following distinctions are usually made: conflict of information (based on incomprehension or misunderstanding), of interest (financial or material), personal (one's private life), psychological (pertaining to an individual's mental health), of identity (ethnic, of

4 M. Guillaume Hofnung, *La médiation*, Paris, PUF, 2012.

TABLE 0.1 Inventory of mediators

International political institutions
UN Mediator in Conflict Resolution
UN Mediator for the WIPO (World Intellectual Property Organization)
European Mediators
International Mediators
Political and administrative institutions
Mediators for the Ministry of Tax and Finances (MINEFI)
Mediators for the French Equal Opportunities and Anti-discrimination Commission (HALDE)
Mediators for the National Education (Éducation Nationale)
Mediators for the Family Allowance Fund
Mediators for the Health Insurance Fund
Mediators for the Caisse des Dépôts et Consignations (Financings of Public National and Local Policies)
Mediators of the National Centre of Scientific Research
Mediators for Postal Services (La Poste)
Military Mediators
Energy Mediators
Employment Mediators
Public Health and Hospital Mediators
University Mediators
Environmental Mediators
Judiciary and legal institutions
Civil Mediators
Family Mediators
Penal Mediators
Mediators in Administrative Courts
Social institutions
Community Mediators
School Mediators
Intercultural Mediators
Social Mediators
Citizens Mediators
Economic institutions
Commercial Mediators
Corporate Mediators

TABLE 0.1 Inventory of mediators (*cont.*)

Work Mediators
Banking Mediators
Insurance Mediators
Complementary Health Insurance Mediators
Housing Mediators
Internet Service Providers Mediators
Financial Markets Authority Mediators (FMAM)
Mediators for Transport Companies (Trains, planes)
Agriculture Mediators
Consumer Affairs Mediators
Media and cultural institutions
Cinema Mediators
Radio Mediators
TV Mediators
Press Mediators
Internet Mediators
Publishing Mediators
Cultural Mediators

acknowledgment), of values (ideological, religious), or structural (in terms of power or social class). This diversity demonstrates that conflict is inherent to human relationships even though these are not all conflictual.

These conflicts are not always visible, as we excel at the art of hiding them to simplify our social interactions. Our sensitive experience gives us many examples of relationships we make viable thanks to myriad individual strategies: flight, renunciation, indifference, magnanimity, underestimation, excuses, and various rationalisations allowing us to preserve our tranquillity and save our energy. On the opposite side of the spectrum, we sometimes call for conflict for reasons that aren't always understandable. Certain behaviours are known for provoking negative reactions from others: insults, aggressivity, humiliation, oppression, lack of consideration or of respect, spreading defamatory rumours, ignoring, setting expectations too high to be met, not respecting one's obligations, being overbearing and intrusive. However, such behaviour isn't enough to provoke conflict. The other party's sensitivity to this behaviour is an additional requirement and a key element. Otherwise, this search for conflict may fail.

This proves to us, if proof ever was needed, that conflict is constructed, and that it is the result of an active process wherein the parties involved add ingredients, either to avoid it or to make it happen. Its development and fulfilment involve a succession of sequences and a series of cognitive distortions destined to simplify the complexity of reality. This 'honeymoon conflict'[5] can be illustrated as follows:

- A blurred initial context with no details, difficulties in communication
- A triggering event that can be more or less circumstantial
- Placing the blame on an adversary
- The adversary's retaliation
- The reciprocal disqualification of the 'other'
- The selective reconstruction of the story, which entails common disagreements
- The invocation of a transgression which is not only a personal interpretation, but is also a reference to universal laws, morals, and customs
- The construction of certainties (convictions must be justified by tangible elements, which are carefully selected, and even when isolated, these can be moulded into generalisations)
- Perpetuation of this conflict sequence by all the protagonists: without an adversary, conflict stands the risk of dying out

At this stage of its evolution, conflict arrives at its peak. It can possibly slip out of the adversary's control and develop in an autonomous way. This is when it potentially becomes particularly destructive. If some expressions of conflict appear healthy, one does not need to be a conflict specialist to understand others are devastating. Drawing a line between the devastating conflicts and those that are healthy and fertile is not an easy task. Ancient Greek philosophers had this distinction between *stasis*, war between parents and fellow men, and *polemos*, war with strangers, people that were not from Greece. Some authors defend the *polemos* and consider that a state of peace does not exist, that, to quote Clausewitz, peace is nothing but a way of continuing war by other means. Far from being harmful, these 'conflicts with exterior groups strengthen the cohesion inside the group'.[6] On the other hand, the *stasis* is generally viewed as destructive, because 'the closer the relationship, the more violent the conflict',[7] the smaller the social distance between the opposing sides is small, the more sudden and violent the conflict can be. The

5 M. Monroy, A. Fournier, *Figures du conflit. Une analyse systémique des situations conflictuelles*, Paris, PUF, 1997.

6 G. Simmel, *Le conflit*, Editions Circé, 1992.

7 L.A. Coser, *Les fonctions du conflit social*, Paris, PUF, 1982.

'internal conflicts in which the feuding parties no longer share the same fundamental values on which the legitimacy of the social system depends' are the ones that 'threaten to collapse the structure'.[8]

These principles of division are, however, not so rational. It is not always so easy to objectively consider the possibilities and the dangers that come with conflict. Our diagnosis often depends on the point of view we prefer, on the interests and values we align with, on the phobias that taunt us; as well as our perception of time, the moment of observation, the evolution of the interaction between the protagonists, and the exterior influences that affect them. What is true at an individual level is also true at a collective level. Each of us will see conflict through the prism of our subjectivity. Only conflicts in relation to actions that are fundamentally forbidden by society, 'strong bonds of the collective awareness' as Durkheim called them – crime, incest, child abuse – achieve a social consensus nowadays.

After the analysis of the functions of conflict, the question of its treatment arises instantly. Must we let it flourish? Or die down slowly? Is it necessary to resolve it quickly? Find a medium-term solution to it? It all depends on the way we see its importance, be it at an individual or collective level, on the consequences we expect or dread of it, on the context of which it is part of, and on the institutional, social, material, cultural, and intellectual resources available to guarantee its regulation.

2 Pacifications

Peace is often presented as the opposite of conflict. In reality, a society without conflict is difficult to conceive, and would probably be fatal. Peace can be conceived in a conflictual context, as long as the nature and intensity of these conflicts is contained within an acceptable perimeter, or as long as their expression is ritualised, institutionalised. The concept of peace isn't easy to grasp: several forms and expressions exist. These range from the *pax romana* which is imposed by force, to the *pax americana*, produced by a political and military hegemony, to a 'just peace', which is established by several parties that mutually recognise each other and accept common, conjointly elaborated rules.[9] Between negative peace, which is at most an absence of war or violent conflict, and can be imposed by terror, and positive peace, character-

8 Ibid., p. 84
9 P. Allan, A. Keller, *What is a just peace?* Oxford University Press, 2006.

TABLE 0.2 The logic behind conflict resolution

	High stakes	Low stakes
Weak relationship	Cooperate (mediation, conciliation)	Give in (submission)
Strong relationship	Fight (use of strength or the law)	Avoid (flight)

ised by a state of tranquillity, equity and social justice,[10] a plethora of intermediary situations exist in which measures of security, control and protection of civil liberties coexist harmoniously.

Anthropologists, sociologists and political scientist have identified innumerable ways to make peace: vengeance, sacrifices, rituals to designate a scapegoat, reparation ceremonies that are magical (theft of birds, duet of Inuit singers) or rationalised (commissions of truth and reconciliation, various trials), outlets that are more or less codified (carnivals, hullabaloo, sport competitions), and diplomacy. All the social systems have had a wild imagination when it comes to preserving themselves from the sprouts of their own destruction, to 'harmonise differences' and establish society. Their evolution limits them to always invent new peace-making processes, more adapted to the transformation of political and economic logical reasoning, or of ways of life and thinking. All this always centres around staging rituals and releasing a certain type of necessary speech.

Since the time that Simmel published his work on conflict, all those who have worked on processes of appeasement come under three main categories: those who adhere to strength, to judgement, or to reconciliation. In the first case, it is a victory by means of violence or ingenuity which is secured by one of the protagonists over the other that smothers the conflict. In the second, it is the law or the system of codified norms that stops the quarrel, and in the third, the warring sides themselves resolve it through dialogue and the elaboration of an agreement. Western democracies establish a hierarchy of these conflict-regulating methods. They endeavour to refuse the use of power by invoking the supremacy of law. As such, they consider that legal norms, as a cohesive and rational set of rules promulgated issued by a public authority, represent the highest rung on the ladder of social norms and peace-making strategies. However, anthropological analysis shows that African and Far-East

10 J. Galtung, *Essays on peace research*, Copenhague, Ejlers, 1975.

traditions do not rely on the law to maintain social order and justice. It is even said that, in China, law can only settle disputes with 'barbarians', meaning foreigners or criminals, whereas social modes of peace-making must be followed as a rule to resolve domestic conflicts.

In a world that refuses dichotomy, old traditions seek consensus above all else to ensure a sort of conjunction of the opposites. One cannot consider physicality without spirituality, rationality without sensibility, order without chaos, or good without evil.[11] The objective of social preservation dominates any consideration of means.

The discontinuation caused by the arrogance of legal rationality intervenes only recently in the history of our societies. It happened in correlation with the construction of modern states. The law appeared in our collective imagination as an expression of state sovereignty. It was and still is considered inherent to and constituting the state's institution. However, this idealised hegemony of the Law and of the State was challenged by philosophers and legal sociologists who emphasised the existence of a diversity of legal systems that relate differently, sometimes antagonistically, to the legal system imposed by the political authority. They consider that a sub-law exists, qualified as living, vulgar or spontaneous,[12] providing global legal regulation without necessarily referring to positive law, but which draws its foundations in sub-culture, customs, folklore, and professional practices. The solution to a dispute depends less on a set of predefined rules than on choices made by the group to ensure its future.

It is in this framework that ADR, or alternative dispute resolution, falls into. Since the 1970s, individualistic ways to 'make peace' have emerged outside of courts, and sometimes without lawyers. The increasing use of negotiation, arbitration, conciliation, and mediation or any other hybrid forms is not just a way to compensate for the deficiencies of the abstract, bureaucratised and saturated legal systems. The metamorphosis of legal regulation also represents, as clearly demonstrated by the resistance it provokes, the questioning of both the supremacy of legal norms (and of its professionals) and the role of the State in handling social conflict. This political dimension is probably expressed most potently in the development of mediation.

---

11 N. Rouland, *Aux confins du droit. Anthropologie juridique de la modernité,* Paris, Odile Jacob, 1991.

12 Pour faire un point complet sur cette perspective voir A. J. Arnaud (sous la direction de) *Dictionnaire encyclopédique de théorie et de sociologie du droit,* Paris, LGDJ, 1993, 2ème édition.

3 Mediations

People sometimes say that mediations are as old as time, but it all depends on what one puts under the umbrella of mediations. Even in exemplary forms of customary law, such as the African assemblies of the 'case à palabres' (meeting house for discussion), or the Indian *panchayats*, how can we be sure that they respected the ethical principles on which the contemporary practices of mediation are founded? Although they are based on community standards, they are closer to the forum arena than the horizontality on which mediation's philosophy is based. The nostalgic and third-world romanticism which seeps into many approaches of mediation comes from the fact that what we generally mean by mediation is all non-institutional modes of conflict resolution. But in reality, mediations are the product of the modern legal forms of regulation and of the informal ways found in old practices.[13] They can be inspired by some of their aspects but can under no circumstances be related to them in the large variety of legal, institutional, and social contexts. To be convinced of this, one needs to look no further than our current Western ways of handling conflict, which assert the supremacy of individual responsibility, whereas the methods used in traditional societies rely on collective responsibility.

In all societies, one can notice the existence of a dialectic interplay between imposed and negotiated order. In the book of Genesis, imposed order finds its source in 'an exterior, superior, omnipotent and omniscient force'.[14] As societies have become more secular, this transcendental power of guaranteeing social order falls in the hands of the State. Negotiated order frees itself of this sacred dimension, of this verticality, and establishes a world organised by social stakeholders. All societies are familiar with these two modes of social regulation: one distant and imposed by the law, the leader's charisma, and the legitimacy of the assembly of the elders or experts; and the other close, defined by communication and dialogue within the mediations and conciliations, which are woven in human interaction. The combination between the two orders depends on a multitude of structural or conjunctural factors. The more authoritarian the political regime is, the more imposed order takes on an important part. The more effective democratic principles are, the more negotiated the social order becomes. In effect, variations between the two

---

13 C. Cunneen, 'Reviving restorative justice traditions?' dans G. Johnstone et D.W. Van Ness (sous la direction de) *Handbook of restorative justice*, Tavistok, Willan Publishing, 2007, 113–131.

14 E. Le Roy, *Le jeu des lois. Une anthropologie dynamique du droit*, Paris, collection 'Droit et Société', LGDJ, 1999.

types of order function similarly to a hydraulic system, adapting to the necessities of the power in place or to those of social cohesion.

The sudden contemporary surge of mediation programmes is, in my point of view, the sign that society is searching a new way to govern and create cohesion with new benchmarks of action. It represents a specific way of handling hypercomplex societies,[15] composed of a multiplicity of cities,[16] in which a diverse and accelerating flux of images, norms, objects, and people transform the conditions of collective action. The collapse of the State's guidance capacity of these blurred social groups requires that social processes be 're-designed according to the multiple flexibilities they have'.[17] Collective action, which was once manoeuvrable from the position of static structures, is now possible to be steered through a variety of networks, mobilities, flows, nomad trajectories and vanishing lines.[18] The rhythm of these concepts adapts itself to our 'sociétés d'impatience', which oblige all communication forms to subscribe to a register of compressed temporalities.

I have already written about the mediation of the 'dynamics of the fluid',[19] named after a 'liquid modernity' used by Bauman to describe a historical context devoid of certainties and solid social forms.[20] This metaphor seeks to show that the binary logic of repressive systems cannot alone establish the legitimacy of a public authority. This legitimacy emerges from the capacity to produce movement, to create new intermediary spaces where micro-adjustments are made. The necessity to bring about passages between tangled spaces and temporalities leads to the conception of flexible and adaptable modes of regulation. It is precisely with their plasticity that mediations are destined to establish flows, movements, bridges between heterogeneous entities (the bridge not only connects two pre-existing banks, but it also creates and gives them a new identity by connecting them). Following the laws of the movement of fluids, and emancipated from institutions, mediations spread like water, seeping into diverse social and institutional contexts.

---

15 N. Luhmann, *Politique et complexité. Les contributions de la théorie générale des systèmes*, Paris, Cerf, 1999.

16 L. Boltanski, L. Thévenot, *De la justification. Les économies de la grandeur*, Paris, Gallimard, 1991.

17 J. Urry, *Sociologie des mobilités*, Paris, Armand Colin, 2005.

18 G. Deleuze, F. Guattari, *Mille plateaux. Capitalisme et schizophrénie*, Paris, Editions de Minuit, 1980.

19 J. Faget, *op.cit.*, 2005, La fluidité de la médiation ne désignerait pas seulement ses vertus instrumentales d'écoulement et de régulation mais la dimension magique (le fluide c'est aussi une énergie occulte, mystérieuse, émanant de personnages charismatiques) d'une recherche de sens.

20 Z. Bauman, *Liquid modernity*, Cambridge, Polity Press, 2000.

The question then arises of whether mediation's task should be considered capable of generating mutations or as homeostatic. A functionalist approach would probably state that their institutionalisation constitutes one of the ways in which the integration and complementarity of different parts of the social system is ensured. A systemic and autopoietic (from auto, the self, and poiesis, creation) approach, which considers that social structures are stable on a long-term basis, would more likely presume that mediations bring to the concerned systems the matter and energy they periodically need to regenerate and perpetuate themselves. Lastly, the interactionist perspective observing the turbulent nature of the exchange processes would depict an insecure social order, repeatedly negotiated between its different stakeholders by means of a mediation process. This process would ensure the sustainability of the system, while transforming it by promoting more cooperative and friendly social interaction, as well as a more democratic way of expressing and defining the world. We shall investigate empirically how these different models can or cannot relate the social customs of mediations. But first, several obstacles that have obstructed both the interest of mediation researchers and the thought process of practitioners, need to be overcome in order to move on.

4 Analytical Barriers

To be aware of the extent of mediation's growth and bloom, and to be able to scientifically study its political and social stakes, it is necessary to be well informed on the topic, not give in to irrational temptations, and untangle the strands of the many practices that stem from it.

5 Obstacle 1: A Wrongly Identified Social Object

We all think we know what mediation is. This obviousness of that notion is the source of much confusion, which is why it is useful to outline it. Dyadic processes, which consist of two people or their representatives finding a solution to their conflict, must be distinguished from triadic processes, in which a third party is involved. However, this third party may have a different status depending on whether the mediation is endured and they impose an end to the discord (judge), or whether it is chosen and they offer a solution (referee). These decision-making third parties are on the opposite side of non-decisional third parties, such as conciliators who try to bring the involved parties closer together, potentially proposing solutions, or as mediators who

TABLE 0.3 Nature of the different conflict handling processes

Process	Decision-making	No decision-making
Dyadic	Negotiation	Natural regulation
Triadic	Judgement	Conciliation
	Arbitration	Mediation

help, in a less directive way, people communicate and to co-create a solution themselves.

However, this subtle distinction is not always easy to make. On the one hand, negotiations assisted by a third party exist. It then becomes difficult to differentiate them from conciliations and mediations. Mediations are also frequently qualified as a negotiated process and can in this case be seen as a technical modality of social negotiation. What is even more confusing is that the first mediators borrowed much from the Harvard model of 'reasoned negotiation'.[21] The blur between concepts comes from the existence of cross strategies stemming from two competing epistemic communities, each developing its own rhetoric of encompassing the other's field; negotiators using the argument of the anteriority of their practices to justify seeing mediation as one of negotiation's tools, and mediators using their new specificities to show how they differ from old practices. In effect, any attempt to clarify this distinction is illusory. A diversity of models and fields of application of negotiation and of mediation exists, and with it a variety of meanings put behind the two fields.

Thus, the Fisher and Ury model was strategically conceived to oppose the rustic model of problem-solving, which brings with it a mechanistic view of conflict resolution. The field of mediation is plural, and full of opposed theoretical streams. Next to the initial model built with the materials of reasoned negotiation model, myriad models appeared, one of these being the transformative model.[22] The latter went through a profound paradigm shift, no longer defining mediation as the search for an agreement, but as the transformation of the perspective conflict is seen from. If the contrast between negotiation types such as problem-solving and transformative mediation is blatant, the distinction between 'open' negotiation dealing with conflict and

21 Fisher, Roger; Ury, William; Patton, Bruce (2011) [1981]. *Getting to Yes: Negotiating Agreement Without Giving In* (3rd ed.). New York: Penguin Books.

22 R. A. B. Bush, J. P. Folger, *The promise of mediation*, San Francisco, Jossey Bass, 1994.

'closed' mediations focused on disputes is less clear cut. (I will come back to this question in more detail in chapters 3 and 4).

On the other hand, the distinction between conciliation and mediation has triggered many controversies. Amongst experts, some use both terms interchangeably, while others give them characteristics that are diametrically opposed. The public remains extremely confused.[23] This confusion is kept alive by the uncertain naming of some conflict-handling activities, and these names seem to be chosen more because of trends than a desire to be conceptually rigorous and accurate. The distinction between the two notions is delicate in practice. Only a detour through etymology might be able to help us. Conciliation comes from the Latin word *conciliare* meaning 'to unify', where as mediation has its roots in the word *mediare* 'to be in the middle'. This difference explains the fact conciliation defines itself mainly by its objective, whereas mediation is chiefly defined by its methods. We can deduct from this that the conciliator, guided by the objective of an agreement's signature, can propose solutions to the opposing side. This is an opportunity that a mediator, representing a third party, does not have.

Lastly, the polysemy of the term mediation does not make the analyst's task easy. In public speeches as well as in social practices, three overlapping approaches to mediation can be distinguished. They are presented as follows from broadest to most restricted.

- The *nominalist approach:* Mediation is what we name as such. All affiliated programmes enter this field, such as mediation of learning,[24] cultural mediation,[25] or therapeutic mediation.[26] It is evident here, but also in other instances, that the term mediation seems to be used to authenticate the innovative nature of developed projects. Adopting a nominalist approach has the advantage of avoiding the complex debate on the line dividing what mediation is and is not, and of having a global view on the uses of a term which owes much of its popularity to its imprecision. Confusion then becomes part of the analysis, at the cost of making it unclear.
- The *substantialist approach:* The term mediation is used generically to identify all the non-vertical ways (as opposed to strength, judgment, arbi-

23 The most recent example is the creation (decree of the 30 March 2015) of a military mediator (general inspector of the army), who gives his/her opinion on the disputes s/he is referred to.

24 Method of acquiring knowledge based on the intervention of an intermediary who prioritises the learner's process of knowledge appropriation.

25 All professions aiming to bring art and artists closer to the public.

26 Type of therapy based on props (asinotherapy or donkey therapy, object creation, ...) that uses and reveals the potential of the patient.

tration) to handle conflicts or to establish communication. All processes that participate in the harmonising of opposites, and that facilitate the production of a common world are hereby named. The term is often confused with negotiation, compromise,[27] conciliation, and regulation. This approach that defines mediation by its objectives considers it as the production process of a certain vision of the world whose function is to maintain cohesion, to produce something global in a scattered society. From this point of view (largely adopted by political scientists), the State is a mediator, and its elected representatives fulfil both a cognitive (they help us to understand the world, make it intelligible and give it meaning) and normative (they define under which action criteria the world is to be transformed) function. The public policies are qualified as 'a social mediation process' whose aim is to 'take in charge the asynchrony between one sector and other sectors, or even between a sector and global society'.[28] Even if this substantialist and flexible use of the term mediation, which is close to the concept of governance,[29] refers to the topic of contractualisation of governance methods,[30] is in itself relevant, it is of no help to analyse mediation practices that are socially or institutionally labelled.

– *The normative approach*: This approach associates the term mediation with social practices that correspond to ethical criteria determined by practitioners and scholars. This doxa[31] bases mediation on the posture of the third party. It is a consensual process of construction or mending of the social link and of conflict handling in which an independent and impartial third party, with no decision-making power, attempts through the organisation of dialogues between people and institutions to help, to improve or to establish the relationship or to solve a conflict. In this restrictive conception all practices that disregard these ethical principles are disqualified; and the concept of mediation, including all the intervention techniques linked to it, is unwavering no matter its institutional and social niches.

---

27 O. Nay, A. Smith (under the direction of), *Le gouvernement du compromis*, Paris, Economica, 2002.

28 P. Muller, *Les politiques publiques*, Paris, PUF, 1994.

29 B. Jouve, C. Lefevre, 'De la gouvernance urbaine au gouvernement des villes en Europe? Permanence ou recompositions des formes d'action publique', *Revue française de sciences politiques*, vol 49, 1999, nr 6, pp. 835–853.

30 J. P. Gaudin, *Gouverner par contrat*, Paris, Presses de Sciences Po, 1999.

31 This idea is represented in France by J. F. Six, *Le temps des médiateurs*, Paris, Le Seuil, 1990 et *Dynamique de la* médiation, Paris, Seuil, 1997, J. P. Bonafé-Schmitt, *La médiation. Une justice douce*, Paris, Syros, 1992, M. Guillaume-Hofnung, *La médiation*, Paris, PUF, Que sais-je, 1995, 1ère éd.

The mediator's posture is strictly the same in all fields of mediation and does not fluctuate along with their fragmentation.

To privilege one or the other of these definitions completely transforms the analysis one can make of mediation. To enable the undertaking of research and to define the fields of observation that are coherent, the nominalist approach must be eluded, which details the strategies behind labelling social practices, but does not give us insight into their content. The normative approach is more interesting, as it allocates the specificity of the impartiality of the third party to mediation. Some of its characteristics, namely the absence of decision-making power the mediator has, are unique to it. Therefore, the normative approach allows us to categorise different practices around this variable. However, its small scope is a disadvantage. On the one hand, it spares itself the reflection on how the doctrine that justifies it is constructed, and on the other hand, it excludes hybrid forms of regulation from its field of analysis. Their institutionalisation erodes the authenticity of their third-party nature, but their philosophy still fits into the same dynamic.

The whole point of the substantialist approach is its wide scope, encapsulating both mediations seeking to handle conflicts, and those whose aim is to establish or re-establish a connection, communication between populations ignoring each other, institutions and their users, and between institutions themselves. This scope is nonetheless dangerous when it leads to conceiving mediations without a mediator, to qualifying as mediation all politics and institutions protecting public interest and producing a shared world, and to often confusing mediation with negotiation.

In the end, only a perspective that relies on the normative approach, but is open to a substantialist dimension, grounded within the empirical observation of both the practice of mediations that are named as such, and with the work of mediators who identify with that name, seems promising to me. This perspective alone, by relying on identifiable and sometimes comparable indicators, allows both the singularity and the globality of the practical stakes of mediation.

6 Obstacle 2: A World Full of Believers

Naïve idealism can often be perceived in certain mediation discourses. I've often been confronted by the animosity of activists who are irritated by my critical view of their practices. Many times, I must have frustrated young or not-so-young researchers composing their memoirs with proselyte dedication. It is true that the world of mediation is full of generous people who view the practice as a way of re-establishing harmony and fraternity between human beings. If we investigate the past, and look at the pioneer experiences of mediation, the activist or religious dimension of mediation is plain to see.

Indeed, the Mennonites and the Quakers did initiate the first criminal mediation programmes in the United States and in Canada. Many of those who became interested in and implanted mediation in Europe had a strong religious education: 'Family relationships, or if not affinity or connivance links, are formed between this emerging social practice and the socio-religious orientations extolled by Christianity: the notion of reconciliation, the restoration of the relationship, the utopia of communion…'.[32]

Furthermore, left-wing activists have imagined community, social or civic mediations, as part of a global strategy of promoting participative democracy, fighting against the institutionalisation of social practices, and re-appropriation by communities of the power to manage conflicts 'stolen'[33] by the judicial institution.

All in all, the majority of North American literature on mediation is produced by believers, scholars or practitioners. Its reception in Europe was not very critical and French, Italian and Spanish publications are apologetic and justify a romantic vision of mediation. It then becomes apparent that mediation practices are above all based on values, which doesn't naturally allow an objective approach to it. This means that all analysis of mediation with scientific pretence must also be carried out introspectively, and researchers must imperatively question the reasons behind their interest.

7 Obstacle 3: Multi-faceted and Overlapping Uses

Social practices of mediation are difficult to classify due to the fact the disciplines in which they intervene (from state administrations to companies to the extent of the neighbourhood area) and their objectives (solving or handling of conflicts, creation or re-establishment of communication, development of collective projects, social control). The existence of a multitude of models has already been mentioned (problem-solving, reasoned negotiation, or the transformative, narrative, therapeutic, educational, and legal models). The common denominator these models all have is the fact that they all encourage the intervention of an impartial third party.

---

32 J. Palard, 'Médiation et institution catholique', *Archives de sciences sociales des religions*, 133, janvier-mars 2006, pp. 9–26.

33 N. Christie, 'Conflicts as property', *British Journal of Criminology*, 1977, 17, pp. 1–15.

These practices are rarely autonomous. Most of the time, they overlap with complex decision-making processes, which can be akin to negotiation and judgement, and can rely on existing law texts or bring forth a normative and unbridled creativity. The same way negotiation can be called from strikes, diplomacy on war, mediation can be practiced in parallel with trials. If this is not the case, the 'juridical imaginary' is omnipresent in some mediations when the protagonists refer to the decisions that could have been made the same way by courts. Like negotiation,[34] there is often a virtual mediation in parallel with the real mediation. This means that mediation seeks less to come to an agreement than to gain time, to show its good will in order to influence a judge taking a decision on another aspect of the conflict, to obtain a more favourable agreement than promised or expected by case-law, or to recover the reputation of the parties involved as well as of their social network.

We also notice numerous cases of fragmentation of conflict, of which one part will be taken up by mediation (for example, its relational aspect), and the other part will be taken up on the legal scene. The separation of family members can simultaneously be taken up in mediation for the custody of the children or visiting rights, and in the civil court for the distribution of possessions and assets. It is not impossible to imagine a space where both can overlap. In this case, it is useful that the mediator reconstitutes the puzzle as loyally as possible, so they understand the real stake of what is happening in front of them.

8 Obstacle 4: Sectorial and National Visions

Most research and published works on the topic of mediation adopt a local vision, without replacing their analysis in a broader context. Yet, the cartography of mediation practices gives us valuable information about its real nature. For example, it tells us that its origins can be traced back to north America (the United States, Canada), that a first wave of the discipline travelled rapidly to other Anglophone countries such as the United Kingdom, Australia, and New Zealand, and through the Francophone province of Quebec, it arrived in France. This exportation is valid for three main branches of mediation that are familial mediation, judiciary mediation, and community mediation. A second wave spread mediation to the north of Europe (Scandi-

34 L. Mermet, 'Place et conduite de la négociation dans les processus de décision complexe. L'exemple d'un conflit d'environnement', dans G. O. Faure, L. Mermet, H. Touzard, C. Dupont, *La négociation. Situations et problématiques*, Paris, Nathan, 1998.

navia) before reaching Benelux and central Europe more slowly (there is a strong legal culture in the Netherlands, and especially in Germany), and arriving in southern Europe with difficulty. The weight of political history and religion probably delayed its arrival in Italy and Spain. Mediation exported itself in a third wave, touching countries of South and Latin America. Argentina was the first to welcome this wave, and Mexico and Columbia followed. Mediations were met with much enthusiasm, because of the high degree of mistrust towards formalism and the alleged corruption of legal institutions. Finally, a fourth wave is currently reaching Eastern European countries, without reliable institutions since the collapse of the Soviet Union, and where it is necessary to create ways of regulating that are immediately effective. Mediation has started to appear in civil and commercial affairs in some Arab countries (Lebanon, Jordan, Algeria), but its effectiveness has yet to be proved.

Thus, we can see that mediations appear in the Western and 'Northern' democracies but are not very present in Africa or Asia, which shows they are correlated with a certain type of political regime and with economic development. The spread of mediation is not random, but can be explained by certain linguistic, religious, political, legal, and commercial variables, which interact in complex ways. Moreover, they differ by type. If familial mediations enjoy success in countries affected by the liberalisation of public morals, the instability of familial structures, and the egalitarian legal status of women, community mediations concern most of all countries in which traditions of participative democracy exist.

The exercise of keeping a broad outlook on the world of mediation has the linguistic, financial, and material obstacles that are common to all international undertaking of research. Because of this, my analysis will sometimes be only approximative, even though I speak and understand a few languages, I've trained students from all continents and I've been lucky enough to be invited to many conferences (in Japan, Canada, Mexico, Brazil, Israel, Algeria, Finland, Norway, Russia, Poland, Hungary, Italy, Switzerland, Germany, Spain, Belgium, the Netherlands, Portugal, Slovenia, and Luxemburg) and to have new experiences throughout the world.

Far from making me renounce, the different obstacles mentioned above have solidified the purpose and intent of my approach. I consider mediation as a great indicator of the metamorphosis of contemporary social and political regulations. I will touch on the socio-political construction of mediation in part one, before moving on to its normative construction in the second part. Finally, I will devote part three to the different workshops where, far from the political and media hype, new forms of collective well-being are created, voicing the search for a more participative conception of democracy.

PART 1

The Social and Political Construction of Mediation

The *homo mediator*, in the broad sense the philosopher Duss Von Werdt[1] gives it, has always existed. Since the dawn of time, individuals have stood up to stop quarrels, reconcile rivals, and mend links between people. Even so, can they be considered as mediators? From a substantialist perspective, certainly. However, from a more normative standpoint, the role of our contemporary mediators is new, namely because of the institutionalisation of social practices that were previously less formalised. This means we avoid tracing the historiography of mediation back to primitive societies or postpone its beginnings indefinitely. The way mediation was constructed in Western societies from the 1970s onwards leans more on ideological roots rather than on its instrumental preoccupations (Chapter 1). This is affirmed by diverse factors that have helped it spread to countries confronted with a fundamental reconfiguration of their modes of political, institutional, legal and social regulation (Chapter 2).

---

1 Joseph Duss-von Werdt, *Homo mediator. Geschichte und Menschenbild der Mediation*, Stuttgart, Klett-Cotta, 2005.

 | DOI:10.1163/9789004734067_003

CHAPTER 1

The Origins of Mediation

The first conceptualisation of mediation can be traced back to 1681, with the publication of a book named *l'Ambassadeur et ses fonctions,* written by Abraham de Wicquefort (1606–1682), a diplomat from Holland. In one of the book's chapters, named *Of mediators and mediating ambassadors,*[1] the author proposes, based on concrete examples taken from his experience, elements of deontology which are surprisingly still relevant: maintaining one's impartiality, refusing to take on a role other than that of a mediator, for example that of a referee, not taking part in any way of the conflict, assuring the parties of the confidentiality of their words in order to earn their trust, never making propositions and not judging those formulated by the parties, believing that the latter are able to reach an agreement themselves. This text is the first attempt to define the role of a mediator.

One must then wait until the The Hague conference in 1907 for mediation to reappear in political conflict resolution jargon.[2] The convention to which its results are devoted stipulates in its title II and article 2 that in case 'of serious disagreement or dispute, before an appeals to arms, the Contracting Powers agree to have recourse, as far as circumstances allow, to the good offices or mediation of one or more friendly Powers'. Article 4 then defines the role of the mediator as 'reconciling the opposing claims and appeasing the feelings of resentment that may have arisen between the States at variance'. A few years later, an article written by Nicholas Politis named *The Future of Mediation*[3] states that to successfully handle a mediation, it is necessary for the mediator to earn the trust of both parties, and for the latter to recognise the mediator's impartiality and wisdom. The fact that these qualities are difficult to find made the author think that 'most of the time', the mediator 'remains nowhere to be found'.

Because of the two world wars, the mediation of international conflicts was no longer a conversation topic. The term was mentioned in the 1950s in rela-

1 Abraham de Wicquefort, *L'Ambassadeur et ses fonctions*, La Haye, J et D. Stencher, 1681.

2 Convention for the pacific resolution of international conflicts, which took place in the Hague on the 18th of October 1907.

3 Nicolas Politis, « L'avenir de la médiation », *Revue Générale de Droit International Public*, 1910.

 | DOI:10.1163/9789004734067_004

tion to work conflicts but was not really put into practice. It was only in the 1970s that it appeared again in other contexts, such as the social, domestic and penal spheres. Their emergence reveals that mediation practices are less justified by the necessities of social engineering whose aim is to oil jammed social machinery than by social upheavals and alternative visions of the world born in the intellectual atmosphere particular to the 1960s and 1970s.

1 A Foundation of Values

The historiography of mediation highlights the names of a few individuals or pioneer groups, whose characteristics and motivations, be they religious or political, are diverse, but they are all characterised by the idea of acting based on values. This is the case of the first experiences of penal mediation (*victim offender mediation*), community mediation, scholar mediation and family mediation, created with the theoretical and technical framework given by the *Alternative Dispute Resolution* movement.

2 A Religious Perspective

The first mediation programmes conceived in the early 1970s in North America were put into place by Protestant minorities such as the Mennonites and the Quakers, guided by their non-violent philosophy.

In 1974, the Mennonites started the first mediation experiment in the penal field. In the town of Elmire (located in the Canadian province of Ontario), two young men pled guilty to the charge of material damage they had inflicted on 22 victims during the course of a drunken evening. Mark Yantzi, the probation officer charged with preparing the pre-sentence report, suggested that the judge, outside of the legal sphere, encourage them to meet their 22 victims, and the judge accepted the proposition. He placed them under probation and demanded that they reimburse the cost of the destruction they caused, which they repaid within a few months. Strictly speaking, this legendary event does not constitute a mediation but illustrates what a remedial sanction can look like. He simply shed light on the necessity to involve and give more responsibility to individuals in the orchestration of penal responses. It is in the same spirit that the Mennonites created the first *Victim Offender Reconciliation Program* that same year in Kitchener.

This Christian Protestant movement appeared in Switzerland ca.1520, and is qualified as Anabaptist as it does not follow the principle of baptising children and reserves it for adults who are then conscious of their engagement.[4] The Mennonites were forced to migrate to North America, where they founded rural communities in order to escape political persecution. Heavily influenced by their non-violent philosophy, the young members tried to avoid military service. The Mennonites were for a long period of time characterised by their propensity for withdrawal and quietism, before they found new ways to give life to their pacifist convictions by funding schools, universities and social organisms. The pacifist human is from thereon no longer not someone who seeks peace (*shalom*) away from conflicts, but someone who interacts with conflict with a view to resolve them. Investing in mediation is a way to put into practice this active task of reconciliation. The Mennonites do not preach to people in conflict but try to create a connection between them, to transform the perception they have of one another. They are the starting point for the restorative justice practice, of which Howard Zehr[5] defines the key points.

The founding principle of this movement is to advocate reform. Instead of brushing misdeeds under the rug and distributing zero-sum sanctions which will satisfy neither the perpetrator nor the victim, and which will not protect society as the rate of recidivism is high, it is necessary to promote new judicial responses that are different from the punitive and rehabilitative methods that have shown their limits.

Punitive responses stigmatise individuals and rush them into delinquent paths; social responses do not help delinquents gain their autonomy. The end goal is to avoid formal procedures in penal justice, which are complex, long and frustrating and 'rob' the actors of control over their conflict. Thus, the Mennonite's objective is not only to settle conflicts, but also to be architects of peace by encouraging reconciliation and harmony between community members. This implies a change in the perception these members have of conflict and of one another.

The Quaker movement has also, in diverse ways, actively participated in the development of mediation. This is the case of the Friends of Philadelphia, which created one of the first community mediation programs. This movement, symbolised by a black and red star, dissident of the Anglo-Saxon Prot-

---

4 This movement appeared in Holland and the north of Germany and is centred around the figure of Menno Simons, who gave his name to the movement in the mid 17th century, 'Mennists', which later became 'Mennonites' after they met the Anglo-Saxons. Today, there are approximately 1,500,000 Mennonites around the world. They are very spread out, and present notably in North America (Canada, US), and South America (44 per cent in Bolivia and Paraguay), in Africa (36 per cent in Congo), Asia and Oceania (16 per cent) and a few in Europe.

5 Howard Zehr, *Changing lenses, a new focus for crime and justice*, Herald press, 1990.

estantism in the 17th and 18th centuries,[6] received the Nobel Peace Prize in 1947 (the English Friends Service Council and the American Friends Service Committee) for their actions favouring peace and the reconciliation of peoples. The Quakers refuse military service and any act of violence, preaching tolerance.

During the time of William Penn, Pennsylvania was the only state to allow Native Americans to live in peace (without the intention of converting them) and to welcome Europeans of any faith. Penn wished to establish a theocracy which would have allowed all faiths to coexist in peace. They gave material aid to many countries in war, without ever taking part and have always been adamantly anti-slavery.

They are also very active in the prison environment and provide support to prisoners. Amidst the founding fathers of peace studies, Kenneth Boulding, who created the *Journal of Conflict* in 1957 and the Centre for Research on Conflict Resolution, is often cited. More precisely, the movement has employed the field of mediation in international political conflicts in the 1970s (conflict between India and Pakistan,[7] then the conflicts in Nigeria, Rhodesia, Sri Lanka and the Middle East). School mediation between peers has become the backbone of their strategy to educate on peace.

The adepts of non-violent philosophy are in general fervent defenders of mediation. Popularised as early as 1921 by Ghandi, this philosophy has inspired many people, such as Martin Luther King in the US, Adolfo Pérez Esquivel in Latin America, Nelson Mandela in South Africa and Aung San Suu Kyi in Myanmar. In France, it inspired Lanza del Vasto, who created the 'Communauté de l'arche' in 1948. Whereas some consider non-violence as a form of individual asceticism, others, like the philosopher Jean-Marie Muller and the Movement for a Nonviolent Alternative, interpret it as a political and social action which manifested itself in the 1970s, both by a symbolic fight led by conscientious objectors against obligatory military enrolment and by social movements opposed to the extension of the Larzac military camp.

---

6 George Fox (1624–1691) was the apostle of inward light, as opposed to the Anglicans who were attached to dogmas and Puritans who were attached to the Scriptures. In Quaker meetings, this 'inward light' can manifest itself by improved speeches, but also by fervent trembling, or *quaking*. Quakerism is characterised by the rejection of all dogmas, prefabricated credos, all forms of religious hierarchy, formalism, sacrament or ceremonious rituals. In Quaker assemblies, there are no altars, platforms or music. There are no priests or pastors either, anyone can take on this role if he/she feels empowered by the Spirit of God. The Quakers were never very numerous. Today, around 300,000 are part of this movement, of which 120,000 in the US.

7 Yarrow C.H., *Quaker experiences in International Conciliation*, New Haven, Yale University Press, 1978.

Nonviolent activists are opposed to violent strategies (military repression or police brutality, court cases) of conflict resolution, which have the effect of crystallising conflict. They prefer to contribute to promoting peace beforehand and favour regulation methods that preserve the space necessary to dialogue and negotiation in the conflict's aftermath. But they refuse to be labelled as pacifists. Nonviolent action supposes the very real exposure of the activist to conflict and does not exclude the collective expression of strength and the construction of power dynamics when it comes to defending human rights or re-establishing justice. Nonviolence is thus a global approach to conflict which is expressed in interpersonal relations, but also in social conflict and in international relations. Its methods of action are diverse (pedagogical, conflict resolution, collective mobilisation, civil disobedience) but mediation in its diverse forms (social, educational, familial) is one of the central methods.

In France, the Non-Violence Actualités magazine has been the vector of this Christian obedience movement since 1978. The activist dimension of this movement goes largely beyond the religious sphere. Non-Violence Actualités shares experiences which emphasize respect for others as well as democracy and citizenship.

3 A Political Vision

In the 1960s, the US saw the rise of social activism concerning civil rights and the Vietnam war. Although this movement was American, it was heavily inspired by German philosophers (Marx, Engels, Max Weber, the Frankfurt school), Italian philosophers (Antonio Gramsci) and French critical philosophers (Michel Foucault, Jacques Derrida). This critical perspective was shared and spread by people of different social categories: black people, university students, scholars, women, members of the LGBTQ+ community, hippies and artists, and emerged on campuses all along the east coast of the US and more specifically in California. These social movements fought against bureaucracy, discrimination, poverty, the arms race, colonialism and defended freedom of expression, minority rights, environmental protection and direct democracy. It was expressed in different theories (feminist legal theory, critical race theory, critical legal studies, peace studies) but also in many experiments that spread across the West.

3.1 *Commitment to Legal Access*

All over the US, then in Canada, Australia, and rapidly in Europe, first in England, new legal practices were born. They continued the work begun in the

1920s and 1930s by the legal realism movement in America, which considered the social context of the law and the effects that the social situation of the judges had on the nature of their judgements. In the late 1980s, these new practices were grouped under the generic name of 'alternative dispute resolution' (ADR). This structure had one common denominator: settling conflicts outside of the judicial system, which was considered too slow, too costly, too rigid and bureaucratic. However, this alternative approach did not produce a coherent set of practices (arbitration, negotiation, conciliation, mediation). Some were very coveted by the business world for their instrumental performance, speed, flexibility, and low cost. Others were used in a more symbolic way by a countercultural movement, whose aim was to de-professionalise and de-institutionalise the management of conflicts, and to return this responsibility to citizens. Mediation, more than other modes of diversion, became the emblem of this democratic and relational conception of legal and social regulation.

3.2 *Neighbourhood Justice Centres* and the *'Boutiques de Droit'*

Lawyers representing poor people, women, racial or ethnic minorities, denouncing an iniquitous legal system that does not recognise their rights, associated with magistrates, activists from diverse associations (trade-unions, consumer organisation, associations protecting tenants, women, parents, immigrant workers, students, teachers) took the initiative to establish for them specific places of access to legal information. Thus, *neighbourhood justice centres* appeared in the US, in infrastructures such as community houses or community action centres present in working-class neighbourhoods. This practice spread in different ways in England (*lawshop*), in Belgium, in the Netherlands and in France under the name of *boutique de droit*.

These neighbourhood justice centres were founded at the beginning of the 1970s by activist jurists to ensure the free and 'comprehensive' defence of the oppressed. They were first oriented toward defence in justice of their clients, then became quickly aware of the need to develop pedagogical actions of legal and judicial understanding, and then progressively of the necessity to invent modes of conflict resolution outside of the courthouse.

Naturally, even though most of these actors (jurists or social workers) were volunteers, the rise of this type of activity brought about the question of its independence and its funding. Some centres received funding from foundations, firms, and individuals. Others gradually accepted partial public funding. The federal government's pilot project was initiated in 1978 in Kansas City, Atlanta and Los Angeles, and allowed these centres to become relatively institutionalised. Certain states even integrated this principle via legislation; there is no unique model of NJC. The actors' backgrounds at these organizations are generally varied, and the spheres of action can be diverse. Most were initially specialised in providing a nearby judicial service (defending people, giving judicial information), and little by little, many become involved in developing actions, promoting a culture of peace in schools, creating peer mediation, victim offender mediation or community mediation programs, on the model mentioned below, which was initiated in San Francisco.

This movement was continued in Leuven, Amsterdam, London and in a few French towns from 1974 onwards (Paris, Strasbourg, Bordeaux, Angers) under the name of *boutiques de droit*.[8] It then became part of a larger movement opposing institutional practices and developing alternative methods, such as the free clinic in the medical field or parallel schools in the educational field.[9] Their objective was not to propose a charity service to the poor or to fill the gap left by the public policies' in matter of access to the law. In fact, their ambition was fourfold.

The first objective was to bring judicial support to minorities and to people living in working class neighbourhoods. It is important to bear in mind that the way in which legal knowledge in these centres is provided is atypical; instead of giving mechanical answers, the goal is to collectively brainstorm on the true nature of the legal request, to promote a critical and strategic way of legal education, and to create actors in control of their legal matters, not consumers.

The second objective was to stimulate thoughts on the most relevant conflict resolution methods, on extrajudicial balance power, non-judicial conflict resolution modes, and the type of strategy most adapted in court.

The third objective was to collectivise these actions in order to create a more equal power balance, facing a system that individualises problems, and organising discussion groups for all individuals confronted with similar problems (women in the process of divorcing, victims of domestic abuse, anti-militarists, tenants, consumers, ecologists, agricultural workers, immigrants, former prisoners).

The fourth and more ambitious goal was to settle by law the zones described as *lawless zones* (such as hospitals, barracks, prisons, schools, administration) which reify individuals and make an attempt on their fundamental liberties, most of the time by a series of arbitrary microdecisions.

---

8 Christian Revon (Dir.) *Boutiques de droit*, Paris, Solin, 1979.

9 Pierre Lascoumes, 'Consultations juridiques et boutiques de droit. Une critique en acte du droit et de la justice', *Déviance et société*, 1978, vol. 2, nr 3, pp. 233–259.

It is obvious that these social practices attempted to strike a blow at legal and judicial ideology, hence the hostility they received from judicial professions, whose monopoly they contested. They fought to give back to citizens the ownership of their conflicts and recommended resolving it outside of jurisdiction, either by creating power dynamics by collective actions, or by communication (through conciliation, mediation) between the individuals concerned. The strategic use of the judicial scene was, however, recommended to demand the recognition of the oppressed party's rights and when judicial logic could be circumstancially favourable to the vulnerable party's interests.

3.3 *The San Francisco Community Boards*

Penal mediation (Kitchener) and domestic mediation (Atlanta, 1974) signalled the beginning of judicial alternatives. However, their projects turned out to be reformist and not always driven by a true political vision. This was not the case of the community boards pioneer experiment conducted in 1976 in San Francisco, which in its own way, continued a long tradition of social experiments, namely illustrated by Saul Alinsky,[10] aiming to empower the poor. Community boards had the particularity of being exclusively devoted to mediation, whereas the structures bearing the same name found all over the US, or the NJC s mentioned previously, had the more general functions (access to rights, participation of citizens in public decisions). The rhetoric of the community boards' promoter, Raymond Schonholtz, stems from a severe critique of the judicial system, framed as formalistic and indifferent to people's feelings. It denounces professionalisation, which deprives people of their conflicts. In this context, community boards had the ambition of breathing new life into neighbourhoods and of developing a culture of tolerance and respect.

Mediation's cooperative dynamic is in this case a tool for transforming social relations and a vector for participative democracy. In order to achieve this, it is necessary to train the largest number of people possible on the practice of mediation, people of all social backgrounds, of all races (the participation of black people, Latinos and Asian people is very valued and meaningful) and of all ages. The independence of these boards from judicial and social structures is particularly important. Financial support is brought by private foundations or by users, and most of the demand for mediation comes from community members, while cases referred by the police or the courts are rare.

The internal functioning of these boards is coherent with the philosophy that drives them. Indeed, the number of professionals present is low; they

---

10 Saul Alinsky, *Manuel de l'animateur social. Une action directe non violente*, Paris, Seuil, 1976.

essentially have the role of training or coordinating. Volunteers have very extensive roles. They visit the opposing party to listen to their points of view, explain the process, encourage them to participate, practise mediation themselves, follow up with each case, spread these ideas within the community, recruit new members and participate in their mediation training.

This type of initiative, coupled with a rapid investment in the academic peer mediation programs, spread throughout North America, then in Australia and in New Zealand before reaching Europe via the United Kingdom. Even if the adopted models were not always independent from institutions, most of them granted a primary political role to community participation and the deinstitutionalization of conflict resolution.

4 An Intellectual Context

These social practices are the result of an intellectual dynamic from which they draw their inspiration. The rise of mediation must be contextualised with all the scientific works of this era, which focused on the critique of legal ideology and developing a new approach to communication and interpersonal relations. Among them, it is important to highlight *critical legal studies*, as well as the influence of the Palo Alto school and the interactionist works of the humanistic psychology movement led by Carl Rogers.

4.1 *Critical Legal Studies*

Within the tumultuous radical movement questioning the traditional values of the American way of life, a deconstructive movement of legal analysis was established in 1977, encapsulated by the expression *law is politics*,[11] to demystify and delegitimize existing law.

However, this 'left-wing' movement cannot be summarised by a homogenous and monolithic way of thinking, given how much it was affected by different movements. Behind a common foundation of denouncing the law's oppressive function of serving the elite, notable differences exist between those who are devoted to questions concerning gender (*feminist legal criticism*), race (*critical race theory*), or those which support sexual minorities, poor or indigenous people.

11 See for example Mark Kelman, *A guide to critical legal studies*, Harvard University Press, 1987 and Roberto Mangabeira Unger, *The critical legal studies movement*, Harvard University Press, 1983.

The main tenets of critical legal studies can be summarised as follows:

- Judicial ideology frequently refers to an impersonal legislator that is supposedly the source of all laws. This proposition does not stand up to sociological vision. This conception does not function in a sociological context; this legislator is just a myth obscuring the fact that laws are the product of a socio-political context and cannot be understood independently from the analysis of its context.
- Legal texts are presented by liberalism as universal, but this is just a trick. In reality, they constitute a political ideology that defends the interests of the political and economical elites and not the values of most members of society.[12]
- The legal system is homeostatic, it ensures the status quo and the perpetuation of established power. It only represents a collection of beliefs and prejudices which hides social injustice under a mask of legitimacy.
- Legal reasoning is not the fortress of objective rationality it pretends to be, but is rather a fragile structure, full of contradictory and arbitrary categories, which are constantly redefined and reworked to perpetuate the domination of the powerful, namely the domination of men over women, rich over poor, and majorities over minorities.
- Legal norms are abstract. They do not consider particular needs and classify disputes into previously established and stereotyped legal categories.
- The judicial institution isolates individual claims, posing an obstacle to the expression of collective claims.
- The judicial system destroys interpersonal relationships instead of building them. The contradictory procedure aggravates conflicts, because the need for designating a winner and a loser makes the search for an agreement impossible.
- Formal justice provides retrospective judgements without worrying about repairing or rebuilding what has been broken.

The theoreticians of CLS call for a radical change of social structure. The law is one of the ways to achieve this 'institutional reconstruction'. But their words

12 This instrumentalist perspective was later nuanced by Pierre Bourdieu's work, which considered the legal field as 'a place of rivalry for the monopoly for the right to speak the law which contributes…to the system of legal norms appearing, to those who impose it and those who are subjected to it, as completely independent from the power dynamics it sanctions and establishes.' The conflictual nature of this field explains the law's hybrid nature, which is the result of a compromise, meaning it never completely expresses a particular group's values.

Pierre Bourdieu, 'La force du droit. Eléments pour une sociologie du champ juridique', *Actes de la recherche en sciences sociales*, 1986, nr 64, pp. 40–44.

do not refer to a Marxist-Leninist revolutionary ideology. Quite the contrary, they wish for individuals to be able to emancipate themselves from the power of the structures that alienate them. Unger thus considers a super liberal state in which categories that usually separate and divide people (sexuality, race, politics, class) are abolished, allowing values to be shared and collective relations to be more harmonious. He pleads for an *empowered democracy* in which the government and the economy would be largely decentralised.

Naturally, this movement was qualified as utopic by jurists and by the establishment. Both rejected it vehemently, but even with virulent opposition, these doctrinal positions did have an effect, as a great number of activists drew inspiration from it to develop innovative programs in terms of access to law and conflict resolution.

4.2 *The Palo Alto School and Interactionism*

One cannot talk about the emergence of mediation without referring to the intellectual climate that characterised this period. Human sciences, starting from the first works of the Palo Alto[13] school in the 1950s up until the interactionists of the 1960s, broke off from both psychoanalysis and institutional sociology. They offered an inter-relational approach to human relationships, opposing both subject-focused perspectives and macrosociological visions.

Grouped together in the early 1950s, in the wake of the anthropologist Gregory Bateson, at the heart of a small town south of San Francisco, a few researchers with varied scientific backgrounds developed a systemic approach to human relationships. They overturned the doxa of the time by positing that the behaviour of each element in a system obeys a set of relations specific to this system. Thus, to understand the logic and identify the problems encountered by its members, it is preferable to be centred on the relations between the different elements of the system more than their 'individuality'. A reciprocal action exists, a communication loop within which each element takes on the stimulus and response role depending on the behaviour of the other element. However, this feedback also depends on the context in which it is taking place, namely the set of elements present in its environment which affect its nature.

The family is one of the most tackled systems in the Palo Alto school, whose work inspired the pioneers of family mediation. It would be vain to seek to untangle domestic conflicts without taking into account the entirety of the interactions which link all the members of the system. Its contributions have

---

13 See for example Edmond Marc, Dominique Picard, *L'école de Palo Alto. Un nouveau regard sur les relations humaines,* Paris, Retz, 2000.

also been significant in multiple organisational contexts such as institutions and companies. Mediation is perceived as a tool for treating 'pathologies' of the communication model and not individuals, because the latter are members of a system that determine the relational context. Some practices, like brief therapy or problem-solving therapy, have some relation with mediation. They highlight the positive function of the presence of a third impartial party, and differ from psychoanalysis by neglecting the unconscious, libido or the subject's story. They focus their action less on the disappearance of conflict than on transforming the perception of it.

The interactionist movement, largely influenced by the work of the Chicago school, was also attentive to the nature of the relationships between people that determine the meaning they give to reality. The construction of reality is the result of a dynamic process of interaction during which, to continue theatrical metaphor started by Goffman,[14] the actors develop representation techniques to avoid losing face. From thereon, the definition they give to their situation depends on cognitive mechanisms they mobilise to produce meaning and to interpret the meaning others confer to them.

Here again, like the researchers of Palo Alto, who had a more curative ambition, it is by working on this interaction that we can transform both the perception the actors have of others and their definition of the situation. Hence the founding idea of mediation: putting the actors in a physical face-to-face position has the power to mutually influence the way that they interpret reality and determine their actions.

4.3 *Carl Rogers' Humanistic Psychology*

Carl Rogers is a reference for mediation pioneers. Distinguishing his work from psychoanalysis and behaviourist psychology, he proposes a fundamentally positive vision of the human being. Indeed, he proposed that people possess resources that allow them to understand and change themselves and to resolve their own problems. 'The only knowledge that may influence the behaviour of an individual are those he discovers by himself and appropriates himself.'[15] However, they may sometimes need a third party to help them become aware of this, though the latter is not an expert. Their role is simply to unlock the potential that a person possesses so she or he can resolve the conflict themselves.

---

14 Erving Goffman, *La présentation de soi (I). La mise en scène de la vie quotidienne*, Paris, Editions de Minuit, 1973 (1959).

15 Carl Rogers, *Le développement de la personne*, Paris, Dunod, 1968 (1961).

His non-directive approach, which excludes any advice or suggestion, aims to favour the autonomy and empowerment of the subjects. The third party adopts attitudes of empathy, acceptance, non-judgement, and only intervenes to reformulate the client's thoughts and feelings. He or she is not trying to solve a problem, but rather to enter into a profound and empathetic relationship with the person, building an authentic and warm relationship different from the psychoanalyst's neutrality. He or she establishes a climate of trust without judgment to encourage the client's free expression. To do this, several techniques are used: reformulation, support in expression, clarification in thinking and aid in decision-making, keeping in mind that the emotional experience is more important than the reconstitution of the past.

All these elements have contributed to shaping the mediator's posture as it is currently defined by doctrine. Naturally, the purpose of the mediator's relationship is different from that of the therapist, as mediation consists in working on the link between people, not on the individuals themselves. However, in Rogers' view, the foundation of the two roles can be easily transposed. Rogers has in fact illustrated this himself during his later days, when he organised peace workshops between the protagonists of the conflicts in Northern Ireland, South Africa and Central America.

4.4 *The Deconstruction Movement and the 'French Theory'*

The emergence of mediation practices must also be put into the intellectual context of the 1960s and 1970s in which all political and institutional domination systems were criticised.

This movement, perhaps characterised too hastily as *French theory*, breaks away from the doxa which, since the age of enlightenment, had represented progress and the rational organisation of social life, and unveils all forms of ideological, scientific and institutional illusions.[16]

Thus, presented in a succinct manner and in no particular order, Lyotard denounced totalitarian mind frames, Barthes analysed and decomposed signs and new mythologies, Derrida advocated for deconstructing language, Baudrillard stigmatised the alienation of consumerism, the 'system of objects' and the media communication which transforms our perception of reality, Debord unveiled a society of spectacle in which image substitutes itself to reality, Foucault highlighted structures of repression and Bourdieu the mech-

16 For a more global vision, see François Cusset, *French Theory. Foucault, Derrida, Deleuze et Cie et les mutations de la vie intellectuelle aux Etats-Unis*, Paris, La Découverte, 2003 et Yves Bonny, *Sociologie du temps présent. Modernité avancée ou post-modernité?* Paris, La Découverte, 2004.

anisms of social reproduction, Deleuze focused on societies of control and the fruitfulness of disorder.

This flood of critical production, transcending the binary principles of the explanation of our world, such as good/evil, nature/culture, man/woman, inside/outside, order/disorder, promotes a new approach to the understanding of reality. Universal beliefs on which the social order was based (religions, ideologies), gave way to more contingent and plural values, and holistic visions gave way to more fragmented and individual perspectives of reality. From thereon, institutions no longer had the function of organising society, but instead to prioritise the emancipation and involvement of people, to recognise their equality and diversity.

Of course, no direct link exists between these theories and mediation practices. However, they inspired a new generation of intellectuals and practitioners who, dreaming of a better society, developed a critical approach to institutional injustice, to the bureaucratisation of social practices, and to the commodification of collective and individual relationships. These ideals manifested themselves in very diverse forms, and the common denominator in this diversity remains the pursuit of a real democracy, one which places the individual at the centre of political debate and institutional practices. The theoreticians of mediation exemplify this ideal by creating alternative ways to address conflict in which individuals and groups can become masters of their own destiny.

CHAPTER 2

The Development of Mediation

Our societies have known considerable upheavals during the second part of the 20th century. Many authors describe them when writing about the passage from modernity to post-modernity (also known as advanced, acute, late or reflexive modernity, supermodernity, hypermodernity).[1]

But not everyone agrees on beginning and end dates. While most people agree modernity began during the Renaissance, at the end of the Middle Ages, and its golden age was the Age of Enlightenment (ideal of reason, strong belief in science, secularisation, split from the universe of myths), it is more complicated to agree on the beginnings of post-modernity.

In my opinion, post-modernity truly begins at the end of the *trentes glorieuses*, in the early wavering days of the welfare state model, when the first petrol crisis arose in 1973, which announced the end of full employment and of the industrial society. Later, in 1989, the fall of the Berlin Wall represented a symbolically important moment, sealing the end of the bipolar world governance model initiated in 1945; but the process had already begun.

Here are a few indicators of postmodernity, with their multiple and tangled causes:

- The 'disenchantment of the world'[2] illustrated by the collapse of the main religious and ideological narratives in Western societies. These narratives were a way of interpreting reality, and they are, namely for the poorest people, a means of rationalizing the injustices they experienced, giving meaning to their existence, transmitting codes of behaviour and proposing ways of regulating conflicts. Their disappearance created the conditions of an uncertain society in which the meaning of human and collective life is diluted.
- The transformation of public institutions and the decreased role of the State in social life, eroded both by centrifugal forces (the creation of supranational political entities, of which the EU is an example) and by centripetal forces, the accentuation of the decentralisation process and the resurgence of regional cultural identities.

---

1 Y. Bonny, *Sociologie du temps présent. Modernité avancée ou post-modernité?* Paris, La Découverte, 2004.

2 M. Gauchet, *Le désenchantement du monde: une histoire politique de la religion*, Paris, Gallimard, 1985.

 | DOI:10.1163/9789004734067_005

- The advent of neoliberalism with the stagnation of the welfare state's resources, the increasing osmosis between private and public sectors, the internationalisation of finance and capital, the deregulation of markets and the logic of economic globalisation.
- The advent of an active social State in which passive individuals dependent on the welfare state are asked more and more to become actors of their own destiny, to be more responsible, and to deserve the subsidies they benefit from.
- Migration phenomena that erode political and cultural boundaries, undermining both national and racial identities and the autarky logic of creating order. These phenomena also contribute to the progressive construction of the word citizenship.
- The development of new scientific and communication technology that upsets our perception of time, dematerialises financial exchanges and human relationships, and ensures the uncontrollable mobility of ideas, information and images.

This avalanche of mutations led to researching other ways to regulate the articulation between universes of diverse and multiple meanings. My hypothesis is that mediation, of which the rise is perfectly concomitant with this evolution, constitutes one of the ways to ensure with flexibility the management of complex societies, which work better with adaptable processes rather than with unstable institutions and territorialised norms.

The necessity of creating bridges between multiple, intertwined scales, spaces and time frames allows for flexible methods of regulation. It is precisely through their flexibility that mediations can establish flows, movements, bridges between heterogeneous entities. The metaphor of fluidity[3] is named after the 'liquid modernity' concept used by Bauman to describe a historical context devoid of certainties and solid social forms.[4] As already explained in the introduction, Bauman's metaphor demonstrates that the binary logic of repressive systems is not sufficient to legitimize a public authority. Instead, legitimacy comes from the ability to create new intermediary spaces where change is possible.

This link between mediation and postmodernity can be observed at different levels: that of the different contextual factors that favour the emergence of these practices, or even that of the social and political reasons behind its development, as well as on the level of the analysis of its development dynamics.

---

3 J. Faget, *Médiation et action publique. La dynamique du fluide*, Presses Universitaires de Bordeaux, 2005.

4 Z. Bauman, *Liquid modernity*, Cambridge, Polity Press, 2000.

1 The Contextual Conditions of Mediation's Development

The spread of mediation around the world is not random. The practice first appeared in the USA and in Canada. A first wave then spread in the 1980s to Australia, New Zealand, England, to Scandinavian countries and France. A second wave reached Latin America (Argentina, Columbia and Mexico first) as well as southern Europe (Spain and Italy), then a third wave saw mediation implanted in Eastern European countries in the 2000s. This spread happened thanks to the practitioners and promoters who shared their ideas. These new adopters of mediation that worked in transnational contexts sparked the spread of pro-mediation public policies. The circulation of their ideas is conditional to the publication of works, the organisation and intervention in international conferences, and the sale of training programmes. But beyond individual initiatives, structural, political, religious, anthropological, judicial, social and tangled variables can explain the speed and intensity of their propagation.

2 The Linguistic Factor

It seems evident that belonging to the anglophone linguistic community has helped the spread of mediation. However, this factor, as we shall see later, must be combined with other variables. France owes the distinction of being one of the countries that received the first wave of mediation to its privileged relationship with Quebec. As one of Ontario's neighbouring provinces, which saw the development of the first penal mediation program (the *Victim Offender Reconciliation Program*), Quebec served as a strong link with the francophone world. A few researchers travelled to the St. Lawrence River to observe these innovative practices and retained some methods of action. This was in particular my case, when I discovered during one of my trips in Quebec an experience called 'conciliation within community' and which inspired the French model of penal mediation. Trainers from Québec came frequently to France, namely to train the first generations of family mediators.

3 The Political and Ideological Context

Different modes of conflict appeasement exist in all societies, no matter their mode of political organisation; however mediation did exclusively develop in Western democracies. Its absence in countries with authoritarian regimes shows that the philosophy of mediation requires a democratic vision of social organisation in order to flourish. Its rare presence in third world countries could mean it is linked to particular economic and institutional contexts, to a point in our democracies' history in which they are confronted with the hypercomplexity of their modes of existence.

I have mentioned previously that the political reference was essential when it came to putting into action the first experiences of mediation in the US. They became implanted in an anti-establishment social context, which, avidly searching for equality and justice, questioned the traditional values of the American way of life. The cooperative dynamic of mediation was conceived in this context as a tool for transforming social relations and as a vector for participative democracy.

In the wake of these first projects in America, a large number of programmes involving volunteers aiming to regulate the conflicts of everyday life of a town or a neighbourhood's citizens appeared in the UK, where the notion of community became more important, as well as in the Nordic countries.

The development of these programs in France, starting in 1983, under the names of *mediation de quartier* (neighbourhood mediation), social mediation and lastly citizen mediation, is more difficult, despite the support of the interministerial delegation for towns (in French, *délégation interministérielle à la ville*). Perhaps this is due to the centralised French state not necessarily being pleased to see the development of modes of conflict regulation out of its institutional control. Because mediation has its roots both in liberal tradition and also in the position of the 'solidarist' republicans, social Catholics and self-managing socialists. All these groups are opposed to the idea of the State possessing the monopoly on the definition of public interest and insist on the necessity of a third sector between the individual citizen and the State.[5]

4 Religion

Mediation practices were born in countries with a largely Protestant culture before spreading to Catholic countries. In principle, Protestantism seems to correspond better to the philosophy of mediation. It is overtly anti-state and defends the idea of a city governed by itself where interactions allow the creation of negotiated truths. The Mennonites, for example, have no hierarchy or supreme authority. Each national conference and local church is independ-

5 V. De Briand, Y. Palau, *La médiation. Définition, pratiques et perspectives*, Paris, Nathan, 2000.

ent. The pastors are not the intermediary between God and the believers, unlike Catholicism in which the Truth is revealed, transcendent, and where a centralised and hierarchical vision of power is cultivated.

However, the interest that the Catholic church has in mediation can be understood as the expression of a political philosophy which glorifies the existence of intermediary parties, which are barriers against totalitarianism, and the principle of subsidising which holds that conflicts not be necessarily treated by the state but by qualified social actors.

Some examples showing the Catholic church's interest are the activism of the Vatican community of Sant'Egidio, the meditative interventions of the clergy in the Chiapas conflicts, in northern Spain and in the Basque country,6 and the eminent role played by the Catholic theoretician Jean François in the promotion of mediation in France.[7]

So mediation is 'fundamentally linked with power dynamics: power in the very functioning of the religious institution and power in the relations between the religious and political spheres'.[8]

However, only Christian countries have adopted mediation. One is led to believe that its principles, the necessity of a ternary relation, the role given to speech as a way to redeem oneself and to reconcile, and the empowerment of actors are better suited to Christian philosophy than they are to the Buddhist and Muslim visions of the world.

5 Indigenous Communities

Indigenous populations exist in the countries that first developed mediation programs, and these communities have an important symbolic role in these countries' political life.

This is the case of the Inuits in Canada, the Native communities in the US, the Aboriginals in Australia and the Maoris in New Zealand.

Faced with inadequate institutional responses to conflicts within these communities, the idea of restoring the traditional modes of regulation (which were often in decay), and of relying on an implicated community arose. This was the case during the development of penal mediation (victim-offender

6 X. Itcaina, *Les virtuoses de l'identité. Religion et politique en Pays Basque*, Rennes, Université de Rennes, 2007.

7 J. F. Six, *Le temps des médiateurs*, Paris, Le Seuil, 1990.

8 J. Palard, 'Médiation et institution catholique', *Archives de sciences sociales des religions*, 133, janvier-mars 2006, pp. 9–26.

mediation), of domestic conferences and of sentence determination circles which were the backbone of restorative justice practices.[9]

6 Legal Culture

Common Law countries (England, the US, Canada, New Zealand and former members of the Commonwealth) in which the judicial system is essentially built on jurisprudence, which gives them more flexibility, have been more welcoming to ADR than countries with Roman-Germanic written law (Germany, Spain, France, Italy), which rely on the cult of the written rule. In the former model of judicial culture, the relatively modest number of professional magistrates and lawyers, and even slightest amount of weight they can put on political instances, can have an impact on the inclination to resort to negotiated and non-institutional modes of conflict regulation. The influence of powerful and organised judicial corporations in public debates would indeed overdetermine the use and influence of the judicial path. The tendency to avoid trials could then be explained by the less legal character of national culture as seen from a continual historical perspective.[10]

However, even countries with written law become, inevitably because of the asphyxiation of jurisdictions, more open to all forms of mediation, be they commercial, work-related, civil, family, or penal. Their introduction was simply delayed, and their impact more limited.

7 The Legitimacy of the Judicial Institution

One may think that the bigger the defiance, or the dissatisfaction of the public regarding the judicial institution, the more the public is keen to use extrajudicial modes of conflict regulation.

The legitimacy of the judicial system is indeed largely based on the representation that the social actors have of its symbolic and instrumental performance. However, the symbolic function of justice is only rarely contested, demonstrating the incredible progression of the social demand for law and the legalisation of social problems.

---

9 R. Cario, 'Changing lenses. Autour de l'œuvre d'Howard Zehr', pp. 45–58, J. Faget, 'Reintegrative shaming. A propos de la théorie de John Braithwaite', pp. 59–70, *Les Cahiers de la Justice*, 2006, nr 1.

10 E. Blankenburg. 'Cultures juridiques comparées', Droit et société, 1990, nr 16, pp. 321–333.

The judicial system has indeed seen an increasing number of requests from domains that were unknown to it in the past. The dilution of the existing means of conflict regulation comes first. When the neighbouring organisations are no longer able to prevent and regulate conflicts, complaint becomes the dominant way of expressing distress.

We are also witnessing a large demand for justice to regulate the excesses of the political world, to outline medical responsibility, to moralise sports or the business world, to address school violence, to define sexual morals. All this is happening as if law and justice were becoming a 'safe haven',[11] satisfying all the needs of the individual uncertain of capitalist havens, lacking ideology and beliefs, in order to make social, political and technological change accessible and understandable to the individual. When neighbourhoods or local communities are no longer able to prevent or regulate conflicts on their own, the courts become the dominant arena for the expression of harm or pain.

This plethoric demand for law, however, leads to the asphyxiation of the judiciary system, which seems to function more and more anachronistically (obsolete formalism, the long duration of procedures in a context of accelerating human and commercial exchanges, difficulty adapting law to modern mobility). Faced with mediocre instrumental practices, the orders of the new public management force are to obey orders to be faster and more profitable. This mediocrity is indicated by the production delays in civil judgement, the number of cases dismissed in the penal field, and by the return rate of cases before the jurisdiction.

Management rationality is progressively taking over all other considerations, but these quantitative orders impose themselves on a demand for quality. The bureaucratization of the resulting activity naturally erodes the symbolic function of the judiciary services and thus their legitimacy.

This trust crisis can have multiple consequences: the renouncing of citizens to assert their rights, the temptation of 'acting' themselves, and the drift (a phenomenon already largely practised in the corporate and commercial world) of entire work sectors towards regulation modes independent from the state, that are more flexible, quicker and cheaper.

Resorting to mediation falls into this dynamic, sometimes organised by judiciary actors themselves to alleviate their workload (penal disputes), other times practised by individuals answerable to the law who are discouraged by the methods used by the judiciary system and the cost of resorting to it (civil and in particular domestic disputes).

---

11 A. Garapon, *Le gardien des promesses. Justice et démocratie*, Paris, Odile Jacob, 1996.

Bypassing the judicial system can also be a politically motivated act. Many mediators justify their affinity with mediation by the corruption that touches judicial actors (Latin America), or by the lack of both stable, reliable institutions and trained and competent personnel (Eastern European and ex-Soviet Union countries).

8 The Cultural Context

One might think that conflict representations vary depending on the cultural context. Anthropologists teach us that when conflict threatens to destroy primitive and fragile societies, the latter put into action cooperative regulation processes to restore the broken equilibrium, whereas societies that are more solid can afford the luxury of conflict. More recent considerations have led to the observation that the societies of northern Europe have a stronger tendency to search for consensus than societies in southern Europe. This is probably due to a number of historical, climatic and psycho-sociological factors, and the fact that mediation 'comes from the north' must be put into perspective with this cultural difference in conflict. Research shows that in Chinese culture, respect for harmony is reflected by an aversion to conflict because in Chinese philosophy, influenced by Taoism, opposites don't reject each other, they help to create balance. This explains why conflict and the object of negotiation are only dealt with indirectly or alluded to with indirect games and masked strategies.[12]

Mediation's doctrine is built on individualistic values particular to American society. It involves the optimistic, and in certain aspects naive, principle of an autonomous, rational, responsible, and engaged actor. These societies with an 'individual identity' are opposed to more traditional societies with a 'collective identity', in which the individual is not defined as a free and independent subject, but as belonging before anything else to a family, a group, an ethnicity and a culture that surrounds it.

Western models of mediation seem in this sense ill-adapted to societies or belief systems that favour the collective over the individuals that compose it.

The development of family mediation is emblematic of the importance of cultural and political factors in the rise of mediation practices. One can only imagine it being put into practice in countries where domestic split is possible

---

12 G. O. Faure, 'La négociation internationale: un transfert de technologie en Chine', in G. O Faure, L. Mermet, H. Touzard, C. Dupont, op.cit., 1998, pp. 59–103.

and where women are recognised as having equal rights to men. This means letting go of the weight of religion and tradition.

The fact that certain countries share structural characteristics does not necessarily mean they have observed the equal quantitative and qualitative propagation of mediation practices, as national particularities affect mediation being put into practice.

To continue my reasoning, which is probably influenced by Pierre Bourdieu, the way a certain practice has been imported depends on the power and exchange dynamics existing in their field of work. In other words, the integration of 'what is done elsewhere' does not only obey spiritual reasons. Those who promote these actions can have different goals in mind, for example that of obtaining a prestigious or influential position in that given field by breaking away from old practices and from those who have monopoly over their functioning.

All this to say that ideas do not spread autonomously. They encounter pre-existing structures that individuals developing preservation strategies, or strategies to obtain dominant positions, gravitate around.

9 The Sociopolitical Reasons for the Development of Mediation

Mediation constitutes, among many others, an indicator of the transformation of the way societies are run. Its virtues are most frequently analysed as functional.

Mediation serves as a link between fragmented societal institutions, as a way to restore lost regulations.

Those who argue in favour of mediation programs often talk highly of their regulative functions, they proclaim not only the objective of resolving interpersonal conflicts but also of repairing ineffective communications between institutions, between different parts of an institution, and between the institutions and the public.

The word 'regulation' helps to stay away from the idea of an omnipotent central actor and to express the fluidity and the adaptability of the processes that orchestrate the social play, motivated by the search for an unobtainable balance and order in a state of perpetual change. These regulations are numerous and distinguishing their diverse categories must not lead us to believe in the existence of specific rationalities.

In reality, all these modes of regulation (be they political, institutional, social, or judicial) are closely interwoven, moved by the same current, without it being possible to clearly distinguish the prevalence of one over another. This distinction is made even more difficult by the fact they are handled the same way by the building sites of postmodernity.

10 The Metamorphosis of Political Regulations

To evoke the idea of a metamorphosis, as Jacques Commaille and Bruno Jobert did when talking about political regulation,[13] is to affirm the existence of a change from an old order based on a super-powerful State, which imposes its vision of social order in an authoritarian and hierarchical way, to more complex and interactive production modes of society.

The weakening of sovereignty and of centralized State power requires compromise and legitimation strategies that are rooted in negotiated processes. Political regulation proceeds by interweaving rationalities, by intersecting '*top down*' and '*bottom up*' strategies, and by favouring the emergence of intermediary piloting systems.

Chevallier highlights the shift from a traditional State to a postmodern State[14] in which the government modes are always less vertical and authoritarian and always more formalised and consensual.

The legitimacy of the traditional State is made fragile by the tension created by the development of political and above all economic globalised regulations and the emphasis put on the decentralisation and localisation processes. This 'glocalisation' is not always synonymous with the State growing weaker, but more with the transformation of its intervention modes. Instead of being a primary resource, the State's intervention is organised when the mechanisms of social regulation aren't functioning, thus taking on a secondary function. This means that the foundation and source of this legitimacy is shifting more and more from the State and the institutions to the individual. In a universe affected both by the State's failure and the market as the regulators of complexity, the resolution of problems must be organised on a citizen level (proximity rhetoric), as the social actors are associated with the conception and the application of norms (partnership rhetoric). Of course, numerous resistances can sometimes reaffirm state intervention, which still has the upper hand in many sectors and greatly benefits from its legitimacy. However, its modes of action are changing and the 'political spirit of mediation', whether it be regu-

13 J. Commaille, B. Jobert, *Les métamorphoses de la régulation politique,* Droit et société, Paris, LGDJ, coll. Droit et société, 1998.

14 J. Chevallier, *L'Etat post-moderne,* Paris, LGDJ, coll. Droit et société, 2003.

lating political, environmental, intercultural, public liberty or interpersonal conflicts, is part of this transformation.

From this point of view, the rhizome metaphor,[15] which introduces the dimensions of complexity, disorder and incoherence, seems to be more adapted than those of the pyramid and the tree[16] to fully account for the metamorphosis of public action.

Whereas the tree is one and develops in successive dichotomies, the rhizome establishes links between random points. The tree is genealogic and rationally structured, whereas the rhizome is made up entirely of dimensions, moving directions; it has no end nor beginning, and its nature is constantly changing. As it is a perennial underground stem which grows roots and aerial sprouts, it is essentially composed of stratification lines, which can be seen as lines of rupture or vanishing lines.

Within the rhizome, multiple secondary roots graft themselves onto the main roots. These secondary roots develop so much they cover up the main roots; the system no longer has a pivot. Even if the unity of the ensemble persists, the space's layout cannot be centred or enclosed.

The shift from a traditional conception to a rhizomatic conception of public action can be symbolised by highlighting different pairs of opposites between the two models.

Far from being radically opposite, these conceptions articulate themselves dialectically to create a transformative dynamic during which these methods of action perpetually redefine themselves.

TABLE 2.1 Models of public action

The tree model	The rhizome model
State	Society
Imposed order	Negotiated order
Vertical relationship	Horizontal relationship
Principle of organised connexion	Principle of random connexion
Homogeneity	Heterogeneity
Law	Contract
Result	Process

15 G. Deleuze et F. Guattari, *Mille plateaux. Capitalisme et schizophrénie*, Paris, Editions de Minuit, 1980.

16 J. Faget, *Justice et travail social. Le rhizome pénal*, Toulouse, Erès, 1992.

These models, far from being radically opposite, articulate themselves dialectically, but their interwovenness remains conjectural. It depends on centralised political traditions of the countries in question, but also on the difficulties that the decision makers have in proving the legitimacy of their action.

Thus, the rhizome model used to describe mediation relies on particularist action principles which affirm the singularity of subjects interacting horizontally in order to eventually create contracts they write freely. This institutionalisation process makes the distinction between these two models less precise. Furthermore, the use of mediation represents, for the moment, a way to work around institutional blocks and to adapt to complex realities, rather than a radical transformation of the principle of public actions, which remains stamped with the seal of verticality.

One example of a hybrid model that concerns the global analysis levels is international mediation, or even more specifically, the management of internal political conflict or the making of political decisions.

The shift from a world articulated around nation-states, endowed with its own institutions and producers of territorialised norms, to a globalised world which struggles to elaborate the principles and norms of common action and whose modes of functioning are progressively deterritorialized, is the source of great complexity.

Naturally, this process is even more spectacular on the economic relations level. The absence of a global normativity and the traps of its elaboration encourage, in order to push back the turmoil of the savage deregulation of markets, the search for new flexible ways of regulating under the form of conventions, ethical codes or contractual clauses of mediation.

This evolution is also sensitive in terms of interstate conflicts. Traditional diplomacy does not suffice anymore to assess the transformation of power dynamics in a multipolar world, or the mutation of forms of expression of political conflict. We are moving from interstate conflicts that have scarred history to territorialised conflicts, that, with the guerilla terrorists' action mode, sabotage international equilibrium. Faced with a powerless United Nations, which is more oriented towards peacekeeping, a large number of important NGOs have appeared, often organised in international networks (for example, the Federal Negotiation Network, which groups together the Carter Foundation, the universities of Harvard, of Uppsala in Sweden, and George Mason University, and the World Conference on Religion and Peace), and which build a sort of parallel diplomacy. These modes of regulation, often subsidised by a group of states, can be analysed as the functional complement of unproductive official diplomacies. But their relative autonomy, because of the diversity of funding and of their contrast status, could likely illustrate the advent of a 'world without sovereignty'.[17]

Cases in which hypercentralised States accept to transform their habitual action methods to find solutions to internal political conflicts do exist. This was the case of the French government, led by Michel Rocard, who, in order to 'exit' the New Caledonian crisis between the Kanak independentist population and the Caldoche loyalists, decided to resort to mediation. This practice was led by a team composed of three state workers but also three representatives of the most present spiritual groups in the territory, specifically the Freemasons, the Protestants and the Catholics.

This mediation resulted to the signing of the Matignon agreements in 1988, which recognised the Kanak identity and the other populations present on the territory, and elaborated the foundational concept of a communal destiny between these peoples. This represented a shift from the French vertical and authoritarian political tradition; however, it did not last long. It continues to meet great resistance as public action always relies on the principle of an integrating State arbitrating and guaranteeing general interest. However, it has had the merit of enriching, in the collective imagination, the range of possibilities for social pacification.

The making of political decisions is also inspired by the rhizomatic model. The political, unionist and associative representation is in crisis (low rate of electoral participation, high percentage of protesting votes, erosion of political parties, of structured activism). The principle maintains itself for lack of a better alternative, but the citizens are prompt to denounce the faults of their elected representatives and to question how representative they are and their capacity to act. 'The democratic individual does not tolerate the limits and constraints imposed by the institutions well… the *homo democraticus* tends to think it can be represented by itself'.[18] Because of this, even if traditional political structures remain important, a new form of public space takes shape, in which the principles of delegation and hierarchical subordination make way for more direct commitments. Thus, numerous signs of new public debate areas are becoming visible, as well as the introduction of a 'negotiated public action'[19] to accept the challenges posed by environmental protection and the development of science and technology.

---

17 B. Badie, *Un monde sans souverainetés*, Paris, Fayard, 1999.

18 D. Schnapper, *La démocratie providentielle. Essai sur l'égalité contemporaine*, Paris, Gallimard, 2002.

19 S. Allain, 'La médiation environnementale comme système politique de régulation. Application au gouvernement de l'eau', dans Faget, op. cit., 2005.

TABLE 2.2 Modes of political decision-making

	Democratic model	
Transformation	Co-decision (*mediation*)	**Participative democracy**
	Dialogue	
	Consultation	
Legitimisation	Information	**Representative democracy**
	Authoritarian model	

More and more frequent collective mediations are put into practice under diverse names (consensus conferences, hybrid forums,[20] cores of citizen participation) for conflicts linked to environmental problems (construction of a motorway, of a bypass, implantation of a waste treatment site, of a wind turbine field, creation of ecological protected zones), or linked to urban development (location of an education centre for young delinquents, of leisure equipment) or linked to the use of public space.

Admittedly, these mediations are only rarely brought about by political stakeholders; they are most often induced by activist movements, namely ecological, but they demonstrate the formation of new types of political decision-making.

Authoritarian decisions made by elected representatives, rationalised by expert knowledge and the legitimacy of public office, are sometimes substituted by more actively democratic principles in which all of the concerned actors are at least informed of the ongoing projects, if not consulted during the thinking process, and in the most successful cases, these actors participate in the decision-making.

If the information and consultation procedures often constitute a strategy of legitimising preconstructed political choices, the higher levels that are dialogue and co-decision, however, constitute a real split in political practices. The numerous actors and interacting rationalities involved are the best illustration of the rhizomatic conception of public action.

20 They are called forums as they are spaces open to debate, and hybrid because the problems discussed are varied (they can be ethical, economic, technical...) See M. Callon, P. Lascoumes, Y. Barthe, Agir dans un monde incertain. Essai sur la démocratie technique, Paris, Seuil, 2001.

11 The Decline of Institutional Regulations

Mediation can be analysed 'both as a symptom and a remedy',[21] a symptom of the increasing influence of bureaucracy over public and social life, and a remedy because of the implementation of both democratic opposition forces and efficient problem treatment methods. The best illustration of this is given by the institution of the ombudsman[22] created in 1809 by the king of Sweden, initially to control how the administration applied his laws.

It was only during the 20th century that the institution was able to regulate the conflicts between citizens and the administration and became a way for them to control the arbitrary side of bureaucracy. From then on, it developed a rhetoric of independence regarding the political and financial powers and built an ethic of intervention based on impartiality and confidentiality. This ombudsman model spread with no resistance throughout the Western world, starting with Nordic countries, then those of the Commonwealth, and in almost all democracies under different names, *médiateur de la République* in France (1973), *defensor del pueblo* in Spanish-speaking countries, *provedor da justiça* in Portuguese-speaking countries. It started to appear in developing countries, specifically on the African continent. Its success is such that many ombudsmen or mediators appear in local or regional politics, in multiple administrations, or in specialised fields of the private sector such as banks, telecommunication, transport, insurance, energy distribution, television or even newspaper companies. Naturally, not all mediators have the same status, they do not obey the same ethical principles with regards to their independence, their competence or their investigation and proposition powers.[23] Whereas some are real white knights, the backbone of a strategy aiming to democratise administrative functioning, considered invasive, opaque and arbitrary, others resemble a political gadget destined to give the institutions the legitimacy they lack. This risk is often denounced when they are nominated by the political or administrative power, of which they have to handle the conflicts or the maladministration.

Except in the cases in which he/she is only the gadget of the mandating institution, the ombudsman is less of a mediator than an agent of moralisation and of institutional change. Indeed, his/her decisions create precedents, par-

21 J. De Munck, 'De la loi à la médiation', in France: les révolutions invisibles (collectif), Paris, Calmann Levy, 1998, pp. 315.

22 J. Faget, 'Ombudsman', M. Bevir (Dir.), Encyclopedia of Governance, vol. II, Thousand Oaks, CA, Sage Publications Ink, 2007, pp. 633–634.

23 P. Magnette, Entre contrôle parlementaire et 'Etat de Droit': le rôle politique du médiateur dans l'union européenne, Revue française de science politique, vol. 51, nr 6, décembre 2001, pp. 933–948.

ticipate in the construction of a guide of 'good practices' and spread a philosophy of 'good' administration. In the end, this 'mediator' is not only there to repair deficient communications between citizens and the administration but also exerts real political control and constitutes a vector for democratisation. The intensity of the ombudsman's impact depends on the person's status and degree of independence.

The success of the ombudsman policy shows the harm done to our administrations, mined by an extreme bureaucratisation, by a more and more present division into sectors of practices, by a segmentation of skill sets. More flexible and efficient forms of regulation are then sought after, the new public management has been fervently devoted to this search for a few years now. The idea of reducing the weight of public intervention and of transforming management methods (tracing them on those of the private sectors), is becoming more and more essential. The integration of mediation into certain institutions can probably be explained by the sovereignty of managerial rationalities[24] in Western democracies. However, this vision cannot account for all the institutional dynamics on its own. The organisational contexts, professional cultures, and the peculiar nature of the social mission given to the institutions, make the evolutions vary. Perhaps becoming aware of the necessity to humanise blind administrative mechanisms and to rebuild a 'lost' relationship with the users[25] can be a powerful driving force for innovation.

This problem concerns the *street level bureaucracies*[26] in another way: these institutions' agents (teachers, police agents, jurists specialised in the access to law, social workers, institutional agents giving out financial aids, employment centres) have a direct relationship with the public.[27]

These institutions have resorted to 'mediators' to improve the contact they have with their users. Because of the crisis of the traditional regulations of proximity, the counters in public services buildings have become a place where people express their dissatisfaction and distress more and more. Violence being omnipresent in the complaints that are expressed[28] there, it is

---

24 A. Crawford, La justice de proximité: appels à la 'communauté' et stratégies de responsabilisation dans une idéologie managériale, in A. Wyvekens, J. Faget (sous la direction de.), La justice de proximité en Europe, Toulouse, Erès, 2001, pp. 37–64.

25 A. Wyvekens, J. Faget (2001) op. cit.

26 M. Lipsky, Street level bureaucracy. Dilemmas of the individual in public services, Russel Sage foundation, 1980.

27 J. Faget, 'Street-level Bureaucrat', M. Bevir (Dir.), Encyclopedia of Governance, vol. II, Thousand Oaks, CA, Sage Publications Ink, 2007, pp. 935–936.

28 V. Dubois, *La vie au guichet. Relations administratives et traitement de la misère*, Paris, Economica, 1999.

understandable that numerous institutions have resorted to action plans to manage this conflict.

From another point of view, we have been able to consider that mediation could constitute a response to the decline of social institutions. Its development would be a consequence of the work crisis on others, in the medical, educational or social work[29] fields. Whereas the traditional social work, figurehead of the welfare state, is founded on a vocational dimension and on the principle of individual relationships, the political, economic and social evolution demands a more technical and territorialised action, imposing partnership practices and privileging acting on groups.

This disqualification of 'classical' social work would be reinforced by the many situations of exclusion, rendering the traditional treatment of marginalisation obsolete.

The increase in tension with teenagers and young adults, particularly foreigners, sheds doubt on the efficiency of the educational institutions and stimulates the research of new modalities of intervention.[30] The resistance social workers have regarding mediation, which they often consider as a war machine against their profession, shows this tension. However, the desire of minority to follow various training courses in mediation indicates a process of redefining the tools and the ethics of social work.

Lastly, mediation seems to compensate for the lack of social institutional control when the local communities call on social mediators to facilitate the integration of foreign populations or to secure spaces that are deserted by traditional social control agents such as national or municipal police officers or even social workers (local social workers, specialised educators). Although significant, the institutional resort to mediation must not be overestimated. Indeed, the attempts to modernise public services have often stumbled on the internal resistances to change, and the observations of institutional practices show that mediation practices limit the intervention to the institutional borders without threatening the hierarchical structure and the work organisation principles.[31] The mediators assigned to these missions are 'plumbers' of hardly productive service relations rather than actors bringing life to new networks of public action.

29 V. Dubois, *La vie au guichet. Relations administratives et traitement de la misère*, Paris, Economica, 1999.

30 J. Faget, J. De Maillard, *Les agents locaux de médiation sociale en quête d'identité*, Etudes et documents, IHESI, Ministère de l'Intérieur, 2003 et « Les Agents locaux de médiation sociale (ALMS) en quête de légitimité. Déficits de reconnaissance et oppositions professionnelles », *Les Cahiers de la sécurité intérieure*, 2002, nr 48, pp. 127–147.

31 Ibid.

12 The Collapse of Traditional Social Regulations

Many have argued that the function assigned to the process of mediation was to compensate for the progressive disintegration of the socialisation modes and of conflict regulation.[32] It is true that the role played in this domain by the clan-like family, the workers' movement, the political parties, the trade-unions, the churches, has notoriously declined. They gave meaning to collective existence, a way to understand reality, they transmitted behavioural norms, the affiliation to these different groups brought with it a certain vision of the world, drew horizon lines and favoured the production of collective identities. Because of the social control they exerted on their members, these different authorities would anticipate the start of conflicts, particularly endogenous conflicts.

Because of the legitimacy their representatives benefited from (head of the family, mayors, priests, patrons) they were able to offer diverse modalities of conflict regulation or of support in adversity. The obsolescence of these socialisation and social control modes to the profit of more institutionalised forms of collective conflict management would have been fertile soil for mediation.

This analysis must however be enriched by a quick sociological detour which complexifies this affirmation. We are part of societies in which individuals are more and more autonomous (etymologically, elaborating their own norms) and claim, in the wake of a human rights movement, the benefit of liberties (liberty of thought, speech, reunion, of faith, ownership, of vote and of participation to public life). These liberties were conceived as a barrier against the arbitrary State and claim certain rights (right to education, to healthcare, to work and to social protection), which bind the state to act in favour of individuals.

This constant aspiration leads them to search for meaning within their own destiny in a constant state of crafting and tinkering; and to question, as previously mentioned, the representation principle and to always demand more 'transparency' and 'proximity'.

These new words of citizen rhetoric express the rejection of passed transcendences and the demand for equality between governed and governing.

This disengagement of all norms and external references, to the profit of 'individual reflexivity' makes identity the result of a permanent reflexive attitude, everyone being ceaselessly called to make choices concerning many aspects of existence that were previously influenced by customs and imposed social norms.[33] A whole conception of organisation of social relationships

---

32 J.P. Bonafé-Schmitt, *La médiation. Une justice douce*, Paris, Syros, 1992.

33 A. Giddens, *The consequence of modernity, 1990*. Cambridge, Polity Press.

would then exert social pressure on individuals to make decisions and commit.[34] This permanent call to responsibility, to be oneself, would represent a mental health risk for individuals who are insecure in their identity and could then become depressed.[35]

This collective process of individualisation does, of course, make the process of elaborating a social contract linking all citizens arduous, as no society can subsist without a common project. The question of knowing how to sustain social links then emerges, the notion of sharing within collective identity, in societies based on autonomy and the sovereignty of individuals. The challenge is especially important when migration flows are more and more substantial and less controllable, when the feeling of insecurity occupies a large part of public debate, when interethnic conflicts are multiplying, and spatial and social segregation phenomena threaten collective harmony and favour the withdrawal of communities and urban planning based on affinity. In multicultural societies faced with growing and intense mobility (of people, capital, information, images, objects)[36] which are more organised in moving, complex and interwoven networks rather than in stable structures, separating and push factors are probably more numerous than pull factors that unify members of a same political community.

The evoked emancipation of individuals is for the moment far from being accomplished, and it is probably in this incompleteness that the development of mediation finds its meaning. Paradoxically, the individualisation of social relations creates a growing need for institutions to compensate for the void it creates.

When an individual obtains freedom from a stable domestic model on which traditional society relies on, in the name of a search for sentimental authenticity, he or she creates conditions in which judges, social workers, psychologists and mediators can intervene.

The individual then needs social help, paradoxically, to defend his or her relational autonomy.

In other words, the autonomy of the individual from family and the market comes at the price of his or her dependence on the State at the institutions. From this point of view, we may wonder if mediation does not constitute one of these crutches which allows the individuals qualified as sovereigns of post-modernity to learn the autonomy they claim but that they do not necessarily

34 U. Beck, *Risk Society: Towards a New Modernity*. London, Sage, 1992.

35 A. Ehrenberg, La fatigue d'être soi. Dépression et société, Paris, Odile Jacob, 1998.

36 J. Urry, *Sociologie des mobilités*, Paris, Armand Colin, 2005.

have the capacity to fully take responsibility for. Mediation could also represent a transitional space to shift the passive mechanisms of the welfare state to those of an 'active social state' in which institutional protections are still available for those who provide proof of commitment.

13 The Legal and Judicial Regulation Crisis

I have already mentioned the criticism expressed by the *critical legal studies* movement that contest a legal rationality centred on the production of general and impersonal norms.

Incapable of taking into account the complexity of social relationships and emotional and human stakes of certain situations, these norms unveil the ideological dimension of a law which hides its true nature by showing itself as the expression of general will.

Many observers have continued pointing this out since then: the legal regulation crisis because of their inability to 'bring order' to the world.

Diverse symptoms can be observed: internationalisation, inflation, ineffectiveness, dissatisfaction.

- The trap of developing an international normativity able to regulate the globalisation of economic exchange and spatial mobility of populations concerns all those whose workplaces and means of expression escape political borders.
- The powerlessness of nation-states in accompanying the social and technical evolution very often leads the latter to put wool over the population's eyes with a plethoric legislative production, which is not very rational, and full of incoherences and contradiction. Because of this, the law, persuaded that no one should misjudge it, becomes an inextricable and incomprehensible group of texts.
- This legislation, often motivated by political tactics, is often marked by ineffectiveness when it is put into practice because of the absence of applicational decrees or budget restrictions. Devoid of their instrumental dimension, these laws rapidly lose their symbolic weight.
- Such a context stirs up the increasing dissatisfaction that the users have regarding the judiciary system and its formal, costly and long procedures (judiciary time seems more and more disconnected from social time). Legal transcendences no longer complete their symbolic task of producing meaning and the instrumental performances are not adapted to individuals' real needs.

However, these diverse failures have not altered citizens' thirst for justice. The judicial system is invested by an increasing number of requests from domains that were unknown to it in the past.

We are witnessing a large demand for justice to regulate the excesses of the political world, to outline medical responsibility, to moralise the business world or sports, domesticate school violence, define sexual morals. This request seems irrational as the fact the institution and its abilities are overloaded is evident.

All this is happening as if law and justice were becoming a 'safe investment'. Thus, the claim to rights and the aspiration to justice would express a need for transcendence when the principle of explaining the world no longer exists.

This massive call to the judiciary institution could be considered as proof of institutional trust; however it is at the same time the essential factor of its crisis, because this is an institution asphyxiated by an intense demand which obliges it to develop management logistics[37] and to privilege quantitative rationalities. The development of short treatment ways favours the resort to guidelines on a civil level, to the sentence grids and guidelines on the penal level, which restrain the share of individualisation within the treatment of cases. The audiences are neither places of individual speech, nor debate spaces. Judicial time is constrained, and the actors' speech confiscated by professionals. Judicial decisions treat disputes without resolving conflict, as show the high rates of return in front of the judge.[38] Even worse, judiciary intervention sometimes worsens conflict and contributes to 'adding fuel to the fire'. In domestic matters, 'when relationships between spouses are conflictual from the start, they often tend to deteriorate during procedures and appear more difficult after the trial'. This observation can be verified, no matter how grave the conflict is.

It would seem that 'the more the conflict is severe, the less the judiciary solution seems adapted to the different parties' situation'.[39] The high repeat offence rates following a penal sentence demonstrate this as well. Lastly, the effectiveness rate of justice decisions stays relatively low and many of them cannot, for various reasons, be enforced.[40]

---

37 C. Vigour et A. Hastings-Marchadier, 'L'économie budgétaire de la justice pénale', J. Danet, *La réponse pénale. Approche empirique et pluridisciplinaire du traitement des délits*, Rennes, Presses Universitaires de Rennes, 2013, pp. 422–494.

38 3 out of 5 divorcees return to see the Matrimonial court judge in M. Juston, 'La médiation dans le contentieux familial: un changement de culture judiciaire', *Gaz.pal.* 2006, 12.

39 P. Noreau, 'La superposition des conflits: limites de l'institution judiciaire comme espace de résolution des conflits', *Droit et société*, nr 40, 1998, pp. 585–612.

40 43 per cent of food pensions are not or very badly paid.

Faced with the limits of the judiciary system, a new approach of conflict regulation developed. A pluralistic vision characterized by an increasing resort to alternative (or amiable) approaches to conflict resolution succeeds as a modern tradition in which the State is considered as the sole producer of a norm fixed both in its form and its contents.

The commission of European communities ensured the promotion of these alternative conflict resolution modes (ADR, or alternative dispute resolution) in 2002 with the distribution of a green book, and most states have now integrated the content of their legislation. The argument is the following: faced with congested courts, the cost of the procedures, the legal issues in transboundary conflicts, it is necessary to develop these ADR s to favour, by means of more flexible, less expensive, quicker and more consensual processes, the citizens' access to law and justice.[41] Naturally, their emergence is not meant to undermine the foundations of legal regulations. Bridges exist between different regulation systems.[42] The alternative modes are still most often practised 'in the law's shadow,'[43] in a sort of porous legality based on contextualised and variable microadjustments. However, it would be naive to consider that they are only complementary with the legal and judicial regulations. In reality, there is a cultural conflict between two conceptions of the management of social conflict, which mobilises new knowledge and new professions. Faced with the traditional conception of the jurists, according to which law is seen as the ultimate way of regulating society, ADR can be seen as a solid objection to the imperial and dominating model[44] of universal and stable law, to which they object the principle of the existence of multiple and interwoven rationalities.

The concern that the European authorities have shown to ensure a satisfactory level of judicial quality and security can be seen in the European Parliament and the council's directive regarding civil and commercial mediations,[45] dated 21 May 2008, showing the organised research for a new regulation mode.

---

41 Commission des communautés européennes, *Livre vert sur les modes alternatifs de résolution des conflits relevant du droit civil et commercial*, COM (2002).

42 F. Ost, M. Van de Kerchove, (under the direction of), *Le jeu: un paradigme pour le droit*, Paris, LGDJ, coll. Droit et société, 1992, E. Le Roy (1999), *Le jeu des lois. Une anthropologie dynamique du droit*, Paris, LGDJ, 1999.

43 C. Harrington, *Shadow Justice. The ideology and institutionalization of alternatives to court*, Westpoint, CT, Greenwood Press, 1985.

44 F. Ost, 'Jupiter, Hercule ou Hermès, trois modèles du juge' in P. Bouretz (under the direction of), *La force du droit. Panorama des débats contemporains*, Paris, Esprit, 1991, pp. 241–272.

45 The European Parliament and the 21rst of May 2008 Council's 2008/52 directive on certain aspects of mediation concerning civil and commercial domains.

The generalisation of contractual clauses, both on a civil and on a commercial level, which make the passage through mediation obligatory before resorting to the judicial authorities, shows the initiative to take a new direction. The ADR should not only 'not be considered as a secondary solution compared to judicial procedures',[46] but would, from now on, become the principal mode of conflict treatment, whereas the judicial system would intervene only as a last resort when all negotiation, conciliation and mediation attempts have failed.

The ethic of mediation illustrates these dynamics perfectly. It represents the shift of a judiciary imaginary world relying on collective values to a democratic imaginary world which gives everyone the possibility to produce law. Conflicts must not be resolved with regards to a transcendent norm (ready-to-wear solution) but by an agreement signed by the stakeholders (made-to-measure solution).

This criticism of the perception of the law as an expression of general will upsets the professional identities of the judicial world. The role of a judge is more and more limited to orienting cases and producing a legal framework. It involves decision-making less and less, the judge only controls the validity of the agreements submitted to him/her and makes them enforceable. This evolution, more evident in civil law than in penal law, does not give the judge a referee function, but rather the role of 'notary of social commitments'.[47]

It illustrates the progressive shift from imposed order to negotiated order.[48] The lawyer's work also becomes transformed because mediation refuses the principle of representation and privileges the direct expression and personal commitment of individuals.

Moreover, the substitution of a consensual logic to a conflictual logic leads to renouncing the dialectical principle of judicial battle to adopt a more pedagogical stance.

This mutation of practices and professional identities explains why jurists did not favourably view the arrival of mediators on a scene over which they previously had a monopoly. The jurists' progressive adaptation to this change, following mediation trainings, and by the development of the concept of *collaborative law,* contributed to the mistrust regarding judicial regulations. Indeed, collaborative law proposes to resolve conflicts (in particular domestic ones) outside of court, by the cooperative work of the opponents and their respective lawyers.

---

46 Ibid.

47 Antoine Garapon (1996) op.cit.

48 Etienne Le Roy, *Le jeu des lois. Une anthropologie dynamique du droit*, Paris, collection Droit et Société, LGDJ, 1999.

The link between imposed and negotiated order

Imposed order is available for all those who wish for their rights or their dignity to be recognised on a public scene, whereas negotiated order is available for those who want to search for a pacific and mutually satisfactory solution in a private setting.

The choice between the two orders depends on the nature of the conflict (anthropological regulation principle, where law intervenes in heterogeneous conflicts, between different protagonists, and negotiated principles prevail in endogenous spheres of conflict, between similar protagonists.)

The choice between the two orders depends on the fate one wishes on the relationship between the protagonists. Negotiated order is more justified when one wishes to preserve this relationship (emotional, contractual, commercial) as judicial competition accentuates antagonisms.

The choice between the two orders depends on how the protagonists evaluate the respective performances of alternate modes of conflict resolution and of judicial intervention, in terms of cost, speed, consideration of 'judicial unpredictability'.

14 The Dynamics of Mediation's Development

The history of mediation details the difficult emergence of social practices based on values and ideals confronted by overt hostility mainly from jurists or political and trade-union movements. Mediation was then impacted by slow, overly bureaucratic judicial engineering and the necessity of adapting to an increasingly unregulated globalised world.

Thus, the development of mediation depends on the moving power dynamics between three idealistic, pragmatic and critical movements. The logic behind these movements either end up colliding or combining.

However, the way the practices have spread also ensues from the internal evolutions of the field of mediation. This is how and why we can distinguish three processes of fragmentation, institutionalisation and commercialisation, and the modalities of these processes depend, for the most part, on the mediators themselves.

TABLE 2.3 Three visions of mediation

Idealistic	Pragmatic	Critical
– Spread of peace culture – Restoration of communication – Work on otherness – Actors' accountability – Improvement of the individuals' skills – Promotion of cooperative logic – Rise of direct democracy	– Speedy and economical process – Discretion of negotiations – Immediate efficiency of decisions – Avoidance of judicial unpredictability – Compensation of legal voids – Reduction of judiciary flux – Preservation of social and economic relationships	– Erosion of the State's legitimacy – Neoliberal deregulation of social relations – Threats on the weakest individuals' rights – Individualisation of conflicts – obscuring political relations of domination – Reproduction of power inequalities

15 Fragmentation

All the mediation initiatives that developed in the 1980s appear splintered, without any real relationship between them or overall strategy. This empirical splintering is doubled by a conceptual splintering, each one based on a specific theoretical corpus.

This means that we are not observing the construction of one field of mediation, in the broad sense of a coherent set of practices, speeches, actors or institutions in objective interaction around the same activity and exercising a control over its limits and content. On the contrary, a fragmentation in myriad small fields or sectorial references can be observed. Each fragment obeys its own logic and to its political, institutional, economic and social stakes which present themselves in different forms.

There is a great divide in the work of mediation. Few mediators are adapted to all terrains of mediation, or have a panoramic vision of the stakes of all mediation practices. On the contrary, a pronounced specialisation can be noticed, although the general principles of mediations are generally the same. Each type of activity, in all countries, has a tendency to generate its own national authority. This is especially the case for domestic or corporate relations that have their own associations, publications, and conferences. I have chosen these examples because they reflect a profound cultural disconnect between the mediators involved in social and human problems and mediators implicated in the production and organisation world. Those who have developed a hybrid specialty, family mediation in the corporate world, for example, are rare. Some fields of mediation totally ignore each other and are more defined by the field in which they intervene than by their method of intervention.

The components of the activity of mediation are similar to that of the Mexican army. If it is difficult (even with several attempts) to organise authorities that federate all mediators, it is notably because many of them also work in other fields. Mediators in the corporate world are often consultants, referees, negotiators, coaches, trainers. Family mediators can also be psychologists, couple counsellors, lawyers, social workers. This professional versatility, however, poses recognition problems, halts the construction of a professional identity, and adds to the feeling of the profession being scattered. If we add to this the fact that the fields of practice are still largely helped by the activist actions of volunteers, as is the case in communal and citizen mediation, the landscape of mediation does seem quite muddy.

Theoretical foundations common to all mediation practices do not exist. A few authors have assembled a corpus of knowledge themselves with the heterogeneous set of tools, both conceptual (sociology of the state and of social control, conflict theory, law anthropology and sociology, postmodern philosophy) and process-driven (game theory, interactionist work, experimental psychology, communication theory).

However, most references are methodological and transpose the external contributions to the narrow frame of the mediation process. This literature, almost always sectorial, was written by practitioners and scholars 'interested' in the promotion of their activity that is based on pre-existing theoretical corpuses to make their practices legitimate. Besides, observation has shown that many practitioners are ill-informed about the theoretical resources available.

This ignorance is sometimes due to the brevity of the training courses available (this varies a lot depending on the country and specialty) but can also be due to the fact that the theoretical fields concerned are not foundational to mediation practices, but support them in retrospect.

16 Institutionalisation

The experimental phase is not yet finished when the statement of a progressive and general institutionalisation of mediation practices must be made.[49] This institutionalisation is sometimes autonomous when the slightly disorganised practices become more and more organised and adopt stable action modalities, but can also become dependent when the institutions provoke the creation of mediation practices themselves.

Moreover, these two processes can be combined when the only chance of ensuring long-lasting innovation is to enter the institutional practices' directory.[50]

The methods of action of auto-institutionalisation can be deconstructed into different phases likely to succeed, to overlap and sometimes to invert each other. This type of analysis corresponds particularly to the way family or penal mediation[51] have evolved.

1. Normally, everything starts with the initiative of a handful of people inspired by a collective thought process or foreign experience. They exert themselves to create, by successive approximations, a practice model that tries to reconcile the initial 'utopia' with the surrounding social context. During this trial phase, new ways of being and doing are openly experimented on.
2. The fixation of the rules leads to codifying and normalising procedures at the same time as a ritualisation of the activity. A doctrine, or orthodoxy, is developed by those who exert leadership in this field under construction (pioneer practitioners, scholars, foreign experts). This phase is generally accompanied by the production of public speeches (newspapers, interviews, conferences) or scientific speeches (articles, other published work), which legitimise the practice. The normal rhetoric consists in criticising the previous modes of conflict resolution, to stand out from other professions that practise it and to offer another way to proceed.
3. This phase is usually concomitant with a request for public or private funding, which guarantees the long-lasting quality of the experience and at the same time, gives it an institutional legitimacy which the actors pride themselves on. The public subsidisers are mainly interested in the

49 J. Faget, 'L'institutionnalisation de la médiation: réflexions à partir de l'exemple français', in M. Jaccoud (sous la direction de) Justice réparatrice et médiation pénale. Convergences ou divergences? Paris, L'Harmattan, 2003, pp. 227–242.

50 P. Noreau, 'L'institutionnalisation de la justice réparatrice' in M. Jaccoud (2003) op. cit., pp. 209–226.

51 J. Faget, La médiation. Essai de politique pénale, Toulouse, Erès, 1997.

spread of a 'modern' activity model which is considered reliable, as it has not been much evaluated; and in the control of its evolution.

4. The construction of a strong identity is then necessary, this is done by putting into place a test to gain access to the domain by selection procedures based on the integration of rituals, codes and constituted knowledge. This closing of the domain aims to constitute a sort of subculture built around values, a common vision of the world and techniques. The creation of more and more structured professional organisations and the influence of their leaders on the field's evolution reinforce this strategy.
5. The moment has then come to think about the legalisation of these practices. This legalisation is the successful conclusion of a social interaction between the parliament which votes the laws, the services of the ministers and the technocrats who prepare, depending on their own professional culture, the action of the judiciary, economic and social lobbies, and the media's action, which facilitates the conditions of it being set on the public agenda.
6. The last sequence of the institutionalisation process is the professionalisation of the activity. This last step has the consequence of progressively marginalising the volunteers' involvement, creating a paradoxical tension between the initial rhetoric of democratising conflict regulation, a wish to give its control back to citizens and the internal logic of the field's construction. These last two factors close the field to those who are not initiated to it and organise its professionalisation.

The dependent institutionalisation process differs a little from the previous one as it designates the creation by an existing institution of a mediation service within itself. The best example of this institutionalisation are the multiple administrations that have established their mediation and mediators in the 1990s. The reasons that push an institution to resort to mediation are diverse. These can be the consequence of external doorstep enquiring, like educational mediation, where the decision to put mediation systems into practice is the result of activists' patient strategies of persuasion. It can also be the increase of conflicts between an institution and its increasingly punctilious users, or even the effect of rivalry with other institutions, which motivate innovation. The integration of mediation practices within the institution does not mean that mediation transforms the institution's logic.

This institutionalisation can be considered complete when the programs are brought under state control and generalised throughout the whole territory (for example, penal mediation in France, the mediation offices created by the Norwegian government that can be found throughout the country, the generalisation of educational mediation in Belgium and Finland). It can also be partial, when the programs are part of a local initiative (communal mediation financed by the *Disputacio* and the town councils in Catalunya), or may be funded privately.

17 Merchandising

The role of the market is increasing, even more since the State, faced with the increasing scarcity of public resources, has tended to delegate a part of the activities it used to oversee to the private sector. This externalisation strategy concerns all working sectors and results in the privatisation of public action sometimes seen as an indicator of a neoliberal evolution, even if it adheres more to conjectural needs than to the implementation of a real doctrine. The vast majority of the mediation authorities belong to the private sector, whether they are explicitly commercial or linked to the community, and mediation practices become from then on a place of rivalry and competition for the acquisition of this new market.

The idea that mediation is being influenced by marketing is convincing upon seeing mediation offices on websites, or in stands found in global mediation offices where movies, interactive tools, books, posters, modes of action, and training courses are also sold.

This competition has the objective of acquiring financial but also symbolic resources. The fields of mediation in the economic and financial domains are the most profitable, those of international conflicts the most prestigious, those in the family field probably the most gratifying. We are thus witnessing the progressive stratification of the mediation professions around the combination of these two stakes, following the 'homology effect' described by Pierre Bourdieu, depending on the social position of the 'clients'. The prestige of a mediation practice, like all other professions, would indeed depend on the place the users have in the social hierarchy. It can also depend on the quality (in terms of program, teachers' qualification, learning techniques and work on oneself), of the training courses followed, the existence of diplomas and of the requirement levels to obtain them. From this point of view, the qualifications needed for domestic mediation (particularly in France, where a selective training lasting 605 hours, or two years, enables one to start working as a professional mediator) and for political and financial mediations (in particular in some universities or American business schools) seem, for the moment, to distinguish themselves from the lot.

Moreover, the training requirements are continually increasing, which opens a market for teaching. This market includes expert scholars and practitioners, who sell their methods and knowledge, both locally, or as it is the case for some American celebrities, all around the world.

The competitive logic that is put into place differs depending on whether the field is new or marked out by professions that have the monopoly over conflicts or the concerned institution. The terms of this rivalry change from one country to another. In Germany, a court decided that alternative dispute resolutions represent a legal service, and that they are considered a legal service linked to the monopoly that lawyers have. However, the latter are excluded in France, like all legal professions, from the practice of penal mediation, which reduces the competition to social actors. When the market stays open, the conflict between lawyer practices and specialised mediators can be intense. This is the case in civil and family mediation, where the jurists, worried about losing the monopoly they have over the market of divorce and separation between individuals, try to control mediation by developing the idea that one must be a jurist in order to properly understand the judicial and material stakes behind conflicts.

However, mediators, who believe that interpersonal skills are most important in mediation, and that these skills are dependent on 'ordinary practical knowledge and is not established as an esoteric professional knowledge',[52] disqualify jurists, who are in their view blind to the psychological and social stakes of the situations they are dealing with.

52 Philip Milburn, La médiation: expériences et compétences, Paris, La Découverte, 2002.

PART 2

The Normative Construction of Mediation

Over the years, because of its progressive organisation and its practices, the world of mediation has defined an orthodoxy for itself. It now refers itself to a set of values, of ethical principles, but also of deontological rules that allow it to stand out from previous political, judiciary of social practices, and to affirm the specificity of the role of the mediator compared to neighbouring professions (Chapter 3). If these 'fundamentals' of mediation are surprisingly similar regardless of the field of application, there is however a certain heterogeneity of practice models, which reveals the diversity of the actors in mediation, as well as their disciplinary and professional origins (Chapter 4). This variety can be seen inside one field of activity, meaning that instead of referring to the field as a singular entity as one generally does, it would be more realistic to use the plural and talk of political mediations, domestic mediations, penal mediations, and so on.

 | DOI:10.1163/9789004734067_006

CHAPTER 3

The Ethical and Deontological Framework of Mediation

The question of the ethical and deontological principles of mediation is crucial on several accounts. Firstly, it allows the analyst to distinguish mediation from the other types of conflict regulation and to identify the philosophical and political stakes that are specific to it. Secondly, it allows mediators to distinguish themselves from all the other 'peacemakers', to show the specificity and thus the utility of their action. Most of all, it means mediators can unite around a certain number of values, that, when shared, create the conditions for the construction of an entity, and down the line, of a professional structure.

Talking about ethics means not only referring to a world of ideas, but also to contingent uses that confer an identity to those who claim to follow these ideas. All this to say that the construction of ethical principles did not happen 'out of the blue'. They do not constitute a revealed truth, but rather a conjectural conclusion reached by the actors that fight for their vision of the world and the practice they promote to prevail. Thus, the 'doctrine' of mediation has been elaborated by scholars and practitioners, who are mostly white and Protestant, and living in rich Anglophone countries where the State is relatively weak and the judicial model is that of the common law.

Yet, this profile, as well as the ideological substratum that is associated with it, are most often obscured by those who give mediation training courses, and these trainers often present the ethics of mediation as a given.

The reason behind the 'mystery of the origins' comes from the fact that the majority of these trainers share the characteristics described above, which inhibits their effort of reflexivity.

The orthodoxy of mediation is transmitted by the publication of books, the spread of 'good practices', and the organisation of conferences that celebrate the fidelity to common principles and reinforce the sense of belonging to the epistemic community of mediators. It is also transmitted by the organisation of training courses all around the world where practice model 'kits' are distributed to the trainees, by the creation of networks and university or professional diplomas, and lastly by putting into practice selection procedures based on knowledge and mastery of the fundamentals.

 | DOI:10.1163/9789004734067_007

It is not uncommon to observe in those rituals a dilution of deontological ethical rules. The convictions and the principles of the mediator are not necessarily salient. The principles spread through scripts or practice guidelines that are only rarely backed up by scientific evidence. Thus, the 'ideology of mediation' is invisible, the philosophical and political values that feed it disappear behind the engineering of conflict resolution.

Even though deontology is only the toolbox of ethics, it often serves as a creed. The orthodoxy of mediation is more combined with a practical mode than a theoretical one, even though it essentially relies on convictions and beliefs.

In order to properly shed light on this process of ideological obscuration, I shall start with a trip to the philosophical and political regions of mediation. Then, I will present the methodological 'fundamentals' that stem from it. These can be found in specialised literature, their codes developed in specialised national or international sectors.

1 The Ethical Framework

Mediation is not just a technique. It also includes a cultural vision of human beings and a social and political transformation project. It conveys philosophical ideals which value a theoretical representation of mankind as free and conscious. However, mediation's discourse is also ideological as it expresses a vision of human and social relations that concretely determine a series of individual and collective behaviours.

2 The Philosophical Background

Mediation's discourse, far from expressing a universal vision of the human being, consecrates a Western perspective relying on the triple ethic of liberty, equality and fraternity.[1] These words reveal the impact of Christian and humanist[2] values in their construction. This point has been mentioned enough in the historical chapter, and it is not necessary to dwell on it any longer.

1 Isabelle Jues, 'Éthique et déontologie du médiateur familial', *Empan*, nr 72, pp. 40–44.

2 Christian values are often associated with humanist values, whereas they are in reality antagonistic from a historical perspective, as the humanist doctrine consisted in freeing mankind from the grip of any form of belief and theology.

2.1 *The Ethics of Freedom*

To consider the individual as the toy of multiple determinisms would mean to diminish its responsibility and its role in the acts it commits and the commitments it makes. In this sense, mediation does not distinguish itself from legal constructs, which affirm the intangible principle of the autonomy and free will of the subjects of the law. This is the heart of humanist values advocated by Enlightenment philosophers, who argue that man is the supreme value, and must be protected from all forms of political, religious and economic subjugation. Mediation uplifts the right of individuals to make choices, to speak words that are one's own.

This basic premise of people's abilities is at the heart of a process which considers, deliberately optimistically, that every human being can at any moment progress and change, improve their listening, communication and comprehension skills. This ability is sometimes understood individually, and other times collectively. In English, the word *empowerment* is often used to qualify the process of gaining back control over one's life, of developing one's ability to progress, get organised, to defend one's rights, to become emancipated in an alienating situation.

However, the principle of individual empowerment is complicated in societies in which the construction of identity operates on an ethnical or collective basis, and in which the individual is defined by who or what they belong to (son of, member of a certain tribe or ethnicity), and not by himself/herself alone, or by his/her personal worth.

2.2 *The Ethics of Equality*

Mediation cultivates the belief that individuals, independent from their social, cultural and psychological characteristics, can communicate with each other provided that they are allowed to do so. It leans on an egalitarian philosophy. The conception of horizontal relations, in which everyone is considered equal in essence and in speech, is part of the universalist republican vision. This perspective is linked to democratic modes of social organisation, which is however, very different from how stratified societies work, in which belonging to a socio-professional category, or even more to castes or ethnicities, organises society in an inegalitarian way. It is difficult to see how mediation could be put into place through social hierarchies that structure political power relations.

2.3 *The Ethics of Social Harmony*

There is, in the ideology of mediation, an irenic way of imagining the world. By exalting the myth of the encounter with the 'other', of exchange and dialogue, mediation draws a relatively harmonious picture of human relations. It obliges the narcissistic individuals of our capitalist paradise to be less self-centred and become more open to others' perspectives, suffering, and to the divergences in their perspectives. This openness does not mean giving one's convictions or interests up, but rather taking into consideration the diverse ways in which one can see conflict. The underlying idea is always to restore greater well-being between States, groups or citizens, to find more respectful ways of living together. The differences that divide these groups or entities then cease to be sources of violence, instead becoming the vector of tolerance.

3 The Ideological Background

As seen before, mediation is part of the political project of postmodern society in which the 'subject individual' is placed at the heart of social regulation. This project can be transformed in three different ways: as a tool amongst others to promote participative democracy, at the service of new recognition policies, or by valuing the advent of relational individualism.

3.1 *The Promotion of Participative Democracy*

The rise of mediation is has not occurred without controversy, when it amounts to the construction of a political universe which controls electoral politics, when it silences citizens between two elections, and when those elected grant themselves the monopoly over public speaking about subjects that concern people's lives. It is important to remember that the ideal of participative democracy was foundational for the pioneer experiment of the San Francisco community boards.

The ethic of mediation defends the principle of direct participation and of giving responsibility to everyone in the resolution of their own conflicts.

Thus, it condemns the principle of delegation (it is necessary to represent oneself) to a lawyer or any other representative, and in doing this, affirms the necessity of a direct democracy in search of a new form of political and social organisation. This idea is fully expressed in the development of community, social or citizen mediations. These rely on volunteer mediators to regulate everyday life conflicts outside of institutions, and aims to reinforce the empowerment of populations and to develop communities' internal solidarity.

However, the concrete conditions of a democratic culture of participation remain to be created. This is what consensus conferences and dialogue tables try to create when they attempt to establish, with procedures open to debate, controversy, and to the representation of all interests present.[3] The deontological rules of mediation strive to put into practice a communicational rationality which gives everyone the possibility of expressing oneself, but in return demands the other to speak, thus creating a public space which relies on an ethic of discussion.[4]

3.2 *The Rise of Recognition Policies*

Mediation is at the heart of a political dynamic when it poses the principle that self-realisation heavily depends on a process of mutual recognition. The works of Honneth distinguish three spheres of recognition.[5] The first is the love sphere, that of emotional ties uniting a person to another or a small group, in which the solidarity and reciprocity allow the individual to be more confident, and to participate assertively in public life. The second is the legal-political sphere: an individual recognised as a subject having rights and duties can interpret his/her acts as a manifestation of autonomy. The third sphere, that of social esteem, is essential to the realisation of one's self-worth. If one of these three forms of recognition is lacking, the offence, whether it be physical, legal or moral, will be seen by the individuals as a threat to their identity.

Mediation, no matter its field of activity, works on this triple dimension of recognition. Of course, the emotional dimension is more present in domestic mediation, the legal dimension more present in political, legal or company mediation, the social aspect of recognition more present in community or environmental mediation. However, all fields of mediation are concerned with all three, as it is always a case of asserting the relational nature of individuals' construction of identity. For Taylor, this need for recognition is particularly characteristic of our contemporary societies. It expresses itself by the increase of racial, ethnic, sexual and cultural claims, but is also present at the level of the individual. The perception people have of themselves depends, at least partially, of what the others reflect on them. Their multifaceted need to be heard, listened to, and respected proclaims it, as 'recognition is not only a polite attitude one has towards people: it is a vital need'.[6]

The ethic of mediation seems precisely to open this space to listen and appreciate differences, where one accesses self-knowledge by the detour of

---

3 M. Callon, P. Lascoumes, Y. Barthe, *Agir dans un monde incertain. Essai sur la démocratie technique*, Paris, Le Seuil, 2001.

4 J. Habermas, *Theory of communicative action*, Boston, Beacon Press, 1981.

5 A. Honneth, *The struggle for recognition*, Polity Press, 1995.

6 C. Taylor, *Multiculturalisme. Différence et démocratie*, Paris, Flammarion, 1994.

realising the other's singularity. It can help to prevent behaviours that are 'insulting … because they discredit people's ability to develop a positive inter-comprehension of themselves, understanding which is acquired via intersubjectivity'.[7] As mentioned before, the perception people have of themselves depends on the perception reflected by others, and mediators understood this when they catalysed the Nouméa agreements in New-Caledonia in 1998. The final initial chart states in Article 3 that 'the moment has come to recognise the shadows of the colonial period, even if it was not devoid of light'. This wording helped to pave a path of mutual recognition between the Kanaks, who endured the humiliation, colonisation and suffering from the colonisers, the Caldoches, who, often exiled by force from France, participated in the development of a territory to which they progressively and fully identified. The role of mediation is precisely to organise the work that allows the confrontation between the sovereign 'I' and the other and its differences which resists it, and in the end, determines its existence.

3.3 *The Rise of Relational Individualism*

The big narratives of modernity are organised around central ideas of progress, freedom and emancipation.[8] Starting in the 1970s, instead of a narrative of emancipation, the notion of the free, responsible, autonomous individual[9] emerges and becomes more important. This individual only refers to himself or herself, and becomes the measure of all things. Placing the individual at the centre of social regulation is the very substance of the postmodern individualist project.

This individualism, however, is not without risk. It is generally associated with the dictatorship of the market, savage liberalism, and inequality. It is considered a factor of selfishness and indifference, and it is true that the rise of a society of individuals puts into risk the production of a common world. The culture of 'narcissism' results in an incapacity to communicate and the cult of the self proves to be destructive on many accounts.

This emancipation does pose numerous problems: an existence in which choices are no longer dictated from the exterior, in which the landmarks come above all from ourselves and in which the requirement of personal success is permanent, can become extremely trying. Thus, the phenomenal increase in the demand for therapy or the consummation of psychotropic drugs may be a response to the 'tiredness of being oneself' and shows the necessity for sup-

---

7 Honneth (1995) op. cit.

8 J.F. Lyotard, *La condition postmoderne*, Paris, Éditions de Minuit, 1978.

9 D. Martucelli, *Grammaires de l'individu*, Paris, Gallimard, 2002.

port in order to confront the demands of one's freedom.[10] Dubet and Martucelli in particular insist on the hazards linked to this experience lived in contemporary society.[11]

The individual, supposed sovereign, responsible and autonomous, is confronted by permanent challenges, given the fact he or she can now only count on himself/herself. The difficulties of the domestic model becoming increasingly precarious especially highlight this paradox.

'Resorting to divorce is the result of an evolution of customs which has made the individual and the demand for individual success a priority, and put the old domestic institution in the background. It is a form of accomplishment of one's emancipation project. However, it is more and more perceived as an ordeal which radically and profoundly questions an individual's identity. On one hand, divorce does not come without suffering, and on the other hand, the individual alone is responsible for the failure of his or her self-accomplishment project'.[12] It is precisely here that mediation has its place, ordering those who have taken the responsibility to form a couple to assume the task of undoing it. Except that 'the divorcees… do not correspond, momentarily anyways, to the ideal of the autonomous and sovereign individual'. For an individual to implement his or her freedom, he/she must be able to do so. Society then has the paradoxical need to help these 'incapable' individuals to become autonomous, and invents support systems that help to re-establish this autonomy that has faded away. From this point of view, we can consider mediation to be a transitory but paradoxical equipment that transforms dependent individuals into responsible ones. The writings of family mediators, who use the phrases 'the empowerment of people', 'the accompaniment of parents in the search for their own solution', or even 'empowering actors by making them co-constructors of the action', clearly express the objective, but also the difficulty 'of this factory of responsibility'.[13]

Even if it is not exempt from risks, and it meets obstacles, the individualist project 'brings a lot of hope'.[14] It is associated with the progression of human rights defence which places the individual at the heart of the social project. Without individualist philosophy, women would not have been able to emancipate themselves, have control over their bodies, and minorities would not be able to express themselves. Naturally, this creative individualism is not spon-

---

10 A. Ehrenberg, *La fatigue d'être soi. Dépression et société*, Paris, Odile Jacob, 1998.

11 F. Dubet, D. Martucelli, *Dans quelle société vivons-nous?* Paris, Seuil, 1998.

12 A. Ducousso Lacaze, 'La médiation familiale. Le mythe de l'individu et les liens familiaux', *Dialogue*, 2006, nr 170, pp. 17–30.

13 Ibid.

14 F. De Singly, *L'individualisme est un humanisme*, Paris, Editions de l'Aube, 2005.

taneous, it is not the result of political providence, but is rather the conclusion of a conquest. In this perspective, we may consider mediation to be a tool gained from this battle and used for the re-creation of social links: a painful tool that leads to a demanding work in which the individual is no longer defined by institutions of the authorities, but instead is defined by himself or herself, during a process of interpersonal exchange and recognition. This idea surprisingly echoes the works of Paul Ricœur in its more messianic aspects.[15] Thus, when he writes 'the relationship between self and self passes through the other' and 'I cannot esteem myself without esteeming others like I do myself', he introduces this core idea of otherness that is at the heart of mediation practices. With its supportive methods, it helps and allows individuals to shift from a narcissistic individualism to a relational individualism, which enables us to live in harmony with one another, instead of living next to each other.

4 The Deontological 'Fundamentals' of Mediation

These philosophical values, or ideological perspective, even if they are sometimes imperceptible, or in any case unspoken, are at the heart of mediation's approach. They permeate the content of all the texts that organise it being put into practice. The recommendations of the Council of Europe on family mediation (R 1998.1), on penal mediation (R 1999.19), on the alternative modes of disputes resolutions between administrative authorities and private persons (R 2001.9), on civil mediation (2002.10), and the code of European conduct for mediators written in 2004, and the directive of the European Parliament and the Council of the 21st of May 2008 on certain aspects of civil and commercial mediation (2008/52/EC), all refer to it explicitly.

We have feared that the instrumental concern of mediation's promotion, and the wish to surround it with judicial guarantees for users, might trample on the initial important principles. But this does not seem to be the case. The permanent work group of the European Commission for the Efficiency of Justice (CEPEJ), created in 2006, which is devoted to facilitating the implementation of the Committee of Ministers of the Council of Europe's recommendations to the State members of the Council of Europe, is inspired by it. I will succinctly present the crucial points of this abundant production, namely the role of the third party and its specific characteristics, the process of mediation based on meeting face-to-face and on direct exchange between the partici-

15 P. Ricoeur, *Soi-même comme un autre*, Paris, Seuil, 1990.

pants and lastly, a flexible yet firm legal framework which facilitates exchange and communication in a secure context.

4.1 *Characteristics of the Third-Party Posture*

Whereas numerous services rely on a dual relationship (social workers, doctors, lawyers, psychologists) the first constituent element of mediation is the presence of a third party. This third party, qualified as 'reflexive'[16] is based not on universal norms and transcendent rules, but on contextualised norms. It is not a referee or a judge but is also not an educator, couples counsellor, therapist or legal advisor. It occupies a singular place owed to the legitimacy given to it by the actors, and constructed by the respect of the following principles.

4.1.1 Competence

If all texts refer to the third party's competence, the content of the latter is not precisely elaborated on. This training is specific to mediation and a constant recycling on theoretical and practical levels. The institutionalisation process of most practices has led to certain demands, which is why in France, one must have a diploma in domestic mediation (605 hours of theoretical and practical training over two years of training in total) in order to be able to practise family mediation. This is probably the highest requirement level in the world in this domain. Generally speaking, the development of the training market disqualifies all those that cannot justify paying for a diploma or training certificate. It would be absurd to think that the graduates who have followed sometimes expensive training courses would have no asset or predisposition in their job search. Professionalisation progressively does its work and with it, so does its logic of selection, even though in certain sectors, such as community or citizen mediation, the call for volunteers is still privileged.

The debate on competence always joins the debate on legitimacy. Max Weber gave three faces to legitimacy: tradition (the strength of habits and precedent), charisma (personal values considered extraordinary), rational legal legitimacy (judicial and institutional status of function, rationality of one's acts and respect for procedures).[17]

Whatever it may be, legitimacy is not founded on coercion but on the free consent of the subjects. It always has its roots in a belief system, whether they be founded on objective or supposed skills. To facilitate the organisation of

---

16 E. Volkrick, 'Intervenir en tiers aujourd'hui'. *Négociations*, 2007/1, pp. 75–88.
17 M. Weber, *Economie et société*, Paris, Plon, 1971 (1921).

social ties, those who have a protected title (doctor, lawyer, judge) are in principle supposed competent.

The appreciation of this competence can then vary during the interaction between the professional and the client. However, the social collapse of authority figures and the deconstruction of the legitimising systems in postmodern societies make these legitimacy regimes fragile. From now on, actors must conquer their legitimacy, which in the past, belonged to them without question. For example, a teacher's legitimacy is not dependent on succeeding on an exam but is 'won' during day-to-day pedagogical exchanges with students. Mediators cannot pride themselves on having a traditional or charismatic legitimacy, as the field is recent. One might even say that a mediator's professionalisation comes from the overregulation of customary practices and from the disqualification of the mediative functions that were previously filled by priests, doctors, the teacher or the village's elders. Thus, the mediator's legitimacy is rational and technical if they have a protected title (this is the case of the family mediator in France), if he/she is authorised by the authorities (judiciary mediation) or authorised by professional organisations that name them (company mediators). Mediators who do not fall into these cases will have to prove the relevance of their action not only to their users but also most importantly to their prescribers who allow them to practise as mediators. Here, legitimacy escapes the relation between practitioner and user and takes on a social dimension. For mediators, it is not only a case of guaranteeing the efficiency of their actions or their appropriateness to fulfil a collective need, but also of building a globally positive image of mediation in society or in a particular domain in order to gain the social recognition of the practice.

Then comes the question of knowing if the necessity of a skill must be interpreted in a general or specific way. On the basis that the 'posture' of the mediation is the same no matter which domain a mediator intervenes in, I tend to think that a generalised training along with minimal knowledge of particular institutional or social contexts is enough for someone to practise mediation in all domains. But this opinion is far from unanimous and collides with the commercial or identity-based interests of certain sectors. The latter insist on the absolute necessity of having a profound knowledge of the culture and customs of each field. Many jurists, for example, believe mediators need to have legal qualifications. This affirmation probably stems from a confusion between negotiation and mediation, as I can confidently say that my law PhD has never helped me in the slightest to help people communicate. The European group of magistrates for mediation seems to agree, as it stipulates that legal training has always been insufficient for mediation. Mediators are first and foremost human relations professionals and must be imperatively trained in mediation techniques, and in particular in those that favour communication and help re-establish dialogue.[18]

4.1.2 Impartiality and Neutrality

The mediator is forbidden to take sides; this does not distinguish it from other third parties such as judges, as both must treat the participants equitably. However, the mediator's role is more original because it does not involve trying to know who is right and wrong. The mediator must, in a way, 'mourn the truth'. This means the mediator must renounce any inquisitive desire of knowing what 'really happened'.

The mediator's ability to be indifferent about potentially contradictory discourses from the parties involved depends on the practice model that is adopted. Logically, as the etymology of the term mediation suggests and recommends, the mediator must be 'in the middle'. This requirement makes problematic the position of a mediator paid by an institution to regulate the difficult relations it maintains with its users. It weakens, for example, the legitimacy of the mediators whose principal preoccupation is to integrate foreigners in their host country or society, to protect victims of offence, and to support populations in need. It is indeed complex to reconcile a social commitment at the service of the oppressed, or people in suffering, with the ethic of mediation.

The imperative of impartiality, which constitutes the very foundation of the activity of mediation, is not easily reconciled with an activist ideal, except if we consider this ideal as being global, like for example the spread of an ideal of peace and mutual understanding between mankind. All identification processes (to the employee rather than the employer, the citizen rather than the elected, to women rather than men, young rather than old, weak rather than strong, to black rather than white, to the victim rather than the perpetrator, to the atheist rather than the religious, the sympathetic rather than the cynical, the cooperative rather than the rebel) are traps for the mediator's impartiality. Being aware of this difficulty can lead the mediator adopting a distant attitude, to assert he/she is 'neither on one side nor the other'. The mediator's mediation practice then risks being dehumanised and thus becoming counterproductive. To avoid this risk, some mediators prefer to talk about 'multi-partiality' or 'co-partiality', in order to signify that they are 'on both sides'.[19] In this case, the mediator becomes closer to the opponents instead of distancing himself/herself from them, to lead a more fruitful search for trust

18 Court of cassation report, special issue on legal mediation.

19 A. Pekar Lempereur, J. Salzer, A. Colson, *Méthode de médiation,* Paris, Dunod, 2008.

within a warm and balanced relationship. This empathetic climate would then lead to sincere exchanges and would increase the chances of a respectful and constructive dialogue between the participants. I am inclined to think that the talent needed to construct such an atmosphere does depend on favouring one word (multi-partiality) over another (impartial).

Many texts confuse impartiality and neutrality. It is true that the meaning of both words can overlap. When the mediator's neutrality is deemed a myth, and inaccessible, the word 'impartiality' is often preferred to neutrality. However, some specialists claim its use. Being neutral does not express, to go back to Roland Barthes' philosophy,[20] an idea of dullness, blandness and weakness; on the contrary, it expresses a strong and active value. Pekar Lempereur, Salzer and Colson introduce an interesting distinction here. Whereas impartiality qualifies the perception people have of the mediator's attitude, neutrality would be the situation experienced by the mediator (distance from his/her subjectivity, awareness of his/her projections, and of the existing resonances between the mediation situation and his/her personal situation or lived experiences).[21]

4.1.3 Independence

This requirement must be understood from both a personal and institutional perspective.

- The European Code of Good Conduct controls the possible conflicts of interests that the mediator could encounter. Thus, the mediator must systematically inform the opponents in this case of him/her having a personal relationship with one of them, if he/she has an interest, whether it be financial or personal, direct or indirect, in the way the mediation is resolved, if the mediator has previously worked with one of the participants (as can be the case with a lawyer on previous trials). However, these incompatibilities are not total. The mediator is obliged to reveal these conflicts of interest to the participants. If this is respected, nothing forbids the latter to maintain their relationship with the mediator.
- The mediator must resist all pressures he/she might face from external actors and in particular from the institutions that have appointed him/her to organise mediations and who would want to subject the mediation practice to internal imperatives.
- This independence must also be understood as financial. The professionalisation must not lead mediators, because of a conquest or preservation of a

20 R. Barthes, *Le Neutre. Notes de cours au collège de France, 1977–1980*, Paris, Seuil, 2002.

21 Pekar Lempereur et al. (2008), op.cit.

'market', to renounce their ethic, or to mold their practices on purely economic rationalities. The European texts specify they must ensure the promotion of their activity in a professional, honest and dignified manner.

The most effective defence against all forms of pressure and instrumentation remains the construction of a strong professional (or cultural for volunteers) identity of mediator.

This supposes the acquisition and the maintenance of a profound culture of mediation via following training courses, analysing practises and participating in the profession's collective life.

4.1.4 The Absence of Decision-Making Power

The mediator is neither a judge nor a referee, he/she does not have to say who is wrong or right. His/her mission is simply to establish the conditions for communication between the participants. The mediator is in a way the catalyst and the methodological guarantor of a process that does not belong to him/her but is fully at the disposal of the people directly involved in the conflict. Because of this, the mediator does not have to force them into the mediation process and does not have any prerogative to influence the content of the agreement they might eventually sign. Naturally, the question of the absence of power is the subject of many doctrinal debates and separates those who opt for a structuring conception of mediation from those who prefer a non-directive approach that they consider more empowering. The 'power of powerlessness', claimed by a large movement, is opposed to those who, in the name of short-term efficiency, open the possibility for one manipulative manoeuvre alone to favour the signing of an agreement. Whereas some forbid themselves to induce the elaboration of a solution, authors allow themselves to make suggestions. It all depends on the objective one assigns to mediation.

The debate is in fact complex, because if power can take on the obvious forms of threats, brute force, and constraint, it can also be built during an empathetic process, developing the relationship and trust between the actors. One must then speak of legitimacy to designate the competence that the participants grant the mediator. The participants assign such qualities to the mediator that they confer a sort of moral power which conditions their words and acts. Let's not forget that legitimacy depends above all else on belief, which down the line, can lead to power being seen as acceptable, necessary and even desirable in the eyes of those subjected to it. Of course, the philosophy of mediation commends the opposite, but the road to hell is sometimes paved with good intentions. It is fathomable that a gentle and empathetic authority could become legitimate and lead people to renounce it.

Mediators do not only have the power to influence; they also have tangible prerogatives. They have the power to interrupt the mediation in certain cases, for example when the mediator believes the process no longer has any chance to amount to a solution or when the agreement contemplated by the opponents appears 'illegal or unenforceable'.

Such a position is surrounded by controversy given the fact it contravenes mediation's ethic of autonomy and responsibility. Those who, among the readers, have empirical knowledge of mediation can easily understand the doubts or even the aversions mediators can have towards some agreements that can seem unjust, dangerous or impracticable.

However, before becoming a censor, I advise my students to:

- stimulate people's creativity by searching all the possible solutions,
- draw on a paper board a list of the pros and cons of all the imaginable solutions,
- demand a moment of reflection before any commitment, during which it is recommended that the opponents seek advice from any competent person,
- implement the agreement in an experimental and provisional way and arrange a meeting to assess its application.

It is infinitely rare, when the mediator uses one or more of these methods, that he/she needs to adopt an authoritarian attitude.

4.2 *The Characteristics of the Process*

The second constituent element of mediation is the face-to-face meeting of the people directly involved in the conflict, as it is direct communication between the participants that constitutes the objective of the process and the key to its accomplishment. This principle distinguishes the mediator from a simple intermediary, *go-between* or negotiator, that would go from one person to the other to adjust the different perspectives. This position relies on the belief that the physical meeting of the participants holds specific virtues that favour working on otherness, meaning first discovering and then progressively accepting difference (which does not mean sharing the other's point of view).

4.2.1 The Mediation Process Is Communicative

It is based on dialogue between the opponents. Only a face-to-face meeting, with its share of fear and emotions, properly allows participants to work on their differences. Thus, the processes in which the mediator is a messenger between opponents are qualified as assisted negotiations rather than mediations. However, for a few years now, online mediations have started to develop, in particular to help with material conflicts (consumption, insurance) in which the affective stakes are low or non-existent, or to help with conflicts in which the actors live far away from each other, and travelling for the mediation process would be too costly (international family mediation). If it is difficult to qualify mediation as the processes during which the communication channel systematically goes through the mediator, we will probably have to accept the idea of organising mediation practices via video conferences, even if it poses a few technical problems and demands great methodological prudence.

4.2.2 The Mediation Process Is Cooperative

Mediation must allow the participants to work together in search of a mutually satisfactory solution. The objective is to shift out of a competitive mode of conflict treatment, a zero-sum game in which each member tries to assert their rights or their claims to the detriment of the other, and move to a win-win situation. In order to do this, the exchange must have a few basic rules allowing mutual respect. This supposes that the mediator knows how to create an empathetic climate in an adapted environment, to stimulate the expression of people and ensure relative balance in speech time.

Along with this, the exchange also needs to be centred around some basic ground rules, such as the prohibition of physical or verbal violence (insults, vehement ways of talking, recurring disqualifications, derision, scathing humour, physical attitudes indicating contempt or defiance), or interruption of the other speaker.

4.2.3 The Process of Mediation Is Directly Participative

The opponents must be personally implicated during the whole process and actively participate in the search for a solution. Thus, this principle excludes the system of representation via a lawyer or any other representative. The aim is to move away from a logic of assistance, and instead move towards the principle of responsibility, and to ensure that the people are truly actors in the resolution of their conflict resolution, and not passive spectators of a scenario which they did not write.

4.3 *The Process's Legal Background*

The legal principles that organise the process of mediation are explicit in all the national and international texts. Faced with the fear and resistance of the judiciary environment, I myself carried out a legal framework for mediation practices[22] in due time. Because the dangers of mediation are not the fantasies

---

22 J. Faget, 'La juridicisation de la médiation', *Les modes alternatifs de règlement des litiges: les voies nouvelles d'une autre justice*, La Documentation française, Mission de recherche Droit et Justice, 2003, pp. 75–88.

of grumpy jurists, the flexibility of mediation sometimes threatens individual and collective rights. The desertion of the ritual public forms of conflict regulation, to the profit of a multitude of private stakeholders, is denounced as a potential threat to freedom. The privatisation of conflicts would impede their political dimension being taken into account and would be a way to cover up their existence.[23] It would notably be harmful to the interests of the more vulnerable. This risk is particularly denounced by movements such as the defence of women's rights, who are opposed to the use of mediation in cases of sexual violence. It would be a way of denying the seriousness of the social problem and reinforcing inequalities between men and women. The feminist political theory argues that 'deliberation (here, one must think of mediation) can be a mask for domination'.[24] The social fight against domestic oppression and more generally against injustice must take place on the public scene that justice represents.[25] The mediation space must not be 'a sort of place devoid of all culture',[26] and there must be no hesitation when it comes to sanctioning the guilty, because penal sanctions have the function of clearly proclaiming social prohibitions, whereas mediation dilutes responsibilities in the search for consensus.

The same type of criticism is made by the trade-unions about company mediation or labour law. It would have the function of hindering the rise of a collective representation of workers' rights, and thus proceed to a sort of occult deregulation.

These worries fed a number of mediation's 'normalisation' strategies. Thus the goal of the European Green Book was, via the consultation of all the organisations and all the interested fields (governments, universities, judges, the Bars, notary offices, chambers of commerce, professional organisations of mediations, consumer associations), to give 'necessary guarantees so the resolution of conflict by extra-judicial authorities could offer the level of security required in the justice administration', to ensure balance between flexibility and guarantee of the mediation processes' quality, and to search for an articulation which is consistent with judicial procedures. The consequence of this was the adoption of the 2004 Code of Good Conduct which lays down the fundamental principles which mediators must follow.

---

23 R. Abel, *The politics of informal justice*, New York, Academic Press, 1982.

24 Ibid.

25 C. Harrington, *Shadow Justice. The ideology and institutionalization of alternatives to court*, Westpoint, CT, Greenwood Press, 1985.

26 Ibid.

4.3.1 The Consensual Characteristic

The process of mediation must absolutely not be imposed; it relies on the participants' willing adhesion to the process. This principle which mobilises the actors' consent is linked to the contemporary crisis of the regulation systems based on constraint. The postmodern governance of subjects demands that they pledge allegiance to the disciplinary proceedings they are offered. We are assisting the contractualisation of society in which the part of ties prescribed by the law is decreasing to the profit of connections consented to via contracts, where, as Alain Supiot describes it 'heteronomy steps down to the profit of autonomy'.[27] This evolution, during which individuals exert their 'free will' at any moment, can be analysed as a process of emancipation or on the contrary as the 'reactivation of feudal ways of establishing social links',[28] as a subtle mode of domination, and the confirmation, as La Boétie puts it, of a 'voluntary servitude'.

The development of mediation participates in this contractualisation, as it can only take place when all the participants consent to it. However, in virtue of this principle acknowledged by international texts, according to which everyone has the right to a fair trial, mediation cannot lead them to renounce their rights. Moreover, mediation is not conceivable in cases of 'rights and obligations of which the parties cannot dispose of themselves', like for example in family law, the status of persons, the name or parental authority. This consent must be under two conditions: it must be free and clear and can at any moment of the process be withdrawn.

The recommendation of the Council of Europe dating from 1999 specifies that people must not be 'incited in an undue manner to accept mediation'. The 2008 directive gives the right to every judge of the community, at every step of the procedure, to offer the parties to attend an informational meeting about mediation, and if he/she deems it appropriate, to invite the different parties to resort to mediation. But under no circumstances should a mediation be ordered. In the case of 'spontaneous' or 'conventional' mediations this consensual condition does not pose any problem. The 'ideal' case concerns two opponents who take the first step together and contact a mediation service or a mediator in order to start the mediation process. Most of the time, however, only one of the participants starts the process. The mediator then invites (but does not summon) the opponent to a meeting to explain what mediation is and to obtain his acceptance or refusal.

---

27 A. Supiot, 'La contractualisation de la société', in Y. Michaud (dir.), *Qu'est-ce que l'humain?* Paris, Odile Jacob, 2000.

28 Ibid.

The nature of consent can become problematic in the judicial field. Some fear, for example, that a defendant refusing the mediation process can be interpreted as a lack of goodwill on the defendant's part to resolve the conflict and this could influence the magistrate's ulterior decision. In the penal context, one might fear that the parties' consent might be hindered by the strategic analysis of the consequences of a refusal. Thus, in a pre-sentence context (in countries where the principle of discretionary prosecution can be applied), the plaintiff to which the prosecutor offers to take part in mediation sessions can fear that his or her refusal might lead to the case being dismissed.On the other hand, the defendant might fear that his/her refusal could lead the magistrate to open proceedings before the court. Does the weight of a relatively random judiciary decision undermine the liberty of consent? Is this not the case for all types of conflicts brought before court? Does the choice of mediation not always respond to strategic choices?

This question cannot be asked in the same terms in case of defect of consent. The philosophy of mediation demands that individuals be able to speak autonomously, commit, understand the consequences of their acts and their decisions. This supposes that consent is formulated by someone who has all their mental capacity. However, this criterion is not easily identifiable; mental illness, for example, is not always readily detectable. Mentally ill people don't always bear the stigma of their illness and in particular, those with split personalities can appear normal or very healthy, the illness might only appear as the process goes along. The borders drawn by psychiatry only delineate the most extreme cases, leaving those who are intellectually deficient, obtuse, hyper-narcissist and passionate to the extreme in the sane category. The law places too few individuals under guardianship or curatorship and does this under the criteria of the financial risk they face, or that they bring on their loved ones. The Council of Europe's wish (R. 19.99), 'mediation must not be pursued if one of the main actors is not able to understand the procedure's meaning', which prompts mediators to ensure their explanations are properly understood, only constitutes a marginal response. Most of the time, mediators are asked to use their 'common sense', to flush out and disqualify from the mediation process all those who are not mentally sane.

Consent must also be enlightened. There again, the Council of Europe specifies: 'before accepting mediation, the parties must be fully informed of their rights, of the process' nature and of the possible consequences of their decision'. A presentation of mediation must be printed on the letters inviting the parties to meet with a mediator. The latter must speak to the parties in a language they understand, this means that the mediator must adapt his/her wording to the intellectual and linguistic level of the parties. Concerning this last point, the parties also have the right to an interpreter, which brings its own set of problems if the interpreter doesn't translate exactly the words that are being spoken. The mediator must inform the parties that they have the possibility of consulting a legal service or a lawyer at any moment during the mediation. Whether a lawyer can participate in the mediation process with their client or not is debated. Some (especially lawyers and mediators specialised in economic and financial litigations) are in favour of this participation in the name of the protection of individual rights, whereas others (a few 'initiated' lawyers and mediators specialised in interpersonal conflicts) are fiercely opposed. The latter have many arguments. Some invoke the necessity of the empowerment and direct participation of the parties, the fact that the presence of a person other than the mediator could inhibit the parties' emotions and the sincerity of their words, and finally the high level of confidentiality of the process. Could a lawyer resist the temptation of using the words spoken in a mediation session if a later procedure was opened?

4.3.2 Confidentiality

What is said in a mediation session must remain confidential in order to facilitate the sincerity of the exchanges and the commitment of the participants. Of course, it is difficult to forbid the latter to not confide in their close ones or their defenders. The prohibition concerns publicity that could be made around the content of mediation. However, it is prohibited to use what happened or what was said during a mediation session in later legal proceedings if the mediation fails. All the international texts are unanimous on this point. The participants and their lawyers have to resist this strategic temptation, and the 2008 directive specifies that the mediator cannot be forced to produce proofs relating to the procedure's progress. But today, these principles are jeopardized by the possible use of recording telephones during meetings and, above all, by the growing practice of online mediation, which makes it difficult to ensure optimal conditions of confidentiality.

The mediator must tell the participants that he/she is committed to not reveal any of what has been said. This means on one hand that the mediator cannot say to one of the participants what the other has said without the first person's formal consent. This is notably the case when the mediator decides to proceed to separate meetings before organising a joint meeting. On the other hand, the professional secrecy given to the mediator stops him/her from disclosing that a mediation is taking place or that one has taken place (for example, a mediator cannot write a certificate to prove this). Finally, when it comes to judicial mandates, the mediator must not give any information to the representative. The mediator can say if the mediation has resulted in an agreement, and can even specify the nature of the agreement, if those concerned accept or ask for it. But no other information must be given. The only point that is still debated concerns situations in which it is in public interest to reveal facts that threaten the protection of children, or the physical or psychological integrity of a person. Even then, it is not easy to know how to act. Mediators only collect allegations, and have no way of testing their truth, and thus they must be prudent when revealing secrets. Experience does show that some of these allegations are revealed to not be true and were only said, in the conflictual logic of the first phase, to disqualify the opponent or shift the power balance in their favour. These allegations usually stop as soon as the interest in mediation is understood and the process properly started.

4.3.3 The Suspension of Legal Limitation Period

In order to avoid mediation becoming a dilatory tactic that could penalise one of the participants, limitation periods, legally anticipated for civil or penal affairs, are prolonged during the whole mediation process. The limitation period then stops when one party decides to withdraw and interrupt the mediation, or when the mediator decides for diverse reasons to interrupt it (violence, inacceptable pressure, physical risks for one person, manipulation, increase in conflict, revelations contrary to public order).

4.3.4 The Agreement's Legal Value

The agreement is generally assimilated to a transaction and produces the legal effects granted to all these types of measures. The participants can choose to have this agreement ratified by a magistrate in order to make it enforceable or to write an authentic act with a notary. As we have seen, the judge's discretionary power means that he cannot mechanically satisfy this request when the agreement seems, in terms of judicial criteria or equity imperatives, to contravene the rules of public order or dangerously threaten the material or psychological interests of one of the parties.

∴

It can naturally happen, like in any profession, that certain mediators stray from aforementioned values or from the set of fundamental principles presented before. However, with my experience in the field, I can assert that this is probably the characteristic of a new activity in search of professional recognition. The ethical and deontological principles are continually reviewed and reworked during training and practice analysis sessions. The vast majority of mediators is profoundly attached to them, as the justification for mediation lies in their scrupulous respect. To do otherwise would be to disqualify it and undermine its raison d'être.

CHAPTER 4

Models of Mediation

Evoking mediation in a generic way is deceptive, as it is multi-faceted. Many studies assessing the efficiency of mediation, compared to other conflict regulation modes, show a considerable methodological bias. They consider mediation to be a general category; however, there are many ways to practise mediation. This leads us to conclude that the effects of these different practices are not identical. There are diverse models, each presenting specificities, even if they have been for the most part conceived in the ideological environment of North American universities. This variety forms a very contrasted mediation landscape, marked with fractures that are not only methodological, but also represent worldviews that are sometimes radically opposed.

Thus, it is heuristic to evoke the principal models of mediation as they have been presented by their promoters. Firstly, because they mark out the field's story and explain its modes of construction, and secondly because they describe ways of doing in the field, or 'knacks' as artisans call them. Naturally, because the disciplines and fields of intervention are interwoven, these models are inter-permeable and mixed, and certain mediators build their own model by combining elements of multiple models. This is notably the case of those who have an extended knowledge of mediation, but not the majority as the training networks have a tendency to privilege teaching a single and very pragmatic model, as with food recipes, without even informing the 'students' that there are more diverse offers 'on the market'. The promoters of mediation participate in mediation's closure when they sell the models they have conceived and which brought them fame during their training courses, which can be expensive.

Firstly, I will present, briefly as it is well-known, the resolution model known as *problem-solving*. Then, I will proceed in approximately chronological order, the Harvard negotiation model, then the transformative model, the narrative model and finally the systemic models. Finally, I will compare the models between themselves to better highlight their differences in characteristics, function and objectives.

1 The *Problem-Solving* Model

The *problem-solving* or *settlement-oriented* approach is, to this day, dominant in the conflict resolution field. It is most frequently used in the treatment of

DOI:10.1163/9789004734067_008

political and commercial conflicts. This model is strongly recommended by its promoters to avoid costly trials, in cases when it is urgent to sign an agreement quickly and in all situations in which people who don't know each other are opposed in material or financial conflicts.

The name of this method explains its nature, it is focused on the search for conflict solutions by establishing an agreement or arrangement. Conflict is perceived as a problem and rarely as an opportunity with positive functions. The saying 'every problem has its solution' is repeated very often. The role of the mediator is to help the parties to reframe their positions in order to have a common definition of the problem. The objective is to generate a mutually acceptable agreement as quickly as possible.

Mediators are often direct in their desire to arrive at an agreement (the model does not constitute a monolithic bloc, however diverse degrees of directives attitudes do exist). Not only do they control the process, but they also control the discussion's substance. They are focused on consensus zones and soluble questions, and avoid the zones of opposition which threaten the consensus. Their function is to help the actors advance towards the solution step by step, and in order to do this, they do not hesitate to set deadlines to reach certain stages of discussion. Even though the decisions are, in theory, in the hands of the parties, the mediators often play an important role in the development of the agreement's terms and in obtaining its approval. They can sometimes act as referees, offering a solution and the model is qualified as 'med-arb'.[1] This hybrid process starts as a mediation; however the parties agree that, if they cannot find a solution themselves, the mediator will then act as an arbitrator, and they will follow and implement his/her solution. In other cases, these mediators act as experts giving shrewd advice, meaning the process is closer to an assisted negotiation than a mediation.

The search for an agreement happens by mutual concessions. Like in a bargaining game, this positional bargaining involves the actors making a gesture in turn to close the gap between the different claims. Naturally, each actor anticipates their opponent's strategy; the base logic of this model consists in exaggerating it in order to win something from the exchange. As exemplified above, one of this model's flaws is that it promotes competitive logic to the detriment of cooperative action. Its logic of compromise means the parties are never completely satisfied; the final agreement only reduces the differences between their respective positions. This method of 'splitting the difference' means the process makes both parties lose, as opposed to a 'win-win' situation. This is in particular what the Harvard negotiation model is famous for.

1 'Med-arb' is an abbreviation of 'mediation-arbitration'.

2 The Harvard Negotiation Model

International law expert Roger Fisher and anthropologist William Ury[2] oppose the North American pre-eminence of Rambo-style negotiations (*hard bargaining*) in which one must intimidate the opponent to win. Instead, they suggest *integrative bargaining*, a softer negotiating strategy, which serves as a communication channel with the first mediation models. Moreover, the first mediators were largely inspired by the Fisher and Ury teachings, which can explain the confusion that exist between negotiation and mediation,[3] in the representation of the actors in these fields. Inspired by this model, Thomak Fuitak, professor at the University of Minneapolis in Minnesota, adapted his own model, which is more open than its predecessors to the cultural dimension of mediation, and is quite well-known in Europe.

2.1 *The Conceptual Framework of the Harvard Negotiation Model*

This model, conceived within the framework of the *Harvard Negotiation Project* of Harvard University (known internationally as the Harvard model) seeks to stand out from bargaining-based models in which each of the parties adopts a position, presents arguments to justify the position, and makes concessions. The authors argue these concessions cannot lead to a judicious, fair and sustainable agreement. Indeed, the negotiators fight for their positions, defend them and become attached to them more ardently the more they are attacked, do everything to preserve them, to save face. The logic behind searching for compromise leads the parties to exaggerate their initial claims, which delays the development of a solution. This becomes even more complicated when the parties are numerous. The model of Harvard negotiation was invented to avoid the characteristic traps of the *problem-solving* strategy.

The reasoned negotiation model can be summed up in four points:

1. *People's questions and the dispute must be treated separately*

In order to do this, human problems must be addressed plainly. Three levels must be taken into account:

–*perception:* the conflict is 'in people's heads', it is not objective. Putting yourself in your adversary's shoes then becomes essential and represents a kind of power. The difficulties one has are not necessarily due to the adversary

2 Roger Fisher and William Ury, *Getting to yes*, Houghton Mifflin Company, Boston, 1981, (Published in French in 1982 under the title, *Comment réussir une négociation*? Paris, Seuil, second edition en 1991).

3 See Jacques Faget, 'Médiation et post-modernité. Légitimation ou transformation de l'action publique?' *Négociations*, 2006/2, 51–63.

or their intention. Thus, it is necessary to exchange perceptions and make propositions conform to the adversary's principles so he/she can save face.

–affectivity: it is necessary to understand one's own feelings and those of others, to express emotions freely, to avoid replying to outbursts of anger, and to make symbolic gestures (express regret, apologise).

–communication: To avoid misunderstandings, it is advised to listen to others carefully, show understanding, express oneself clearly and ensure you are understood, speak of yourself but not of others ('I am disappointed' instead of 'you disappoint me', 'from my point of view, this is how things happened' instead of 'you are wrong', or 'you are lying'), as advised in all books on nonviolent communication.[4]

2. *It is necessary to concentrate on the interests and not the positions*

Positions such as 'I want this', 'I have the right to', 'I'm right' only serve to amplify differences and lead to unsatisfactory compromises. Negotiation must not be established on divergent positions, but on desires, needs, fears and worries. It is necessary, if possible, to forget the past and look towards the future. Positions can be loud, but interests are the real silent motors of action. When positions diverge, this is not always the case of interests, especially when several interests are at stake.

3. *It is necessary to imagine mutually beneficial solutions*

Fisher and Ury illustrate this point with the famous orange metaphor. Two people covet the fruit but cannot agree on who should have it – they then ask a third party for help. The latter can be tempted to suggest splitting it into two, but this 'common sense' decision can turn out to be unsatisfactory for all parties. If the third party had focused on interests (why do you want the orange/what would you do with it?) and not on positions (I want the orange), the decision and outcome might have been different. The third party might have discovered that one person wanted the juice, and the other wanted its peel to make a dessert, for example. Thus, it is necessary to focus on interests in order to move forward, and to be imaginative and think of as many solutions as possible. It is of the utmost importance to avoid hasty judgements, to think that only one solution exists or that the solutions mentioned are contradictory, in favour of one protagonist or the other; that there will necessarily be a winner and a loser. It is crucial to make common interests emerge.

4 See for example Marshall B. Rosenberg's famous book *Non violent communication: a language of life, Puddle Dancer Press, 2003.*

4. *The result must be based on objective criteria*
To avoid the struggle that is a negotiation position, it is useful to base the agreement on legal or equity criteria, or on a professional tradition, the market value, legal precedents, scientific evaluations, or simply the ease of putting the agreement into practice. For the solution to be sustainable, it must, if possible, be independent from the parties' will.

The authors then evoke a number of questions that help them formulate well-known concepts in the world of negotiation, such as the BATNA[5] concept or Jiu jitsu[6] technique. They specifically concern the relations between negotiators. However, some are useful for the mediator to have in mind, either because they could help his/her understanding of the strategies used by the actors, or because they could help the mediator determine his/her attitude. Via a transposition from negotiation to mediation, elements of reflection about crucial questions such as: Is mediation conceivable when one of the parties is obviously more powerful than the other? What must one do if one of the parties refuses to play the game, is disloyal, lies, gives false information, threatens, exerts pressure, refuses dialogue completely, or makes extreme requirements? Is it possible to talk with terrorists or people who act motivated by religious convictions? How can one adapt his/her approach depending on culture or personality characteristics, or more simply, different types of people?

2.2 *The Harvard Model Adaptation: The Authentic Arena*

The model of the authentic arena, developed by Thomas Fiutak,[7] is the adaptation of Ury and Fisher's model, only it is specifically addressed to mediators. It expresses a very pragmatic American conception of mediation, oriented towards the search for an agreement. For the author, mediation is a form of assisted negotiation, but this link between the two is mitigated by a global humanist vision formed over the course of travels and practical experiences.

---

5 BATNA: Best Alternative To a Negotiated Agreement, which consists in imagining fallback solutions beforehand, evaluating their most unfavourable and alluring aspects, and choosing the best one.

6 Jiu Jitsu recommends that opponents not enter into a conflict position and not resist an attack head-on, but instead use the opponent's energy and deviate their strength to your advantage, like in martial arts.

7 Thomas Fiutak, *Le médiateur dans l'arène. Réflexion sur l'art de la médiation*, Toulouse, Erès, 2009.

2.2.1 The Mediation Cycle Model

This model has 4 phases and a catharsis point:

- Phase I is **What?** People express the perception they have of reality. The role of the mediator is to allow everyone to express themselves and to clarify the situation. Communication is organised essentially between the mediator and the two other parties.
- Phase II is **Why?** It allows the parties to ask questions to each other, test their respective representations of reality. This conversation is the time for them to think about their real interests and needs. Communication is essentially horizontal, and the mediator has the role of encouraging and favouring it.
- Phase III is the **What if** phase? The parties explore the different options while being as open-minded and creative as possible. Having as many options as possible is useful.
- Phase IV **How?** This consists in developing an action plan likely to create a new reality. It helps to choose the option that can guarantee the sustainability of the agreement. When the actors can answer the following questions: who does what, and when? and that they can evaluate the consequences of non-compliance with the agreement.
- The catharsis point is that of the expression of emotions. This moment is a transitory phase between each person's narrative and story, and the search for options. It brings 'transformative energy to the relationship process'.

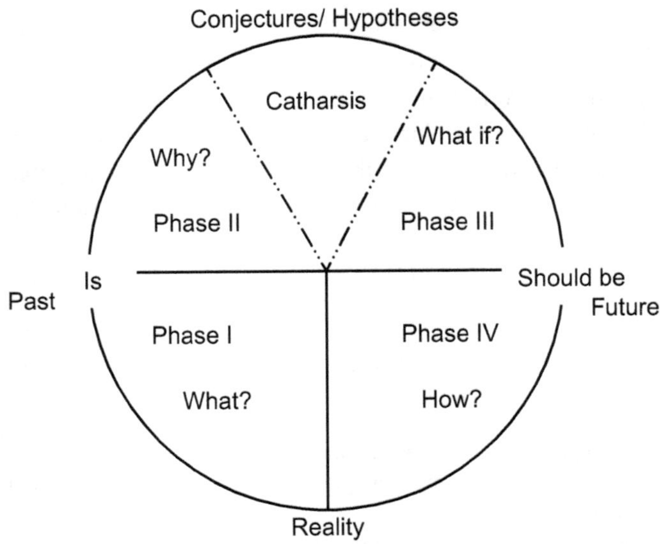

FIGURE 4.1 The mediation cycle model

These phases do not follow each other mechanically. It's not the mediator who decides to move from one to the other, but the parties who express it through with their words and behaviour. The model suggested here is only a dynamic map to describe the rhythm and sequences of mediation. The process can jump forwards and backwards; no mediation follows this theoretical model perfectly. Its ambition is only to help and show where the parties are in the process, and which step can be the next.

2.2.2 The Authentic Arena

Every society creates arenas, courts, 'cases à palabres', churches, stadiums, political or domestic assemblies, dinner tables: these places have the function of helping people interact following a ritualised set of customs and modes of expression. In the same way, mediation is an arena which can sometimes replace that of the court or the family assembly for domestic conflicts. Fiutak defines it as 'a physical and psychological space integrated in a culture'. It is not a closed-off space but a borderless one, where the surrounding world is present even when only two people are present. Historical and social dynamics intersect psychological and emotional dynamics. It is first and foremost a physical space, the most neutral possible, conforming with the cultural representations of the participant. It's a place whose layout is co-constructed by the mediator and the parties. It is also a psychological space where individuals or groups meet each other following a structuring and protective mode. By their presence alone, these individuals show their willingness to change something in their relationships. This space's authenticity comes from the appropriateness that exists between the material and relational space created, and the cultural outlines of the actors. From there on, Fiutak offers his thoughts, ensuring the physical and psychological safety of the people present, and the legitimacy of the arena.

3 The Transformative Model

Faced with the dominance of the *problem-solving* approach, which is essentially preoccupied by tangible results, a movement emerged in the 1990s that constituted a paradigmatic shift in its way of conceiving and handling conflicts. Even though their approaches were developed independently from each other, the following works can be qualified as 'transformative'; those of R. Barush Bush and Joseph Folger on one hand, and those of John Burton, Johan Galtung and John Paul Lederach on the other. Initially, the first two theorists were focused on interpersonal conflicts, such as family or community disputes, whereas the latter were more focused on intergroup conflicts (often based on ethnicity), and on international political conflicts as well. Despite their diverse fields of application, they have many common points.

4 R. Barush Bush and Joseph Folger's Conceptualisation

The work of these American scholars,[8] one of them a jurist (Bush), and the other an expert in communication science (Folger), differs from the problem-solving approach, which aims to generate a mutually acceptable solution to the existing conflict. The only common point with this model is the call for a neutral third party who isn't involved with the conflict. Every other point is different. The *settlement-oriented* mediator explains what the objective of the mediator is and defines the process by which he/she will assist the parties in their search for an agreement. The emotions likely to increase anger are controlled. The non-negotiable questions are avoided. These mediators do not encourage a debate on the past, which could lead to reproaches and could hinder the progression of the process. The parties are more encouraged to focus on what they want for their future. Even though the decisions are, in principle, left in the opponent's hands, these mediators play a large role in formulating the problems and obtaining approval. Moreover, they act more like referees, encouraging the parties to make good progress as fast as possible by sometimes using deadlines to structure the work in progress. Generally, this type of mediation is only considered a success if an agreement is reached.

The transformative model represents a paradigmatic shift from the problem-solving method. It takes its own space in the history of mediation, which has four principal phases. The first part, *satisfaction story*, presents mediation as a considerable proof of progress compared to the other competitive modes of conflict resolution. Firstly, it allows more satisfactory solutions for both parties and not just one of them, as is the case in the adversarial model acknowledged by the legal system. Secondly, it helps reduce the financial and emotional cost of the traditional processes. The second part, named *social justice story*, suggests that mediation is a good way to unite individuals around a single interest more suitable to social justice and the fight against exploitation. By allowing the parties to resolve their problems themselves, mediation reduces the dependence and inferiority of the most vulnerable groups in society. The third part, called *oppression story*, argues that mediation is dangerous

8 J. P. Folger, R. A. B Bush, *The promise of mediation. Responding to conflicts through empowerment and recognition*, Jossey-Bass, San Francisco, 1994.

because of this informality and its consensual characteristic which can lead to the most powerful party manipulating the most vulnerable one. The mediator himself/herself has a large power to manipulate and can orient the solutions according to his/her wishes and vision of the world. Mediation only concerns itself with particular interests and contributes to the disintegration and privatisation of class conflicts and obscuring questions of public interest. Like a success story, the fourth part is the one the authors offer to write, a *transformation story* which allows people to transform themselves by helping them to define their problems and objectives in their own words. This type of initiative progressively contributes to the transformation of society.

The transformative approach does not seek the resolution of the immediate problem, but rather the empowerment and recognition of the concerned people. These two key concepts are defined as follows:

- *Empowerment* is the 'restoration of the individual's sense of value and strength, and capacity to manage and solve the problems in his/her life'. The opponents gain 'more clarity on their objectives (a better comprehension of what they want and why they want it), their resources, their options (awareness of the diverse possibilities available to them, and the costs and benefits that come with them) and their preferences'. They use this information to control the process, the subject of the discussions and to make their own decisions. The process of empowerment is finished when the conflicting parties are acutely aware of their own value and their ability to manage the situation, no matter the difficulty and the exterior constraints they face. This movement can be represented by a shift from a state of vulnerability (someone who is worried, confused, fearful, disorganised, uncertain) to a position of strength (someone who is calm, clear, more confident, more concentrated, and more capable of making decisions).
- The term *recognition* means 'recognition and empathy for others' situations and problems'. This does not mean agreeing with the other person, but simply considering him/her as a human having their own preoccupations. The recognition is achieved when, depending on the degree of empowerment reached, the people involved express a sensitivity to the other's situation and his/her human qualities. The movement helps to shift from a self-centred attitude (an individual who protects himself/herself, and who is defensive, suspicious, incapable of thinking outside their own thought system) to a more sensitive attitude (an individual who is more attentive, open, able to consider the other to be in good faith and to better understand the other's perspective).

These two notions often pave the way to a mutually acceptable agreement, but this is only a side effect. The primary objective is to reinforce the empower-

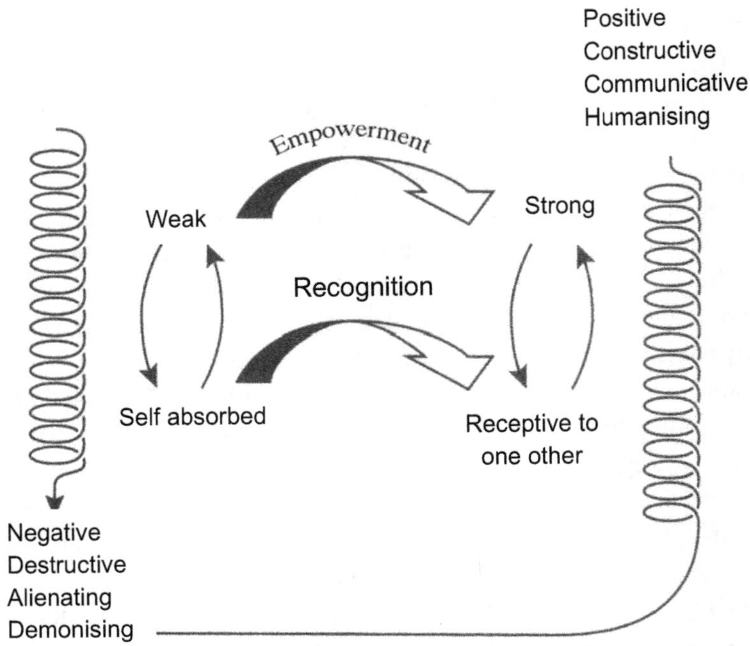

FIGURE 4.2 Change in conflictual interaction
J.P. Folger, R.A.B., Bush, D.J. Della Noce (under the direction of), *Transformative mediation: a source book, Resources for conflict intervention, practitioners and programs*, Association for conflict transformation, institute for the study of conflict transformation Inc., USA, 2010.

ment and recognition ability of the parties to allow them to tackle their present and future problems with more strength, confidence and openness. If they reach an agreement, this is the result of their own will and responsibility. Empowerment and recognition work together to form a virtuous circle and mutually reinforce each other as follows: 'The stronger I am, the more capable I feel of offering my recognition. When I give my recognition, I feel stronger'.

The authors formulate 10 propositions that help to guide the transformative mediator:[9]

1. The mediator describes his/her role and objectives in terms of empowerment and recognition. He/she must explain that his/her task is to help the parties to understand their own interests and opinions more clearly, and, if they want, to better understand their opponent. The agreement is present only as a possible solution to the process.

9 J.P. Folger and R. A. B. Bush, 'Transformative Mediation and Third-Party Intervention: Ten Hallmarks of a Transformative Approach to Practice', *Mediation Quarterly* 13:4 (Summer 1996) pp. 263–278.

2. The mediator must emphasize that the responsibility of the outcome of the mediation belongs to the parties involved. In such a model, the role of the mediator is only to identify the opportunities that favour the empowerment and recognition of the parties.
3. The mediator must avoid judging the ideas and decisions of the parties involved.
4. The mediation process becomes easier if the mediator develops an optimistic vision of the competence of the actors and of their motivations. The more he/she will think they are incompetent or malicious, the more he/she will be tempted to get involved in a directive way.
5. The mediator must allow the protagonists to express their emotions, as they often reveal fears or beliefs, uncertainties or misunderstandings. By encouraging them to find the root of their emotions, the mediator favours both the empowerment and recognition of the parties.
6. For similar reasons, conversations about the past must be encouraged. Debates on people's stories reveal the foundations of their present stances. This jump back in time can clarify their self-understanding and can improve mutual recognition.
7. The transformative mediator must help people explore their uncertainties and doubts. However, the protagonists must proceed to this exploration first by themselves. The mediator must simply favour it with his/her patient and tolerant attitude.
8. This type of mediation requires the mediator to stay narrowly focused on the present conflict and on the words spoken by the actors during the mediation sessions. By paying attention to the conversation, he/she can precisely locate the elements of confusion and incomprehension and thus identify the opportunities to develop and strengthen the actors' empowerment and recognition.
9. The mediator must consider his/her intervention as a simple moment in the evolution of the conflictual process. There is a *before* the intervention and an *after*. He must be conscious of the limits of his action, which helps him to adopt a non-directive attitude and to not be obsessed by the search for an agreement.
10. Lastly, in order to maintain energy and motivation, the mediator must be willing to share with the parties the satisfaction of seeing the degree of empowerment and accountability increase, even if this progress is modest, as 'every little step counts'. Agreements will only be sustainable if they are navigated by those who feel empowered and who accept accountability.

These practise norms, which constitute the foundation of a transformative mediation, ensure that the mediator supports a process which belongs wholly to the actors. The success of such a process can be measured with the progress made, with the growth in the actors' self-confidence and in how attentive they are with others. For Bush and Folger, these norms can be applied in fields as varied as interpersonal, environmental but also workplace and international conflicts.

5 John Burton and Johan Galtung's Theoretical Contributions

We can also mention, within the framework of the transformative model, *analytical (interactive) problem-solving*, initially based on John Burton's[10] theory, and later developed by Herbert Kelman, and those conceived by the Norwegian scholar Johan Galtung. In a more social and humanist perspective than the realistic approaches focused on the role of the States, Burton assumes that conflicts are created by people or groups seeking satisfaction of their basic human needs such as identity, security or recognition. By redefining these latent needs, the parties now find themselves able to redefine the conflict and to search for the right solution interactively, which they previously were not able to do. The focus is on the expression of emotions, mutual recognition of the parties' needs and their empowerment.

Burton's works inspired many *peacemakers* who, in the extension of his model, organised numerous peace-making workshops with the objective of favouring respect and mutual understanding in the context of political conflicts, such as the one in Cyprus. The first of these was Herbert C. Kelman, a psycho-sociologist specialised in social influence mechanisms, whose workshops were organised between 1971 and 1991 on the fringes of the Israeli-Palestinian conflict, and which had a considerable effect on the Oslo agreements (1993). Aside from mediations that mobilise political decision-makers, he gathers influential figures together, from both communities, but not among official political and diplomatic circles. These *people-to-people workshops*, organised *in camera* and on neutral terrain, do not have the objective of searching for an agreement, but are implemented with an analytical and inter-

10 John Burton, *World society*, Cambridge, Cambridge University Press, 1972 et *Conflict. Human needs theory*, London Macmillan, 1990. John Burton was born in Australia in 1915. He became doctor at the London School of Economics in 1942, and then played a key role in Australian foreign politics. In 1963, he taught at the University College London then at Kent University in Canterbury, and he taught at the George Mason university in Virginia, USA in the 1980s.

active process, in the hopes that the participants become the vectors of a transformed understanding of the conflict. Colson and Lempereur proposed a recent application of this in the post-conflict action they lead in Burundi, and in the Democratic Republic of Congo.[11] In both countries, they organised 'formative retreats', gathering key people with the objective of overcoming current disputes, often linked to past difficulties. These five day-long workshops firstly help the participants get to know each other and progressively respect and understand one another. Secondly, they identify the most urgent problems for their countries and where they can exert influence, then they search for solutions together. The mediators play the role of simple facilitators, respecting three fundamental principles: reconciliation cannot be imposed, only the actors themselves can work towards and achieve it; the action of reconciliation is undertaken on site (even if the process is supported by many international partners) and over time (there is a permanent local outpost entrusted to local people and a periodical follow up of the workshops to talk about what has changed since the previous workshop); finally, the effort of reconciliation must integrate all of the conflict's actors, including the most radical ones, as peace can only be made with one's enemies. A certain number of criteria, including gender (at least 30 per cent women), professional, geographical, ethnic and ideological, are met to ensure the participants are representative. The people participating in these workshops are designated by combining different lists drawn up by the political, religious and academic authorities, or by respected members of civil society. Those whose names appear more frequently are invited to these peace-making workshops.

Johan Galtung, creator of the Journal of Peace Research and of the PRIO (International Peace Research Institute of Oslo), is considered the eulogist of irenology, the science of conflict resolutions by non-violent means. His essential ideas can be summarised as follows. If peace is defined as the simple absence of war or violence, it is *negative peace*. We must favour *positive peace,* which relies on the development of constructive collaborative relations between conflicting States or groups. Galtung also highlights the fact that it would be vain to want to resolve conflicts without tackling structural violence, which is the context of the conflicts. What he means by the phrase structural violence is all the mechanisms of political domination exerted by the States, or more generally by the Centre on the periphery, the North on the South, which

11 Aurélien Colson, Alain Pekar Lempereur, 'Un pont vers une paix durable. Reconciliation et médiation post-conflit au Burundi et en République Démocratique du Congo', *Négociations,* nr 9, 2008/1, pp. 13–28.

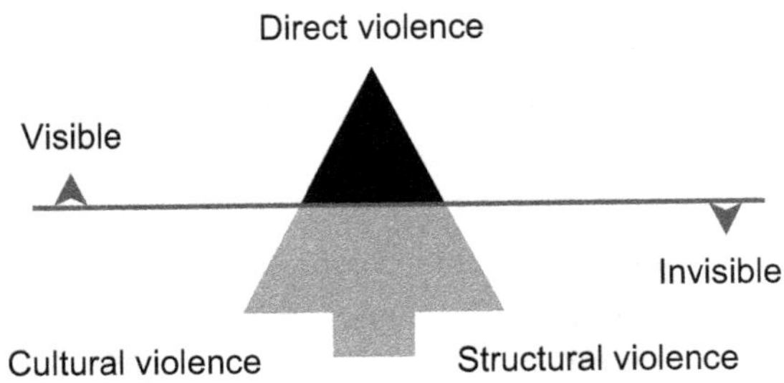

FIGURE 4.3 Galtung's violence triangle

hinder the complete emancipation of individuals. Galtung specifies sexism, racism, ethnocentrism, elitism and nationalism in particular. His conception of peace production is thus demanding and long-term, as it not only supposes arriving to a cease-fire situation, but also fighting the structural causes that determine the class, race and gender oppression.

In 1993, Galtung created the organisation *Transcend*,[12] with which he spread a non-violent method of conflict resolution, whose foundational principle can be defined as follows: Four paths of unsatisfactory conflict resolution exist. In the first one A wins, and B loses; and the other way around for the second path. In the third, neither A nor B are ready to resolve their conflict; in the fourth, a confusing compromise which does not satisfy the parties, and temporarily appeases the conflict, is reached. The fifth path, which is in line with Burton's suggestions, supposes following a win/win logic, the satisfaction of the basic human needs of the protagonists, (freedom, identity, dignity, physical well-being). Via dialogue and empathy, the mediator must help them to understand the problem and to clarify their objectives before they orient themselves towards creative and sustainable solutions which are in harmony with their mutual objectives. These solutions must be reached by the protagonists and not imposed from the outside by a mediator who would have interests in the conflict.

5.1 *John Paul Lederach's Perspective*

John Paul Lederach's[13] work is probably more well-known because it is more recent, and also because it concerns the processes of political peace as well as a more general dimension. The pacifist dimension of Lederach's positions can be explained by his commitment with the Mennonites. According to him,

12 Johan Galtung, Jacobsen, C.G. and Brand-Jacobsen, K.F. (2000) *Searching for Peace; The Road to TRANSCEND*, Pluto Press.

13 John Paul Lederach, *Preparing for Peace: Conflict Transformation Across Cultures*, Syracuse University Press, 1995.

peace is linked with justice, with the construction of relationships and just social structures that respect human rights; it is linked with a non-violent philosophy. This philosophical and religious framework, associated with a lot of experience in numerous violent political conflicts, led him to build the conflict *transformation* model in the 1980s and the 1990s; a model which is opposed to the *conflict resolution* and *conflict management* models that were dominant at the time. His model stands out because it allows a better understanding of the nature of the conflicts. On the one hand, the *conflict resolution* model presupposes that conflict is negative and bad in essence, and holds that it is necessary to arrive at the conflict's end hastily by means of adapted process and solution. The *conflict management* model, on the other hand, holds that conflicts are a long-term process and that they can be directed or controlled in order to reduce the risks, without tackling the real source of the conflict. On the contrary, the transformative model does not present itself as a set of techniques to resolve or regulate conflicts, but rather is part of a more general perspective which replaces the conflict back into the social structure that generates it.

Lederach does not have the ambition of eliminating or controlling conflicts, but of recognising them as they are and of working with their 'dialectic nature'. According to him, conflict must not be considered as a threat but as an opportunity to develop and grow the understanding we have of ourselves and of others. In the absence of conflict, life would be 'monotonous and flat, and our relationships would be sadly superficial'. With this phrase, Lederach highlights conflict's dynamic function, and how it brings about change in human relations and social structures.

As social conflicts alter communication, models of social organisation and the images people have of themselves and others, they can only be transformed by working on the events, the people and relationships that cause them. Because conflict usually transforms perceptions by accentuating differences between people and their positions, the efficient transformation of conflict can only happen with the improvement of mutual understanding. Even when the interests, values and needs of people are different, and appear irreconcilable, progress is made as soon as each group understands the other's positions and logic more precisely. Here, it is easy to see how crucial the role that Lederach gives to dialogue and face-to-face relations is.

The transformative model also implies transforming the way the conflict is expressed. The environment must shift from being competitive, aggressive and violent to non-violent, mediative and cooperative. Favouring such an evolution implies a certain activism to develop the awareness and thoughts of people on conflict and to transform the way they perceive it. This is precisely the objective mediation has, to catalyse 'the shift from mutually destructive modes of conflict to dialogue and interdependence'. A shift like this must take place both on a personal and a systemic level. On a personal level, the transformation of conflict implies a rise in awareness and a will to change things which can operate via the identification of the fear, anger, sadness, bitterness that everyone feels inside. These emotions must be recognised and worked on in every single pacification process. Re-establishing peace also implies a systemic transformation, a process which ensures more justice and equality in the social system. This might imply the elimination of political and social oppression mechanisms, the improved sharing of resources and the promotion of non-violent conflict resolution between groups. Each of these actions reinforces the other. In other words, the transformation of personal relations facilitates the transformation of social systems, and systemic changes facilitate an evolution on the personal level. These two dynamics work together to favour and anticipate reconciliation and peace, seen not as static states, but as a continually evolving process.

All in all, the transformative perspective approaches conflict as being the expression of a vast and complex relational system. Even though it takes the immediate situation into account, it resists the temptation of urgency which pushes to adopt solutions as quickly as possible. Immediate conflict is seen as a window, where one must look not at its reflection, but at what can be seen on the other side of the glass. This approach exceeds the episodic and superficial expression of conflict to concentrate on its historical and relational roots. Whereas in conflict, people feel insecure, do not clearly understand and control what is happening, the transformative model has the object of helping them to better understand and control what is happening via dialogue. It also helps them to voice their needs, the life they want, and their desire for change. This supposes taking into account the identity dimension of conflict, the stories people tell about themselves, who they are, where they come from and what they fear for the future. How they relate to others depends on their perception of their identity. Thus, the challenge of the transformative process is to encourage people to have a positive sense of their identity in relation to others but not in reaction to them, to make sure that people define themselves by who they are and not in opposition to others.

Naturally, some arenas exist in which this transformative ambition is limited and for some conflicts, a direct and quick solution is more appropriate. This is the case when the protagonists do not have a significant relationship, for example in a commercial context when the conflict concerns settling a debt between two people who hate each other and no longer wish to be in contact. In such cases, the exploration of relational and cultural models has a limited interest only. However, Lederach argues that in all situations in which the opponents share a long history and will have a significant relationship in the future, when conflicts between them come back repeatedly and are deeply rooted, a transformative process becomes relevant.

6 The Narrative Model

Based on a theory developed by White and Epson, the Australians Winsdale and Monk[14] argue that conflict emerges more from the social and cultural context than impulses or people's interests. People's stories (metaphorically speaking) are socially and culturally constructed. All visions of the world and knowledge are relative to the moment in time, the place and social landscape in which they were created. Thus, it is necessary to work with these stories in which conflict is deeply rooted rather than pursuing an objective reality, because this supposed objective reality does not exist. Only multiple subjective realities exist. These stories must be placed at the centre of the mediation process, instead of being marginalised as is the case in 'interest-based' mediation models. This is because we live our lives by the stories told to us by others and those we tell to ourselves. These stories are constantly revised, adapted and recreated. This means that people that are involved in conflict are not fixed and rigid but susceptible to change.

The aim of the narrative model of mediation is precisely to organise a partnership between the opponents so that they can understand the stories behind the conflict and co-produce their preferred alternate stories. Mediation is not only a place where the participants' worlds are explored and discussed, but also where these worlds can continue to be created and transformed. The three phases of the process are the following: tell the story of the conflict and its effects, deconstruct this story and the people's positions, create conditions that favour the creation of an alternate story which opens up a space for dialogue and cooperation. The mediator's role, more directive than in the transformative model, is to help the parties create another story. The strategies used, often illustrated by Winsdale and Monk, are the following:

- Establish trust: convince each of the parties that the mediation process can be beneficial to them and that the mediator understands the depth of their distress, without appearing influenced by the other's narrative. By listening

14 G. Monk, J. Winsdale, *Narrative mediation: a new approach to transformative resolution*, San Francisco, Jossey Bank, 2001.

respectfully, the mediator must show that he/she takes each of the parties' stories seriously.

- Using a 'deconstructive' way of questioning: the mediator asks questions which invite the participants to explain how they were impacted in the conflict, with the idea that there is not one way of thinking about things, but many. This method is less polemical that of confrontation or criticism. To illustrate this, let's take the example of a conflict regarding the custody of a child. The father tells the following story: as a father who works and ensures the material livelihood of this family, he thinks he is in the best position to take care of the child. On the other hand, the mother argues that she was the first to care for the child, and gives the child permanent affection, which the father did not. Because of this, she thinks she is the most legitimate to have custody of the child. The father and the mother are having trouble considering the other's position. The father's vision is dominated by this cultural idea that material wealth is the condition of a good education, and the mother's is dominated by the cultural model and ideal that maternal care is primordial. If the mediator takes these affirmations into account as cultural, and not as individual values, he/she can help the parents to deconstruct their positions by exploring the cultural factors that have formed their point of views. The idea is not to ask the parents to analyse their religious or their cultural traditions but to help them to understand their own position as well as the other's. All it takes is inviting them to be curious about their own affirmations and what justifies them.
- Letting 'externalised' discussions develop (this technique overturns the usual logic in psychology, in which one looks for an explanation within the person): the conflict is addressed as if it were an exterior object; as a result, conversations appearing unrelated to the conflict are accepted, and even recommended. This is because 'the person is not the problem, the problem is the problem'. The way of speaking 'around' the conflict deflects blame and guilt. For example, the mediator will not ask the protagonists what the cause of their conflict is, but rather what difficulties the conflict has caused in their relationship, or how it might have impeded on the well-being of their children. Emotions can then be expressed, and resentment, anger, and hurt do not appear as aspects of themselves but as characteristics of their story.

Thus, it is recommended to tell the conflict's story to identify when it started, how it evolved, and how it affects the security, confidence, and well-being of the people that surround the parties. Then it is time to ask them if they want to act in order to change the evolution of the conflict, which opens the door to a different conversation. The mediator must be aware of the cultural constructions that affect his/her way of working (what he/she hears, understands, how he/she proceeds), and how these constructions may affect the end result. For example, some might be tempted, because of their own story, to become defenders of children or women's rights. Even if it is often limited to the domestic litigations, this 'culturalist' perspective is interesting because it highlights that even the more everyday acts are part of a cultural model, of which we are not always aware, yet still determine our actions and ways of thinking. As the conflicts we encounter and go through are themselves a consequence of this cultural model, they cannot be resolved without taking this collective dimension into account.

To clarify their common points and differences, I have put the three different models of mediation presented up until now in perspective in the table below. After having defined them, I will compare these models and their objectives, values and beliefs, as well as the empirical strategies they advocate.

7 The Systemic Model

This model, conceived within the framework of the Palo Alto school,[15] is not strictly speaking a mediation model. This is why I have presented it independently from the previous models, but it more or less irrigates the practices of mediators. It proposes an inter-relational approach to human relationships and is particularly opposed to clinical approaches centred on the subject, and also to all those who, to resolve a conflict, would neglect the context of the interactions between the protagonists. The uses of the systemic model in mediation are usually within the framework of the family, corporate, educational or political field. Mediation work is then seen as a way to treat the 'pathologies' of the communication model and not a method of action on individuals.

Within the family framework, conflict between adults only makes sense in the context of a broad and complex system of relations, that encompasses all those involved in the functioning of the family entity (parents, grandparents, children, substitute parents in the case of stepfamilies, loved ones) and concerns the familial history of each of the parties. Putting into place such a model, as opposed to the narrower clinical conception which only associates the two parties of the conflict, supposes having children participating in the mediation process, as well as other people who play an important role in the system's

---

15 Edmond Marc, Dominique Picard, *L'école de Palo Alto. Un nouveau regard sur les relations humaines*, Paris, Retz, 2000.

TABLE 4.1 Comparison between mediation models

	Harvard model	Transformative model	Narrative model
Objectives	Mediation helps people in conflict shift their focus from their positions to their interests in order to generate mutually acceptable situations.	Mediation helps people shift from self-centred, vulnerable and uncertain positions to a better self-confidence and capacity to understand and feel the other's perspective.	Mediation gives people a better understanding of the cultural dimension of their narratives and helps them to co-construct stories of cooperation and mutual respect.
Values and foundational beliefs	– Conflict is seen as a problem to which one must find a solution. – Individuals act independently and are responsible for their choices. – People pursue their own interests but the adjustment of their common interests is crucial. – People have the capacity to make decisions that concern them and are, as opposed to an outsider, the best placed to resolve their own conflicts.	– Conflict is a crisis of human interaction that can have positive functions. – People are interconnected. They have separate identities but live with ties and relations to one another. – People search for a moral progress represented by empowerment and recognition. – People are the best placed to manage their own conflicts. This means an underlying optimistic vision of their abilities and values.	– Conflict is the expression of the dominant cultural discourse which circulates in the community. – The social and cultural context shapes the positions, attitudes, and the interests of the people and their identities. – The person is not the problem, the problem is the problem. – Conflict comes from a cultural shock between different narratives. Its deconstruction opens opportunities to mobilise people's resources.

TABLE 4.1 Comparison between mediation models (*cont.*)

	Harvard model	Transformative model	Narrative model
Work methods	– The mediator helps separate the people from their conflict by accepting the expression of their emotions and by developing communication and confidence. – He/she directs the process, makes sure the rules are respected, favours the discussions likely to lead to an agreement. – The mediator helps people imagine a large array of solutions. The options and ideas are evaluated and selected within the spirit of mutual gain. An objective criteria is used to evaluate the options such as the value of the market, the law, an expert's opinion, and commercial practices. The parties are encouraged to develop a BATNA.	– The mediator helps people express their emotions and feelings on which the work is organised. – He/she gives individuals considerable latitude in managing the process. He/she adopts a very flexible application of mediation rules and invites reflection with open-ended questions but avoids rephrasing. – He/she concentrates on the here and the now, is attentive to the interactions between people and searches for signs that help him/her to favour empowerment and the comprehension of the other's position.	– The mediator lets people express their emotions, but they are not considered as essential aspects of a person, but more as characteristics of their story. – He/she asks questions, inviting the participants to step out of the story of their conflict and understand how they got caught in the dispute's net. – The mediator stimulates cooperation between people in order to both deconstruct their positions, interests and expectations, and to build an alternative story with them.

functioning and can unblock the situation. This practice, which is far from unanimous in the closed off world of mediation, is used in various domains.

Corporate conflicts can be extremely diverse, opposing both employers to employees or employees between themselves. Whatever their nature is, including behavioural deviances that appear personal such as bullying, the systemic model considers that these conflicts cannot be treated and understood intrinsically. They have to be replaced within the more general context of hierarchy, work organisation, communication channels, and of human resources management.

In the same way, conflicts involving the educational field, which may involve relationships between the school management and teachers, between teachers and parents, between teachers and students, and between students themselves, cannot be worked on without taking in account the effects of school organization. Thus, they cannot be separated from questions such as the overall school climate, the coherence of the pedagogical project and of the team that supports it, the organisation of lessons and activities, the place of parents and of their representatives in decisions and the disciplinary sanction system.

In the political field, the famous *multi-track diplomacy*[16] model can be considered as the heir of Bateson and his disciples' research. Even though this model does not reference mediation and is silent on the fundamental question of the third party's posture, it must be included in this analysis' field as it is important to the training of many political mediators. Diamond and Mac Donald highlight the necessity of rejecting the principle of a hierarchical approach of understanding political conflicts, which only takes into consideration the bargaining between states, governors or diplomatic personnel. They argue that, in order to ensure a sustainable peace, the correlation between nine tracks presented in the shape of a compass must be taken into account (government, professional resolution of the conflict, market, citizens, research, training and education, activism, religion, funding, public opinion and communication).

This 'systematised approach to peace' searches for complementarity between traditional diplomacy, financial and institutional action, partnership with local authorities, women and peace entrepreneurs to develop the implication of the community and improve the local harmony by leaning on local wisdom. As I shall explain later on in the political mediation section, other

16 Louise Diamond, John W. McDonald, *Multi track diplomacy: a systems approach to Peace*, Kumarian Press, 1996.

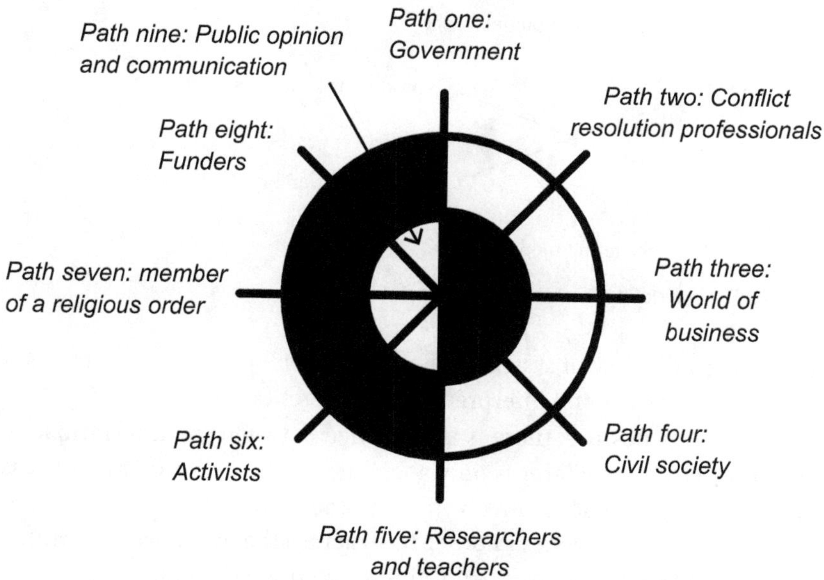

FIGURE 4.4 Multi-track diplomacy

bottom-up models, which cultivate a spirit of peace within conflicting communities, are also inspired by a systemic approach when they do not separate researching a solution to the conflict from more general preoccupations such as the promotion of social justice and the distribution of power and wealth.

8 The Empirical Hybridisation of Models

The models presented gravitate around the 'fundamentals' of mediation, the presence of an impartial and independent third party without any decision-making power, who, through face-to-face meetings, facilitates the communication between the parties of the conflict. However, this 'core business' is filled with tensions which often have the effect of producing hybrid and adaptive practice models, hybrid when they delicately combine the elements of different models, adaptive when the choice of the model varies depending on the nature of the conflict (relational or financial), the parties' characteristics (social and cultural background, emotional charge) or even depending on the phases of the mediation process (establishing communication, searching for solutions). These tensions can be illustrated by a diagram composed of three dimensions: the third party's stance (directive, non-directive), the objective of the mediation (solution, communication) and the mediation's

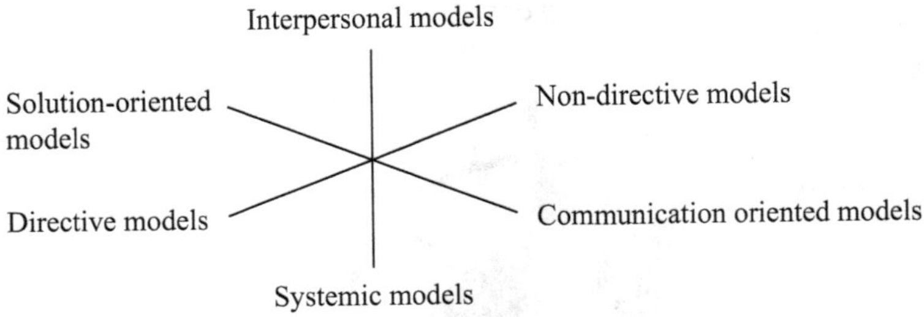

FIGURE 4.5 The multidimensional dimensions of the practice models

field of action (individual or systemic). Each mediator's practice is the result of the way he/she receives and interprets these different tensions.

Concerning this posture, there is a difference between the transformative models, in which the mediator is only a facilitator, and in which the process wholly belongs to the parties involved; and other more intrusive models in which the mediator intervenes in order to structure the exchange and search for solutions, and even to suggest solutions in the more extreme cases.

Certain models centred on subjects coexist with systemic models, in which the conflict cannot be treated independently from the context in which it arises. This larger vision, closer to social psychology, involves different methodologies. In the first case, the mediation work is focused only on the opponents; in the second case it includes either some people or the entirety of the group impacted by the conflict, and its regulation in which they can participate. Amongst the models centred on persons, the question of whether they have a therapeutic dimension remains. This is not the case of the narrative model, which clearly distinguishes the work on the person and on the conflict. This question is especially relevant for the transformative model. Because, although many specialists agree that mediation can have therapeutic effects, it cannot be a substitute for therapy, for several reasons. Firstly, it helps people tackle an isolated and explicit conflict which opposes them to another and not on a personal psychic conflict. Secondly, it is limited in time (in general, practitioners avoid planning more than a dozen mediation sessions in order to limit transference or dependence mechanisms), as opposed to therapy which can be a medium or long-term process. Finally, methodologically, the mediator can only activate communication techniques and not other clinical techniques, such as behavioural. However, certain practitioners put into place hybrid models which spread confusion, and some assert they practise therapeutic mediation.

The third dimension concerns the objective of mediation. It opposes practices which are largely focused on the search for a solution, consider conflict as harmful, and others oriented towards the creation or the stimulation of com-

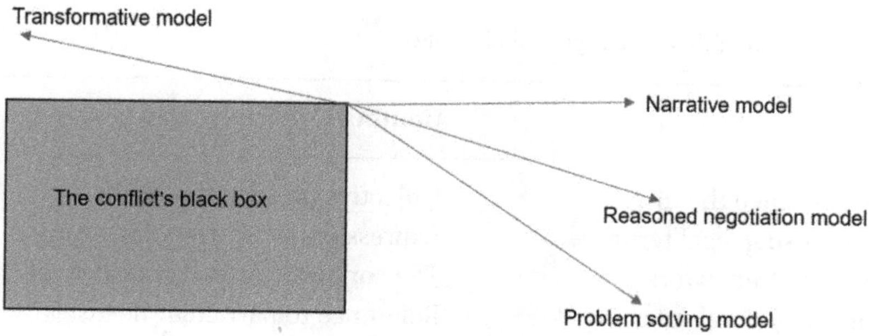

FIGURE 4.6 Opening of the conflict's black box

munication between the opponents and a mutual recognition. This choice leads to very distinct methods of working. Whereas in settlement-oriented models, the mediator seldom opens the conflict's black box, only letting surface the emotions that might lead to an agreement quickly, in the other models, he/she will allow feelings and emotions to be expressed. How open this box is depends on the individual case, the people's competence and the mediator's initial training. All studies on this subject show, for example, that mediators who have a background in law and then trained to become a mediator are more likely to favour a problem resolution type of mediation practice in which the black box is rarely opened. However, mediators who have a background in psychology or humanities in general lean towards more open models which take the latent conflict into account more than the explicit conflict.

The more this box is opened, the more the mediator works on the conflict, and the more the box is closed, the more the mediator is focused on the dispute. Isabelle Gorchs puts forward an interesting distinction[17] on this point. According to her, dispute is often only the translation of a conflict in legal terms and mediation cannot be an alternative to judicial power as the practice concerns non-judicial matters. This distinction is crucial as it is the source of many misunderstandings between mediators themselves, taking into account the variety of mediation models, or between mediators and judicial professions. In reality, they do not all have the same job. Problem resolution type mediations work with disputes, like the legal system. The exchange is overcoded, the positions are legally rationalised, the word 'party' is used, and the idea is to know if someone is within their rights. Laws are referred to, and jurisprudence and the enforced customs are used to calibrate decisions. Judicial competence is then asked of the mediators. On the contrary, in transformative and narrative models (the Harvard negotiation model is a hybrid

17 Gorchs Béatrice, 'La médiation dans le procès civil: sens et contresens. Essai de mise en perspective du conflit et du litige', *Revue trimestrielle de droit civil*, 2003, nr 3, 409–425.

TABLE 4.2 Work modalities on disputes and conflicts

Dispute	Conflict
Objective: resolve the dispute	Objective: resolve the conflict
Expression using legal terms	Expression using everyday terms
Fixed dispute framework	The conflict's framework can evolve
Reference to general rules ('normative ready-to-wear')	Reference to particular needs ('normative tailor-made')
The final decision can resolve the dispute but not necessarily the conflict	The agreement can contribute to resolving the conflict
Legal skills are necessary	Legal skills are not necessary

of both categories), the mediation practice is organised around the conflict. It is talked about in terms of suffering, trouble, injustice and absence of communication, the words 'actors', 'mediated' and 'mediating' are used. The root causes of the situation are searched for, and in this field, it is often thought that 'one conflict often hides another'. People lean on their personal needs to find mutually satisfying solutions. In this case, it is not necessary for the mediator to have any legal skills, but having a penchant for humanities and communication techniques is thoroughly recommended.

The difference between dispute and conflict can also be symbolised by using the iceberg metaphor. Whereas the dispute represents the tip of the iceberg, the conflict corresponds to the immersed part of the iceberg, whose volume is much bigger. Whereas the legal system or the closed models of problem resolution only take into account the obvious dimension of the conflict, the open mediation models tackle the feelings, emotions, needs and values which are at the root of the conflict.

It is easy to understand that what is at stake when using one model or the other is not only theoretical. Those working with disputes (coming from a legal or commercial environment) and those working with conflicts (coming generally from a humanities or social sciences background) do not have the same positions in the social hierarchy and do not have the same financial and symbolic resources. There, behind the conflict surrounding the definition of mediation, and the skills needed to practise mediation, hides another conflict, in which those who protect the monopoly of legal professions oppose those who fight against it. The question of what motivates these people, these motivations can be mystical, ideological, social and financial, does colour the conflict differently but does not modify its political and institutional structure.

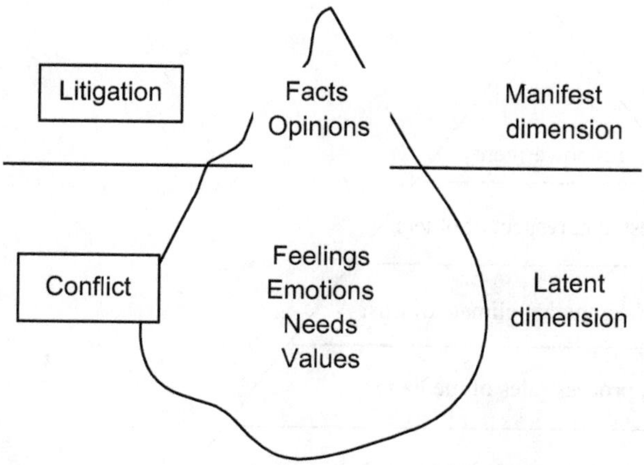

FIGURE 4.7 The iceberg metaphor

Finally, to conclude this chapter, which, without going into the detail in terms of the tricks of mediation, has the objective of encouraging practitioners to have a reflective gaze on their ways of doing their job, Maslow's pyramid of needs can be used and adapted to the 'hybrid' needs of the mediation process.

The first level refers to the individuals' physiological needs (eating, drinking, sleeping, breathing). It highlights the material and above all psychological needs which, for some individuals, can be more appropriately attended to when they are able to regulate particularly destructive conflicts that damage their mental and physical health. The second level (physical, health, work, material security) shows us that people need a sufficiently reassuring environment in order to start a mediation process and become committed. The mediator's structuring role is essential to curb the negative effects of the extremely insecure situation of having to communicate with a hostile or indifferent opponent. The third level (social needs: love, friendship, intimacy) highlight how important the mediator is in creating an empathetic environment (which is not the same as sympathetic), indispensable for the actors to be implicated and sincere in their commitment. The fourth level introduces the need for the mediation process to strengthen the protagonists' self-esteem and respect for others, these two elements being closely connected. This work on otherness demands that the mediator progressively distance himself/herself from the exchange, and leave as much space as possible to the two protagonists. The fifth and last level of the pyramid is personal accomplishment, or as Bush and Folger name it, empowerment, which is expressed both by the capacity to have a relationship with the other actor, as well as by the capacity to face difficulties in a constructive way, for example the establishment of a mutually satisfying agreement.

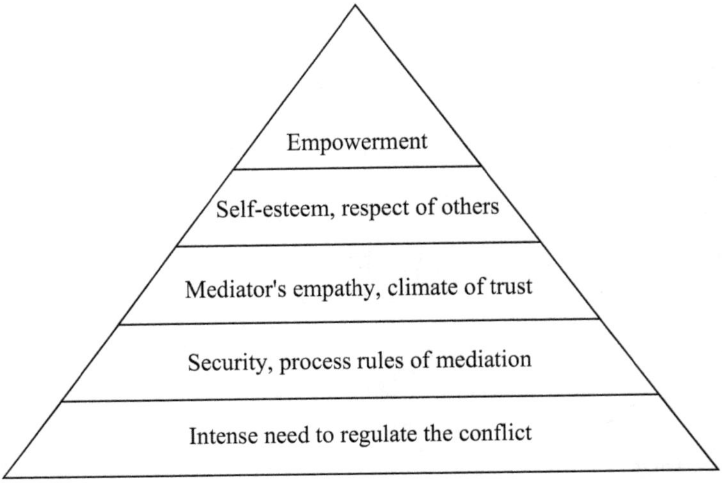

FIGURE 4.8 The hierarchy of needs in mediation

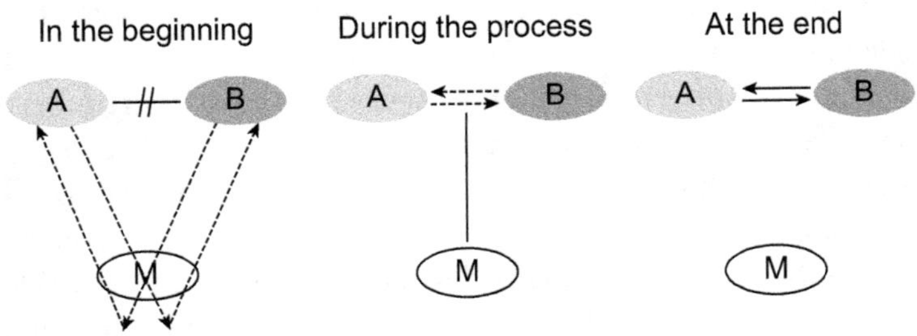

FIGURE 4.9 The progressive distancing of the mediator

PART 3

The Fields of Mediation

In this book, I will not specifically focus on institutional and administrative types of mediation in which so-called mediators disregard even the minimal ethical and deontological requirements of mediation. They manage the relationship between the organisation that pays them and its users, do their best to make the exchanges with clients go smoothly, shed light on misunderstandings, give little-known regulatory information or intercede in the favour of people wronged by institutional practices. They are also committed to defending citizens, consumers, clients, users, and helping them face the challenges that the failure of commercial or administrative life presents. They support people in need, whether they be poor, immigrants, or homeless, to help them through administrative procedures. All these functions that they have linked to helping the various victims of our society are extremely crucial in the humanist perspective of having one's rights recognised and maintaining social relations. However, this does not mean they are mediations, even though they use the same vocabulary, because they do not respect the foundational necessity of the mediator's role, which is to be 'in the middle'.

All types of mediation mentioned in this book have the common denominator of the intervention of a third impartial neutral party with no decision-making power. What distinguishes them from one another is the mediator's level of independence, the specificities pertaining to the institutional or legal world in which they develop, how institutionalised the practices are, the objectives they have, and finally the policies that shape them. The weight of these factors can vary depending on the field of practice, but all the actors know the tensions that determine their own dynamic. Firstly, I will mention organised mediations dealing with general interest conflicts, starting with the oldest one, political mediation, which began in the middle of the 17th century, up until recent environmental mediations. Then, following their increasing quantitative importance, I shall present judicial, family, social, educational, commercial, company and finally sanitary mediation.

 | DOI:10.1163/9789004734067_009

CHAPTER 5

Political Mediation

On the 24th of October 1648, the Münster and Osnabrück treaties put an end to the Thirty Years' War. This peace, named the Peace of Westphalia, was significant in European history as it organised relations between European countries until the dawn of the First World War. It is relevant for us because it was achieved through mediation, in the modern sense of the term, which took place over several years (from 1643 to 1648) and led by Cardinal Fabbio Chigi (1599–1667, he later became Pope Alexander VII), appointed by the Pope and the ambassador of the Republic of Venice, Alvise Contarini (1601–1684). The former's mission was to soften relations between Catholic powers whereas the latter managed relations with Sweden and German Protestant princes. Chigi received the instruction to stay neutral, to apply the *indifferentia* principle (which can be translated as equal treatment to both parties in order to keep their trust), to avoid suggesting solutions to the parties, to keep their secrets unless he had explicit authorisation, to seek religious peace, and to suggest laying down their arms so as to negotiate better. The two accomplices organised an impressive number of meetings and they shuttled back and forth between the protagonists. They conformed to a strict principle of impartiality despite the pressure they were facing to take on the role of the referee, and never accepted gifts nor invited the parties to their table. Duss-Von Werdt held that these two mediators managed to develop political mediation by establishing new requirements between countries and religions, and by respecting the diversity of their traditions and cultures.[1]

After assisting to this mediation, Abraham de Wicquefort (1606–1682), the French King's Dutch ambassador, proposed a first conceptualisation of the mediation project in a book that enjoyed great European success.[2] One of the chapters named 'Of Mediation and mediating Ambassadors' is a proper mediation manual, which I cannot resist quoting as it is such a pioneer for modem problems that mediators encounter in all types of conflict.

> The quality of Mediator is one of the most difficult that an Ambassador has to fill, and Mediation a most difficult task. The Prince he represents

1 Duss von-Werdt Joseph, *Homo mediator. Geschichte und Menschenbild der Mediatior,* Stuttgart, Klett-Cotta, 2005.

2 Abraham de Wicquefort, *L'ambassadeur et ses fonctions,* La Haye, J et D. Stencher, 1681.

 | DOI:10.1163/9789004734067_010

> must be without interest, and his Minister without passion, which is not easy, nor ordinary.
>
> Power is absolutely not necessary to the Mediator […] the word "Mediator" expresses the position very well: it consists in putting oneself in the middle, to bring two parties that have drifted away from one another closer […].
>
> The instructions […] given to the Legate Mediator […] are firstly, that he should be neutral above all else, otherwise his missions would be rendered useless, the Legate would not be accurate and his conduct would be observed as partial.
>
> […] 2. That he should make no suggestions; as he could make one that would be disagreeable to one of the parties, and in doing so, would be rendered suspect and futile, that he should just faithfully report what has been said […] 4. He should gain the trust of both parties, so they can express their real feelings to him. 5. The mediator should keep secrets and not communicate to the latter what the former does not want to. 6. That he should not become a referee […]; as instead of being a mediator, he would become a judge.

The ethical and deontological lessons one can take away from this story are numerous: keeping one's impartiality, not becoming a referee, having no interest in the conflict, having no line of conduct except helping the parties sign a peace agreement, earning their trust by assuring them their words are confidential, never making propositions and not judging those the parties formulate, not having any power, staying 'in the middle'. These lessons were reworked 40 years later by François de Caillères (1645–1717), who as a diplomat and part of King Louis the XIV's cabinet witnessed the signing of the Treaty of Ryswick (1697), which hailed the end of the Nine Years' War. In the work he left behind,[3] he meticulously describes the mediation process and closely analyses the ethical questions that the mediator poses to the power disequilibrium between the parties. He also notes that a treaty can only exist if it is based on mutual benefits, which introduces the modern idea of a win-win process. In the absence of this condition, agreements quickly become obsolete.

---

3 François de Caillères, *De la manière de négocier avec les souverains* (Pour la compagnie, Amsterdam), 1716.

These different contributions seem to have been forgotten for several centuries before being used in contemporary debates. Mediation timidly re-appeared during the Convention for the pacifist resolution of international conflicts signed at the Hague in 1907. In its Title II, Article 2, it states that in case of 'grave dissent or conflict, before resorting to arms, the contracting powers convene to resort... either to mediation's or one or more allied powers' good offices'. Article 4 then defines the mediator's role as 'conciliating opposite pretentions and appeasing the resentment that may exist between conflicting nations'. Article 33 of Chapter VI, which tackles the pacifist resolution of the disputes of the United Nations charter written in 1945, only mentions mediation as a pacifist way of resolving disputes.

This historical background shows us that the emergence of mediation is recent,[4] and concomitant with the evolution of political conflict. Resorting to force became rarer at the end of the 20th century due to the transformation of geopolitical equilibrium since decolonisation, the end of the Cold War, the rise of democracy, and the increasing interdependence of economies. The rise of mediation must also be put into context with the considerable decrease in international conflicts to the profit of intra-national conflicts;[5] these conflicts made it necessary to imagine new strategies, as their regulation did not fall within these diplomats' competence.

Whereas mediation attempts concerned 20 per cent of the conflicts between 1945 and 1962, this number increased to 34 per cent in the period between 1963 and 1989 and later to 64 per cent between 1990 and 1996.[6] These mediations intervened essentially within the field of territorial or ethnic conflict (these two elements can overlap) between geographically close opponents. The proof of the rise of mediation practices is demonstrated by the creation of a support group within the UN's political affairs department in 2007, a group which brings its expertise and logistic support to mediation initiatives.

At the same time, new peace actors emerged. International mediations between 1945 and 1995 gave more than their share to diverse countries (47 per cent) and the UN (23 per cent). Then come the regional organisations (11 per cent), the NGOs (6 per cent), individuals (4 per cent) and mixed medi-

---

4 See Jacques Faget, 'les métamorphoses du travail de paix. Etat des travaux sur la médiation dans les conflits politiques violents', *Revue française de science politique,* vol. 58, nr 2, avril 2008, 309–333.

5 Andrew Mack (Dir.), *Guerres et paix au XXIème siècle,* Presses Universitaires d'Oxford, University of British Columbia, 2005.

6 International Crisis Behavior Project Data Archive, http://www.icbnet.org.

ations (9 per cent).[7] But the mediations accounted for here are not always those defined in this book. Peace studies liken mediation with good offices and all types of interventions led by third parties. Thus, it is probable, even though the quantitative proof is impossible to provide, that the roles of the regional organisations, of the secular or religious NGOs, of the charismatic individuals of foundations and expert scholars, are at least as important as that of the State in the civil and ethnic conflicts that can tear countries apart.

1 The Two Approaches to Political Mediation

Most of the works on political mediation concern mediations led by countries and their diplomats in international conflicts. We can add those initiated by international or even regional organisations to the list. However, other types of mediation exist, such as bottom-up mediations led by less powerful and visible actors. Most of the time, these mediations are concerned with ethnic or cultural conflict internal to the country.

1.1 *Top-Down Mediations*

The first top-down mediation organisation that comes to mind, naturally, is the UN. The general secretary and their special envoys (for example Martti Ahtissaari, who won the Nobel Peace Prize in 2008 for his actions in Kosovo) have always taken on a mediating role in their own way (because the organisation is politically ambiguous). This fact, never negated, was reinforced in 2007 by the creation of a mediation support group within the UN's political affairs department, a group whose aim is to bring its expertise, skills, and logistic support to mediation processes all around the world.

A few regional organisations whose actions are akin to mediation can also be cited. In Europe, the EU (within the framework of the second pillar of the common foreign and security policy (CFSP)) has been involved in Ukraine and South Ossetia, as well as the Organisation for Security and Co-operation in Europe (OSCE), which has taken action in the Baltic states, Abkhazia, Transnistria, Ossetia, and Georgia. Elsewhere, the African Union can be cited, which was involved in conflicts in Angola, Burundi, Liberia, Sierra Leone, Tchad, Darfur, Ivory Coast, Zimbabwe, as well as the ASEAN (Association of Southeast Asian Nations), the League of Arab States, and finally the organisation of

7 Judith Fretter, 'The United Nations and the mediation in international conflicts', in Jacob Bercovitch (ed), *Studies in International mediation*, Basingstoke, Macmillan, 2002.

American States (OAS) for its actions in Honduras, El Salvador, Haiti and Bolivia. Their States and diplomacy complete this inventory.

These mediations have only been studied since the 1970s, and it is only in the mid-1980s that American scholars started making them more visible. Their research generally refers to mediation as 'a conflict management process in which the opponents seek assistance, to tackle their conflict or resolve their differences without resorting to physical force or invoking the law's authority'.[8] Their research also leaves the mediator free to use the posture that seems adequate to him or her as long as he/she avoids the traps of physical constraint and of the law, which opens the door to all sorts of influence and manipulation.

This work is divided between case studies and quantitative research. Many research fellows strive to use sophisticated mathematical models to analyse samples that can range from a hundred to more than 350 mediation cases over a 15-to-50-year period. Others build simulation models with which they test the efficiency of diverse mediation practices.[9] All in all, this work seems heavily influenced by a finalist obsession, in the tradition of rational choice theory, of tracking down the magical formula that would pacify the world.

The tonality of this research expresses a Western vision, often marked by ethnocentrism even when, paradoxically, it evokes the need for the parties' empowerment. It magnifies the peacemaking objective without acknowledging the positive dimensions that conflict can have for dominated peoples. It then predominantly focuses both on international armed conflicts (which concern international equilibrium and thus the great powers' interests), to the detriment of so-called peripheral or national conflicts, and on the actions of the governments, of the head of State and of official diplomacy. This state-centred work is linked to the realistic paradigm of international relations, essentially concerned with high politics. It values the technical contributions of the problem-solving theory, which it uses too mechanically. I will here present a summary of the five most talked-about themes, namely conflict, the parties involved, the mediation's context, the mediator's positioning, and the measure of the mediation's effects.

---

8 Jacob Bercovitch, Théodore Anagnoson, Donnette Wille, 'Some conceptual issues and empirical trends in the study of successful mediation in international relations', *Journal of Peace Research*, 1991, vol. 28, pp. 7–17.

9 See for example, amongst numerous attempts, Alastair Smith, Allan Stam, 'Mediation and peacekeeping in a random walk model of civil and interstate war', *International Review Studies*, 2003, 115–135.

1.1.1 Conflict

Conflicts go through different life cycles and can be broken down into different phases, some of which are more suited to the intervention of a third party than others. Thus, to have more chances to succeed, the mediation should intervene at the right moment. Then comes the question of being able to know when this moment has arrived. For some, there is not one favourable moment, but two. The mediation efforts that take place soon after the dispute would have better chance of succeeding than those taking place after a long period of time. If the conflict is not resolved quickly, the efforts during the intermediary period are probably not as effective, and mediation may even be counter-productive.[10]

Other analysts renounce the notion of conflict maturity, and prefer that of the trigger event which transforms the perceptions and attitudes of the opponents. According to Zartman,[11] a conflict is ready to be resolved when a mutually harmful stalemate arises, when each of the parties realises they cannot resolve the conflict by themselves or when they feel that the conflict's escalation is leading to catastrophe, that the conflict's costs are no longer tolerable. Maturity can also be dependent on political changes internal to the conflicting groups, for example the emergence of new leaders, a contested leadership of a tear within the government, previously united by its warlike objectives. In other words, a conflict's maturity cannot be evaluated rationally, but rather by taking into account its psychological dimension, as well as the nature and intensity of the passions that the actors have. The window of opportunity for mediation to succeed would thus be quite narrow. Even if the factor of maturity seems influential to negotiate a ceasefire or reduce violence between the warring parties,[12] distinct dynamics determine the short – or long-term success of the mediation process.

1.1.2 The Parties

Assuming that the mediation process cannot be imposed and relies on the actor's will, the vast majority of authors hold that this choice is dependent on strategic and tactical considerations, because peace is not always what

10 Patrick Regan, Allan Stam, 'In the nick of time: conflict management, mediation timing and the duration of interstate disputes', *International Studies Quarterly*, 2000, 239–260.

11 William Zartman 'Ripeness: the hurting stalemate and beyond' in *International conflict resolution after the cold war*, P.C. Sternand, Daniel. Druckman, Washington D.C., National Academy Press, pp. 225–250. 2000.

12 Moorad Mooradian et Daniel Druckman, 'Hurting stalemate or mediation? The conflict over Nagorno-Karabakh, 1990–1995', *Journal of Peace Research*, vol. 36, nr 6, 1999, pp. 709–727.

the opponents search for. From this point of view, Richmond[13] highlights the importance of analysing how the mediator is perceived and mediation instrumentalized. It can be used in a cynical way, like a dilatory manoeuvre to gain time (the frequent ceasefires in Bosnia allowed the belligerents to reconstitute their forces before resuming combat), as a strategic option that allows rearmament and the redeployment of troops in better positions (as in the case of Angola), to mask the exhaustion of resources, to profit from a temporarily favourable power dynamic which leads to making the fewest concessions possible. The acceptance of a mediation also allows one to project a good image of oneself, to obtain alliances or even financial fallout. It can even be founded on internal political reasons, such as keeping one's leadership, or replying to the population's demands. This strategic conception of mediation often leads to failure. For example, in the Cypriot conflict, the Greeks and the Turks used mediation to attain incompatible initial objectives.[14] In any event, the choice of mediation, without being completely rational, because the actors do not have all the information (for example, one party thinks the other party has resources they do not have, and wrongly anticipates its demands), most of the time only represents one strategy amongst a complex array of possibilities. It would rely more on individual interests rather than 'common values' or a 'convergence of interests'.[15]

The parties that have long relationships tainted with friendship or cooperation bonds are considered more valuable to protect than those who only have recent relations. Cultural proximity would help the success of the mediation, notably when the opponents share a politically democratic culture.[16] Countries with a multiparty system who engage in mediation have a 35 per cent success rate, whereas only 6 per cent of mediations between single party countries have a favourable outcome.[17] Even the actors contest the effects of 'civilisation shock' dear to Samuel Huntington, because according to them, conflicts between Western and Arab countries, despite an 'intercultural dissonance between the individualistic and collective cultures' do not obtain worse results

13 Oliver Richmond, 'Devious objectives and the disputants view of international mediation. A theoretical framework', *Journal of Peace Research*, 1998, pp. 707–722.

14 Ibid.

15 Thomas Princen, *Intermediaries in international conflict*, Princeton, NJ: Princeton University Press, 1992.

16 Russell Leng, Patrick Regan, 'Social and political cultural effects on the outcomes of mediation in militarized interstate disputes', *International Studies Quarterly*, 2003, 47, 431–452.

17 Jacob Bercovitz, Théodore Anagnoson, et Donnette Wylle, 1991, op.cit.

than conflicts between Arab countries. Only democratic countries are more likely to resort to mediation.

1.1.3 Context

The international context impacts the mediation process from its initiation to its conclusion. The financial and political pressures exerted by other countries which have a direct or indirect interest in the conflict are influential, as well as the attitude of neighbouring countries impacted by the waves of refugees arriving on their territory.[18] The simultaneous occurrence of other events, like the beginning of another conflict or the influential neighbouring countries' change in diplomatic policy, can transform the process.[19]

The presence of peacekeeping forces on the concerned territory may affect a mediation process. If these initiatives, generally developed by the UN, are necessary to avoid the conflict restarting or escalating, they also inhibit the opponent's efforts to search for negotiated solutions. The Cyprus case illustrates this dilemma. The same investigation shows, however, that the presence of interpositional forces can be favourable once the peace agreement is signed. It reassures the opponents and allows them to lean further into the pacification work.[20]

The existence of financial support brought to the mediation process would determine its openness but also its nature. Without Norway's 60-million-dollar investment, the 1993 Oslo Accords would not have been signed. The mediation undertaken by Alexis Keller that amounted to the 2003 Geneva agreements between Israelis and Palestinians would not have been possible without the support, even if it is comparatively modest (1.5 million dollars), of two Swiss foundations. This private origin of this funding ensured a great independence from his government.[21] The mediation organised in Mozambique by the Sant'Egidio community took place thanks to the Vatican and the Italian state's support, the main funding partner in the country at the time.[22] Several authors insist on the organisational conditions favourable to the serenity of the process such as the distance from the conflict's territory or

---

18 Hizkias Assefa, *Mediation of civil wars: approaches and strategies – the Sudan conflict*, Boulder, CO, Westview, 1987.

19 Marieke Kleiboer, 'Understanding success and failure in international mediation', *Journal of Conflict Resolution*, 1996, 40, 360–389.

20 J. Michael Greig, Paul Diehl, 'The peacekeeping-Peacemaking dilemma', *International Studies Quarterly* (2005), 49, 621–645.

21 Alexis Keller, *L'accord de Genève: un pari réaliste*, Paris, Seuil, Labor et Fides, 2004.

22 Jean Louis Marret, *La fabrication de la paix, nouveaux conflits, nouveaux acteurs, nouvelles méthodes*, Paris, Ellipses, 2001.

the necessity for optimal comfort conditions allowing an atmosphere as warm as possible to be created.

1.1.4 The Mediator's Positioning

Most specialists distinguish between three types of mediators: the facilitator, the formulator and the manipulator. The facilitator's role is to be a communication channel between the parties; he/she only has little control over the process (this is the case of the Norwegian mediators Thor Larsen and Arne Anaheim in the Israeli-Palestinian conflict of 1993). It is sometimes referred to as 'the good offices'. He/she can, at the most, organise the logistics of the process, facilitate communication, and pass on messages between the actors if face-to-face communication is impossible. The formulator, meanwhile, brings a more substantial contribution as he/she has more formal control and chooses the place, number and type of meetings, plans the agenda, manages the distribution of information and suggests new solutions to the parties (an example of this type of mediator is George Mitchell[23] in the North Ireland conflict). The manipulator can not only formulate propositions but also use his position and his power, influence and persuasion resources, give ultimatums (an example that illustrates this is Jimmy Carter and the Camp David agreements in 1979). However, only powerful mediators, possibly influential in an international environment, can play this role. Numerous actors consider that the mediator must not stick to one mediator stance, but rather adapt his/her mode of intervention to the evolution of the crisis or conflict.

The dominant doctrine considers the mediator's impartiality as a fundamental condition of the mediation's success, the only way of gaining the opponent's trust, and thus establishing the conditions of the mediator's legitimacy. However, whereas Wehr and Lederach show that trust is a determining element, it is not necessarily associated, notably in certain Central American societies, with impartiality.[24] On the contrary, there would exist an insider-partial and not an outsider-neutral mediator, whose acceptance would be founded not on distance or objectivity but on his/her links with the conflict and trust relations with the parties. These authors stress that this type of mediator can be found in cultural contexts where the face-to-face relations continue to characterise political, financial and social exchanges, and where tradition has not been eroded by modernity. According to Zartman and Touval, imparti-

---

23 Democrat leader in the American Senate, elected representative of Maine, then president of the *International Crisis Group*, he intervened as an American emissary in the Irish conflict and contributed to the signing of the Belfast Peace agreement in 1998.

24 Paul Wehr, Jean Paul Lederach, 'Mediating conflict in Central America', *Journal of Peace Research*, 1991, 98, pp. 85–98.

ality is subordinated to the mediator's possession of power, for example that of giving out *sticks* (negative sanctions) and *carrots* (positive sanctions) or representing a material support.[25] Bercovitz and Houston argue that power is more influential than impartiality and the more leverage the mediator has, the more the parties expect him/her to be impartial.[26] Andrew Kydd illustrates this point of view by arguing that the mediator can reduce the probability of conflict by giving them information. In doing this, he does introduce a bias, but according to a model based on game theory, a biased mediator can seem more credible in the actors' eyes. In other words, impartiality is not required attribute for a successful mediator, on the contrary, the model shows that a certain amount of bias, notably in giving information, is not only acceptable but also necessary.[27]

The notion of the mediator's power provokes numerous debates. For example, Rubin distinguishes six forms of the mediator's power:[28] the power to reward when he/she is able to offer advantages to the protagonists in exchange for the shift in their behaviour; the coercive power based on the threat of sanctions; the expert power that comes from the knowledge and the expertise of the mediator in the matter; the legitimacy power based on authority and the mediator's charisma; the relational power which is based on existing relations between the mediator and the opponents; the informational power which positions the mediator as a messenger between them. Conversely, Quaker mediators value having a low profile and talk about the power of powerlessness.[29] Their intervention is precisely acceptable because they have no power to constrain the parties and do not have ulterior motives or objectives. They only have the leisure of applying a model and influencing the tonality of the exchanges. However, most analysts think that if 'pure' mediators (the so-called Norwegian model) can be quite successful in the preliminary stages when the communication resumes, only powerful mediators can manage to arrive at the signature and enforcement of an agreement. This

---

25 Saadia Touval, William Zartman, *International Mediation in theory and practice*, Boulder, Westview Point, 1985.

26 Jacob Bercovich, Allison Houston, 'Influence of mediator characteristics and behavior on the success of mediation in international relations', *International Journal of Conflict Management*, nr 4, octobre 1996.

27 Andrew Kydd, 'Which side are you on? Bias, credibility and mediation', *American Journal of Political Science*, vol. 47, nr 4, October 2003, pp. 597–611.

28 Jeffery Rubin, 'International mediation in context', in J. Bercovitz, J. Rubin (eds) *Mediation in International relations: approaches to conflict management*, New York, St Martin's Press, 1992, pp. 249–272.

29 Thomas Princen, 'Joseph Elder. Quiet peacemaking in a civil war', in *When talks Works*, Deborah Keble ed. San Francisco Jossey-Bass, 1994, pp. 428–445.

would be the reason behind the failure of the Oslo peace process.[30] This leads us to the recurring theme of the results of mediation processes results.

1.1.5 The Measure of Mediation's Effects

The delicate question of mediation's success is an obsession for the authors even if it raises more methodological questions that it gives answers. It expresses an 'instrumental' perception of mediation which prioritises the objective result in the short or medium term (signature of a treaty, cease-fire, arrangement, beginning of a dialogue, de-escalation of hostilities) over the operation mode and its subjective consequences in the medium or long term (quality of the communication, change of attitude of the populations, construction of common projects). Most analysts are looking for the recipe which will contribute to optimising the chances of success of the mediations undertaken.

According to Dixon, across 220 cases in which the countries have accepted the intervention of a third party, 40 per cent have led to the conflict's de-escalation.[31] These processes always try to identify the factors that favour agreements and in particular the nature of the conflict, the mediator's characteristics, his/her technique, the length of the mediation. When Bercovitch and Derouen[32] assert, after an analysis of 309 cases, that the regulation of conflict by mediation roughly has one chance in three of 'being successful', they take care to distinguish these conflicts depending on their nature because the resolution of so-called traditional international conflicts would be a lot more frequent (about two thirds of the cases) than that of ethnic conflicts (a third). According to them, the mediation process has a 60 per cent chance of succeeding when it is started at the right moment, by experienced mediators (who obtain the largest number of agreements and better-quality agreements) who use directive strategies. Directivity would have a positive impact on the probability of obtaining an agreement and appeasing the crisis. Thus, Siniver, when analysing four mediation cases in the Arab-Israeli conflict (Bunch in 1948, Kissinger for the Yom Kippur war in 1973, Carter for the Camp David agreements in 1979, the Norwegian diplomats of the Oslo agreements in 1993),[33] asserts that the most efficient mediator is the mediator who can mobilise the most resources (this is the case of Kissinger and Carter) to change the opponent's

30 Asaf Siniver, 'Power, impartiality and timing: three hypotheses on third party mediation in the middle east', *Political Studies*, 2006, vol. 54, 806–826.

31 William Dixon, 'Third-Party techniques for preventing conflict escalation and promoting peaceful settlement', *International Organization*, 1996, 50, pp. 653–681.

32 Jacob Bercovitch, Karl Derouen, 2004, op.cit.

33 Asaf Siniver, 2006, op cit.

attitudes. This point of view is dominant, but non-directive postures also have their virtues as they reduce the tensions more sustainably.[34]

All in all, this research which without a doubt presents informative virtues, seems handicapped by considerable methodological biases. The main problem lies in the choice of a very extensive conception of the concept of mediation. All the interventions of a third party in a conflict are amalgamated under this term. Yet, there is an enormous qualitative difference between the pressure exerted by the President of the United States and the non-directive intervention of a Swiss or Norwegian scholar or a small charitable NGO. The propensity of certain researchers to ignore the misappropriation of mediation by institutional political entities leads them to overlook the diversity of peacemaking initiatives. It is true that they are not easy to identify.

1.2 *'Bottom-Up' Mediations*

The unveiling of these political mediations goes against the principle of confidentiality which characterises them. Many mediators hold that the discretion of their approach is a condition which is crucial to its success. The invisibility of the mediation process would be, even more than for the international conflicts treated by traditional diplomatic means, necessary for identity or ethnic conflicts, whose complexity demands time and agility. The inventory of these mediations is probably impossible to do, which invalidates all quantitative methodological pretension. Only a qualitative approach seems relevant when it comes to knowing the small world of political mediators, the way they proceed and the links they have with other arenas of conflict regulation.

1.2.1 Diverse mobilizations

Political mediators have heterogeneous statuses, members of NGOs or foundations, from the biggest to most modest, moral and religious authorities, specialised university centres. They are civil servants or employed by private structures, conflict regulation professionals or volunteers. What unites them is their common belonging to Western democracies. They are majority White and North American, but can also be found in some European countries (Norway, Sweden, Finland, Switzerland, Italy, England, Ireland) or more distant countries (Australia, New Zealand). The reasons for which they invest themselves in this type of activity are generally private, but a small detour through their country's history shows they are linked to political commitment as well

34 Kyle Beardsley, David Quinn, Bidisha Biswas, Jonathan Wilkenfeld, 'Mediation styles and crisis outcomes', *Journal of Conflict Resolution*, 2006, vol. 50, nr 1, pp. 58–86.

as professional action logic; 'professional interest is often not isolated from humanist good will, political commitment or religious ethic'.[35]

The most represented sectors are journalism, psychology and law. Jurists, who are probably the most numerous, are close to both the *alternative dispute resolution* movement which ensures the promotion of informal justice closer to citizens, and to the *restorative justice* movement. These initiatives convey a critical vision of the State and of its institutions, an individualising conception of social relations and an optimistic philosophy of human beings, capable of positive self-transformation through dialogue with others. As these values are more induced than displayed, Sandrine Lefranc sees in this an expression or the depoliticisation of their action.[36]

Nevertheless, as I mentioned earlier, the first American mediators came from a left-wing pacifist and liberal background in the 1970s, hostile to the establishment and the external American policies. The new models of political mediation were built on this countercultural foundation, as illustrated by the case of the pacifist Roger Fisher[37] who, in 1984, created the *Conflict Management Group*. However, it would be very hazardous to read these investments as 'left-wing' today, as the field of expertise of political conflict resolution (this resolution does not always involve mediation) distances itself little by little from these origins and was invested by people with diverse backgrounds.

The second pillar of political mediation is philosophical and religious. We cannot understand the commitment of numerous mediators without referring to their non-violent convictions inspired by Buddhism and Ghandi (as Johan Galtung) or other religious convictions (like Adam Curle). The actions of the Quakers or the Mennonites in favour of the reconciliation of peoples and their non-violent philosophy prepare them almost naturally to invest in mediation. The Quakers did, as early as the 1970s, intervene in the conflicts opposing India and Pakistan,[38] in Nigeria, Rhodesia, Sri Lanka and in the Middle East, whereas the Mennonites invested themselves, at almost the same time, in an active combat for peace, of which John Paul Lederach is the standard bearer.

---

35 Sandrine Lefranc, 'Du droit à la paix. La circulation des techniques internationales de pacification par le bas', *Actes de la recherche en sciences sociales*, nr 174, 48–67.

36 Ibid.

37 Roger Fisher was a jurist at Harvard Law School, known for intervening in the Vietnam war, the taking of American hostages in Tehran, in the Arab-Israeli conflict, in South Africa, in Georgia but also for elaborating the Harvard model, which establishes the win-win principle and which was largely widespread with his bestseller *Getting to yes* (Roger Fisher et William Ury).

38 C.H. Mike Yarrow, (1978) op.cit.

Then, the Catholic movement invested in the mediation field either in an internal way, via religious orders or priests, or externally via the intervention of diverse Christian movements.[39] Thus, the Bishop Ruiz Garcia intervened in the conflict between the Zapatistas and the Mexican government in 1994,[40] the Irish redemptorist priest Alec Reid (who was later solicited in the Basque conflict) had an influential role in the Good Friday agreement in 1998 in Northern Ireland. The community of Sant'Egidio 'the international secular association of the Catholic church', created in Rome 1968, is the most famous example. It progressively shifted from missions fighting against poverty to more political mediation strategies (in Lebanon in 1982 and in Africa in the following years). The signature of a peace agreement in Rome on the 4th of October 1992, which put an end to the 15-year-long conflict in Mozambique, was its most significant success.[41] The interest the Catholic church had in this new type of intervention must be understood by means of a political philosophy which exalts the existence of intermediary bodies, barriers against authoritarianism and totalitarianism, and the subsidiary principle which demands that the conflicts not be necessarily treated by the State but by qualified social workers competent in the field closest possible to their reality.

These initatives, rooted in conviction, were rapidly confronted by the technical and financial necessities of professionalising the mediator's activity of constructing and engineering peace.[42] The original activists had to adopt a distanced and impartial position more linked to the ethic of mediation, to integrate more elaborated intervention techniques, to acquire legitimacy in a competitive context and had to know how to obtain international or national funding. Thus, a large number of university courses, such as from Harvard Law School, from Massachusetts Institute of Technology, and from Eastern Mennonite University, saw the light of day in the US, then in Europe, to train conflict resolution specialists. A field of activity was built, with its diplomas, specialisations, reviews, networks and careers. National and international experts then emerged, experts who help the most modest NGOs as well as large international organisations (for example the Carter Foundation, the Centre for

39 Xabier Itçaina, *Les virtuoses de l'identité. Religion et politique en Pays Basque*, Rennes, Université de Rennes, 2007.

40 Pilar Gil Tébar, 'Entre la médiation politique et la recomposition sociale: l'Eglise catholique dans le conflit du Chiapas', *Archives de Sciences Sociales des Religions*, 1997, nr 97, pp. 63–72.

41 Jean Louis Marret, 'Les ONG et la médiation de la paix: l'exemple de la communauté Sant'Egidio', *Annuaire Français de Relations Internationales*, vol. 1., 2000, 1–11.

42 Sandrine Lefranc, 'Convertir le grand nombre à la paix. Une ingénierie internationale de pacification', *Politix*, 80, 2007, 7–29.

Humanitarian Dialogue in Geneva, the International Crisis Group, the Search for Common Ground) and export the peace conceptions and the management logics that have been instilled into them. However, this structure of mediation activities has, for the moment, not induced the homogeneity of conceptions and practices.

1.2.2 A Wide Range of Action Models

We have seen that the traditional approaches to mediation offer three types of intervention: that of the facilitator, the formulator and the manipulator. In doing this, they neglect the variety of models that the amalgam of social and political mobilisations has provoked. The relative disorder that can be observed between the different conceptions of mediation explains the contradictions and incoherences of a process that began as an alternative and gradually institutionalised, and which keeps its ability to subvert the logics order and vertical regulations. The discourse that exalts the empowerment and autonomy of populations, the deinstitutionalization and the relative dispossession of the elites and the professionals, the transformation of the cognitive relation between groups of antagonist, the discovery of otherness, the multiplication of the deciding practices that respect cultural outlines of the concerned populations, does not have exactly the same objectives as the discourse which is focused on obtaining ceasefires and formal agreements, which values the use of the mediator's influential power and the necessity of slightly infringing the principles of impartiality and independence.

The previous chapter has shown that the number of action models is large. This diversity must be understood not only as a proof of the ideological diversity of the point of view, but also as the consequence of a financial competition between specialists to control the training market and spread their own models throughout the world. Whereas numerous disciples scrupulously apply the model taught from their 'master', many take a different path and build their own posture, combining different models, or switch from one model to another depending on the characteristics of the conflict and its evolution phases.

To summarise, we can roughly see an opposition rising between those who have the objective of resolving the conflict, and others, who, in the manner of Adam Curle, have the project of regulating the conflict and establishing (or re-establishing) communication.[43] Beyond the methodological dispute, two universes are opposed, that of professionals from the business, law and political world on one side, and on the other, the world of scholar-activists steeped in

43 A. Curle, *In the Middle*, Oxford, Berg, 1986.

humanities. A whole conception of peace is at stake. The idea that the peace process is necessarily anchored in official negotiations and formal agreements is opposed to the conviction that it requires a process of relational construction within the civil societies. Thus, according to Roger Fisher[44] and his disciples, it would be vain to ask diplomats to establish and sign an agreement without appeasing the existing tensions and hatred first. The peace process must be committed not only at the level of the high-ranking officials and notables but on all levels of society and culture through which each actor gives meaning to the conflict. This goes back to the distinction Galtung elaborates between *negative peace*, where the violent conflict is simply put to an end (the European movement reproaches the Americans for having a conception of peace which is too superficial and argues that all negotiation or mediation must necessarily allow the actors to work on the profound causes of the conflict) and *positive peace* which involves collaboration, and mutual assistance between countries or social groups.[45]

In order to avoid 'pacification without reconciliation',[46] Lederach evokes the necessity of building sustainable pacific relations by using objective communication experiences, because if the relationships are the source of the conflict, they also become the condition of its resolution.[47] In this perspective, he suggests a work model that takes into account three levels of intervention, which he illustrates with his famous pyramid figure.[48] This dialogue and tolerance learning process would have helped the peace process in Northern Ireland, which was too elite-driven, and not driven by the people who, heavily divided into its communities, remained passive spectators.[49]

1.2.3 Multiple Interacting Arenas

An extreme focalisation on mediation would not make much sense. It would run the risk of overshadowing all the initiatives within which it takes place and

---

44 See John Cana, 'La privatisation de la diplomatie. Une expérience caucasienne', *Critique Internationale*, nr 1, 1998, pp. 169–178.

45 Johan Galtung, *Essays on peace research*, Copenhague, Ejlers, 1975.

46 Nathalie Duclos, 'Pacification sans réconciliation. Les apories de la politique de réconciliation conduite par les Nations Unies au Kosovo' in Sandrine Lefranc (Ed.), *Après le conflit, la réconciliation?* Michel Houdiard Editeur, 2006.

47 Jean Paul Lederach, *Building peace. Sustainable reconciliation in divided societies*, Washington, United State Institute of Peace, 1997 or *The moral imagination: the art and soul of building peace*, Oxford University Press, 2005.

48 Ibid.

49 Elise Féron, 'Irlande du Nord: la paix en haut, la guerre en bas?' *Critique Internationale*, nr 18, 2002/3, pp. 24–30.

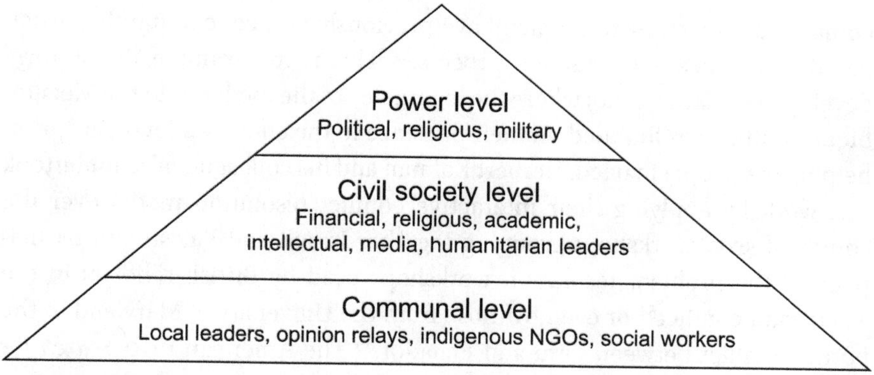

FIGURE 5.1 The three levels of intervention (according to John Paul Lederach's pyramid)

which make it efficient. The analysis must include interrelations between different levels of intervention, which are not always visible. For example, Saunders distinguishes four interconnected and complementary arenas,[50] the first one being stately diplomacy; the second that of individuals or institutions cooperating with governments but without benefitting from authority or an official status (this is the case of Terje Rod Larsen and Mona Juul for the Oslo agreements between Israelis and Palestinians, of Alexis Keller for the Geneva agreements and of the Catholic clergy for the Irish or Basque conflicts); the third is the public dialogue arena in which non-official actors invite influential people to dialogue extensively to understand the nature of the conflict, develop alternative scenarios and take initiatives; the fourth involves civil society more largely throughout peace-promoting actions and education without violence. In order to be effective, the peace process must be continued in a complementary way (comprehensive strategy) in all arenas and build bridges between all of them. This multi-party mediation,[51] which boasts the advantages of coordination, transferring information, and of sharing resources, presents the risk, however, of threatening the necessary trust between the parties, which needs confidentiality in order to prosper, and clashes with the concerns of the non-official actors (track two) of not being mistaken for the official speakers (track one).

In this perspective, it is not a question of limiting the reflection during the mediation process, but of opening it on the ensemble of the interwoven and

50 Harold Saunders, 'Prenegociation and circum-negociation: arenas of the multilevel peace process' in Chester Crocker, Fen Hampson and Pamela Aall (eds.) *Turbulent peace: the challenges of managing international conflict*, Washington D.C., United Institute of Peace Press, 2001, pp. 483–496.

51 Chester Crocker, Fen Hampson, Pamela Aall (eds.) *Herding Cats: Multiparty mediation in a complex world*, Washington D.C., United States Institute of Peace Press, 1999.

complementary strategies which have previously and concomitantly participated in the peace production process.[52] This is for example the strategy developed by Sant'Egidio; where the legitimacy of the mediator in the Mozambique conflict was founded on their presence in the country a few years prior, helping the people in need. Herbert Kalman and his colleagues also undertook this work by applying their interactive conflict resolution model over the course of sixty workshops grouping together Israeli and Palestinian participants,[53] the problem resolution workshops used by British scholars in the Moldavian conflict[54] or even by those from the University of Maryland in the border conflict between Peru and Ecuador.[55] The American NGO *Search for Common Ground* also made this choice, and the NGO's investment in conflict resolution is based on the promotion of a partnership with local communities, the training of local mediators (for example in Moroccan slums), the development of actions favouring intercomprehension of peoples such as the publishing and distribution of magazines, of TV programmes (this was the strategy used by the 'media of hate' in the Rwandan genocide), radio programmes, the creation of pre-schools for bilingual children (Macedonia), peace festivals, football matches in Burundi with young Hutus and Tutsis, holiday camps for children coming from different conflicting groups (Seeds for Peace). Similarly, Peace Brigades International (PBI), which organises workshops on nonviolent conflict resolution for groups of women, unions, teachers, in Guatemala, Columbia, Mexico and Indonesia,[56] can be cited. This is also the process followed by the association Elkarri (Dialogue) in the Basque Country,[57] who considers that a peace process needs to mobilise as many people as possible in order to maximise its chances of success, has organised since 1992 tables for dialogue and listening, debates, and campaigns to raise awareness. All these initiatives support the position Ronald J. Fisher defends. He argues that only a comprehensive approach to the conflict can surpass past trauma and satisfy the par-

52 Ronald J. Fisher, 'Coordination entre les diplomaties de type 1 (officielle) et de type 2 (parallèle) dans des cas réussis de pré-négociation', *Négociations*, 2006/1, pp. 5–33.

53 Herbert Kelman, 'Interactive problem solving in the Israelian–Palestinian case: past contributions and present challenges' in Ronald J. Fisher, *Paving the way: contributions of interactive conflict resolution in peacemaking*, Lanham, MD, Lexington Books, 2005, pp. 41–63.

54 Andrew Williams, 'Conflict resolution after the cold war: the case of Moldova', *Review of International Studies*, nr 25, 1999.

55 Edy Kaufman, Saul Sosnowski, 'The Peru-Ecuador peace process: the contribution of track two diplomacy' in Ronald J. Fisher, 2005, op.cit. pp. 175–201.

56 Peace Brigades International, *Annual Review* 2006–7, www.peacebrigades.org.

57 J. Mansvelt-Beck, *Territory and terror: Conflicting nationalisms in the Basque Country*, London, Routledge, 2005.

ties' basic needs; an argument which can be supported with the example of the Cypriot conflict, where all the 'top-down' mediations failed. The unofficial efforts made since 1996 by the Cyprus Consortium involving hundreds of influential individuals in bicommunal interactions seem to be successful as they build, or re-build, mutual respect.[58]

2 The Political Stakes of Mediation

The fervent supporters of mediation, sometimes guided by messianic logic, give the impression of being the missing link in the chainmail of fraternity. Other promoters are more visibly motivated by power stakes or financial considerations as the field of mediation becomes a market (see the North American companies that practise both political or financial risk-management consulting with politicians or investors and offer mediation services, see also the funding given by governments to international peace offices, amongst these the International Crisis Group, Search for Common Ground). Evaluating the impact of mediation on peacemaking requires giving up on these two positions.[59]

2.1 *A Simple Facelift for Diplomatic Work*

One can be tempted, in observing the development of mediations, to conclude that we are assisting the privatisation of diplomacy in the sense evoked by Béatrice Hibou when she speaks of 'concomitant processes of spreading of the use of private intermediaries for functions previously filled by the State'.[60] The strength of the bonds linking certain American NGOs and the American government would attest to the privatisation of entire sections of American diplomacy. Such a delegation of competences to the profit of politically irresponsible organisms could be interpreted as a strategy to depoliticize the domain of pacification. Then comes the question of knowing if the mediators, and the NGOs to which they belong, are a disguise for stately intervention or not. This hypothesis is particularly plausible for the US, often discredited in its role as an impartial intercessor and eager to obscure their role. The hypothesis can be more validated when these NGOs get their revenue from their own

58 Ronald J. Fisher, 'Cyprus; the failure of mediation and the escalation of an identity-based conflict to an adversarial impasse', *Journal of Peace Research*, 2001, pp. 307–326.

59 J. Faget (directed by), *Mediation in political conflicts. Soft power or counter-culture?* Oxford, Hart Publishing, 2011.

60 Béatrice Hibou, 'Retrait ou redéploiement de l'Etat', *Critique Internationale*, nr 1, 1998, pp. 151–168.

government or are funded by a coalition of Western governments, who share more or less the same vision of the world. The use of mediation would ensure, under a gentler disguise, the maintenance of a form of domination. The exercise of such a soft power[61] would find meaning in a neo-liberal vision establishing the supremacy of transnational networks on countries through the exercise of global governance.

However, the mutagenic function of this 'other diplomacy' depends the degree of independence of the mediators. Admittedly, most of them claim, in their discourse, an autonomy with regard to state strategies, but this autonomy is debated seeing as some of their interventions happen in parallel to or work in a complementary way with stately action. Thus, the 'Norwegian model',[62] even though it is democratic and not very intrusive, is characterised by combining stately actions and NGO representatives, largely subsidised by the authorities. Since 2002, the creation of a structure internal to the Minister of Foreign Affairs, the 'Peace and Reconciliation' section, proves the nationalisation of mediation practices. The same observation of dependence has been made by the Sant'Egidio community, considered as a 'parapublic'[63] actor representing the Vatican's gloved hand. Since 1995 and their joint intervention in the Guatemala guerilla, continuous links exist between Norway and the Vatican. Even if these two countries are particular in such ways that they cannot serve as models to analyse the mutagenic characteristics of mediation practices, one cannot deny that the interwovenness of the pacification, political, financial and humanitarian arenas, as well as a multitude of actors, threatens the autonomy of mediation. The moment when it is put into practice, the modalities of its action and its result depend more on what is happening on

61 Joseph Nye, 'Soft power', *Foreign policy*, 80, 1990, pp. 153–171.

62 There would exist a 'Norwegian model' which revealed itself not only in the Israeli-Palestinian conflict, but also in Guatemala, Sri Lanka, Columbia, Haïti, Santo Domingo, Cyprus, Sudan, Uganda, Eritrea, Somalia, Indonesia, Myanmar and the Philippines. It is characterised by an action which combines stately actors and NGO representatives, a secret process and a conception of mediation based on trust and not power. Norway has created a work speciality in conflict pacification. This can be explained by several reasons. The country is peaceful, has no colonisation history, has a long history of humanitarian aid, a relatively independent international position, benefits from an impartial image and does not represent, because of its size and power, a threat to other countries. Amongst countries, the action of large powers must not obscure the activism of small countries such as Switzerland and Norway, who make promoting peace a constituent of their foreign policy. (Switzerland disposes of a pool of experts for the promotion of peace within the Federal Department of Foreign Affairs (DFAE: Département fédéral des affaires étrangères), and Norway has a 'peace and reconciliation' (fred og forsoning in Norwegian) division within its minister for foreign affairs).

63 Jean Louis Marret, 2000, op.cit.

the other scenes than on the mediator's talent. Thus, 'the sovereignist overbiddings on one hand, and the blocking of repressive stances on the other hand, all of it in a context periodically dramatised by acts of political violence', hindered the clergy's mediation attempt in the Basque conflict.[64]

Even if we hypothesise about the structural independence of mediators and of the organisations to which they belong, one can wonder if their common socialisation in Western democracies and their training in prestigious American and sometimes European universities does not lead them to project an ethnocentric vision on the world that surrounds them. The third-party role of the mediator and the impact of his/her action would not only be to 'resolve conflicts, but also to export an order, via his or her own values and financial, political, social, cultural and normative conceptions of society'.[65] In a perspective which is close to John Galtung's structuralism[66] which unveils modes of reproduction of hegemony of the centre(s) on the periphery (or peripheries), Dag Hareide, in his comparison between old religious missionaries and contemporary peace missionaries (in particular Norwegian missionaries), tells us that 'the old men preached God and salvation, and the latter preach peace and democracy. The old men stayed long in their position, were not paid much and learned the local language, the young men travel a lot, have a high salary and speak English. What is similar between the two is a well-developed sense of macro theories which opposes good and evil... Both have the same creed, even if they do not want to admit it, of thinking that someone from the West can save the rest of the planet'.[67]

2.2 *The Ethical Metamorphosis of the Peace Work*

Without a doubt, the international use of mediation continues to consecrate the government's leadership and only leaves the smallest share to independent mediators and groups representing citizen's interests. However, we cannot elude the impact of the diverse mobilisations that animate the world of mediation. We cannot exclude the symbolic and instrumental force of the discourse of mediation more. In reality, outside of the complementarity model explained in the previous paragraph, other possibilities exist.

---

64 Xabier Itçaina, 2007, op.cit.

65 Richmond Oliver, 'A genealogy of peacemaking: the creation and re-creation of order', *Alternatives*, vol. 26, Issue 3, 2001.

66 John Galtung, 'A structural theory of imperialism', *Journal of Peace Research*, 8 (2), 1971, pp. 81–117.

67 Dag Hareide, 'Peace mediator: the new Norwegian missionary?' http://www.nordisk forum for mediation and conflict management, peace mediation, Norway, 26/07/2003.

Mediation can have an alternative reach as soon as it proceeds to a methodological shift. The transformative model allows, in contrast with the problem-solving method, a medium – or long-term work on the roots of the conflict and the different parties' needs, which takes place by organising dialogue spaces assembling not only the elites but the representatives of all political, social or community forces. This type of method is recommended for the regulation of deep-rooted conflicts, as it produces sustainable results under the condition that the protagonists' identity and participation needs are being properly met.[68] The example of the Northern Ireland conflict is in this case edifying and worth mentioning.[69] The social workers play the role of mediators between the Catholic and Protestant communities close to the highly secure areas where a 'culture of violence' reigns, based on the Manichean and stereotyped representations the people have of the other community. The citizens living in these neighbourhoods are more concerned by unemployment, misery and crime than by the perspective of bettering their relationship with the other community. Thus, it is difficult to mobilise them and give them this objective, as the European programmes or local authorities wish to. Only the social actors, local celebrities or external mediators are legitimate enough to do so. Their strategy is to organise inter-community discussion groups to debate very concrete stakes such as the trajectory of a parade or the access to a care facility. Seeing as the actors are extremely sensitive, the mediators must be very vigilant when it comes to the respect of equity rules that structure debates. It does happen that these groups amount to tangible results, like for example the trajectory of the Londonderry Protestant parade, traditionally a source of conflict. The Catholics consented to these parades following their usual trajectory, even when it entered majority Catholic residential zones; the Protestants agreed to stop the Unionist orchestras from playing and committed to monitor the crowd coming from all around the province in order to avoid fights with the nationalists. Beyond this single agreement, a whole way of living needs to be rethought, and its objective, by the increase in the number of these instances, is to accustom the people to meet and respect each other, to change the mutually demonising view they have of each other. These types of mediation highlight the necessity of working on peace at the citizens' level, and not only at the

---

68 Perry Mars, 'Ethnic politics, mediation and conflict resolution: the Guyana experience', *Journal of Peace Research*, 2001, pp. 353–372.

69 Elise Féron, Restaurer la confiance en Irlande du Nord? La négociation aux interfaces urbaines, *Négociations*, nr 9, 2008/1, pp. 41–54.

leaders' level; in the perspective of a 'mutual recognition policy',[70] involving identities and the sensitivities of communities.

Mediations can also be organised in places and for conflicts in which the state has no interest. Here, an example can be poor countries mined by internal conflicts which present few financial or strategic interests. These mediations which compensate for political indifference are the most invisible and it would be beneficial to develop, in partnership with the local population and NGOs, a research program to identify them.

The fact that political mediations are practiced by NGOs that are often partially financially dependent from the government should not lead us to conclude too quickly that they are subservient to state logic. These NGOs do not constitute a homogeneous entity and they don't have the internal coherence that is sometimes attributed to them. It would be interesting to work on their contradictions, the confrontations between messianic impulses, bureaucratic rationalities and the political motives that drive them. We must also take into account the fact that they are constantly building their network (see for example the Sant'Egidio/ Norway government axis or the *Negotiation network* federation), into configurations whose piloting escapes governments and illustrate the rise of a 'world without sovereignty'.[71]

We can finally postulate that the discourse of mediation produces performative effects. It was and is led by charismatic individuals of diverse allegiances such as Johan Galtung, Roger Fisher, Jean Paul Lederach, who have an important aura both in the mediation field, but also in the field of international institutions with which they have collaborated. Their role was essential in the constitution of an epistemic community which grows more and more influential as it has access to decision-making spheres, and would be at the heart of a 'real industry of democratic promotion'.[72] Because of this, mediation's discourse conveys a set of values; these are political (participative democracy, the self determination of peoples, human rights), ethical (independence, impartiality) and philosophical (praising difference, advocating for tolerance and respect), which gives it a large audience and partly explains the strength of the mobilisations it provokes, favuring the emergence, although fragile, of a new international morality.

---

70 Charles Taylor, *Multiculturalisme. Différence et démocratie*, Paris, Flammarion, 1994.

71 Bertrand Badie, *Un monde sans souverainetés*, Paris, Fayard, 1999.

72 Javier Santiso, 'Circulation des idées et relations internationales', dans Marie Claude Smouts, *Les nouvelles relations internationales*, Paris, Presses de Science Po, 1998, pp. 227–251.

CHAPTER 6

Environmental Mediation

The origins of environmental mediation are usually traced back to the US. The first experiment took place in 1973 and involved the controversial project of building a dam over the Snoqualmie River, a project supported by the state of Washington and by the Ford and Rockefeller Foundations. It was from the 1980s onwards that its growth was most evident, in Canada where it is imposed by the OEPH (the Office of Environmental Public Hearings) as a prerequisite to public debates, then in Australia, New Zealand and Europe, essentially in Austria, Germany, the UK, the Netherlands and Switzerland. It generally concerns conflicts involving the management of water and natural resources, the occupation of space, forestry management, the establishment of energy, rail or road equipment, or pollution. It is now institutionalised in several countries and the profession of specialised mediation has become so structured that professional organizations of environmental mediators now exist, along with their training courses, procedures and qualifications, their publications and conferences. The first European symposium was organised in Vienna in 2001.

The rise of environmental mediation must be placed in the context of the start of different deliberative techniques such as citizen juries, practices such as 'deliberative opinion polls', consultation procedures, consensus conferences or hybrid forums. Consensus conferences are probably the most well-known example of this technique. They began in Denmark at the end of the 20th century. Over 100 juries or citizen panels have been organised in the last 30 years, especially in the US, Denmark and Germany.[1] They resemble mediation in the sense that they resort to an external third party who facilitates the discussion. They group people together more or less by theme, and are most of the time designated by random draw and are regrouped into focus groups, around 15 people in each group, as representatives of civil society but without any particular knowledge on the case or personal interest. In France, these consensus conferences are also called citizen conferences, following the example of the 1998 conference on GMOs, the 2001 conference on mad cow disease and the 2002 conference on climate change.[2]

1 Horming G., 'Citizen's panels as a form of deliberative technology assessment', *Science and public policy*, vol. 26, nr 5, 1999, pp. 351–359.

2 Boy D., Donnet-Kamel D., Roqueplo P, 'Un exemple de démocratie délibérative: la conférence française de citoyens sur l'usage des organismes génétiquement modifiés en agricul-

 | DOI:10.1163/9789004734067_011

The name 'environmental mediation' is not generalised. Some processes are referred to as concertation, facilitation or territorial dialogue, without any specific reference to mediation. Conversely, the term is sometimes used to designate practices that stray somewhat from its fundamentals. Environmental mediation can be defined as a process aiming to establish dialogue between institutions, groups of interest or individuals concerned by environmental problems (management, exploitation, appropriation or protection of natural resources, of landscapes, species or environments) and/or to search for mutually satisfactory agreements for all. It operates with the intervention of an external third party, the mediator, who does not get involved in the conflict and does not attempt to influence the outcome of the mediation. The mediator's only function is to facilitate the conditions of a constructive exchange. This process can be mobilised in two scenarios, either after the event to resolve an open conflict, or before to elaborate projects concerning the management of territory or the environment with the active participation of the concerned actors. Going back to table 2.2 relating to the modes of political decision-making, what distinguishes mediation from all the other modes of participation is the power given to the citizens to elaborate and make the decision themselves. From this point of view, we can argue that it represents a higher level of participative democracy.

Compared to mediation in general, environmental mediation presents a number of specificities which influence its methods and approaches.

1. It involves a large number of participants: professionals and companies, associations, local and regional authorities, administrations, simple users and inhabitants, etc… which means working with different registers of communication, of institutional culture and regional competence. The integration of a considerable number of actors makes the constitutive tensions of the deliberative practice evident. However, the legitimacy of the deliberative processes requires us to involve as many actors as possible, which prejudices almost fatally the quality of the deliberation.[3] As the interindividual communication techniques have been proven to be inadequate in this context, specific communication tools are put in place have been put into place which combine open forums for public debate and mediation scenes, which are more private.

---

ture et dans l'alimentation', *Revue française de science politique*, vol. 50, nr 4–5, 2000, pp. 779–809.

3 John Parkinson, *Deliberating in the Real World. Problems of Legitimacy in Deliberative Democracy*, Oxford University Press, Oxford, 2006.

2. Environmental projects or conflicts are characterized by a high degree of institutional, scientifical and relational complexity. They mobilize multiple rationalities and fields of knowledge, which create large zones of uncertainty in their approach. Mediators must therefore be equipped with methodological tools that, in addition to techniques for leading collective debates, enable them to organize available information, to begin diagnosis, carry out studies or solicit an expertise.
3. Third specificity: the complexity of the stake and the extent of the territory concerned can lead to very long mediations that can spread over several years even if the effective intervention of a mediator is not constant during this period.
4. Finally, the last characteristic of environmental mediation is that it involves questions of general interest and thus constitutes a public stake. In this sense, it is directly political, as its organization constitutes a mode of governance of social problems that threatens political and professional monopolies and aims to replace a single rationality (institutional or technical) into a multidimensional one. This signifies that the general interest is no longer defined by the state or any authority but is the product of a permanent negotiation process between the ensemble of the actors participating in the deliberation.

1 A Political and Institutional Counterculture

These political and ideological stakes allow us to understand the difficulties that come with generalising this type of deliberative process in centralised countries. Moreover, resorting to mediation is rarely a choice made by the government or the administration. This choice is generally made either because of the pressure of social events, depending on the degree of organisation and efficiency of the pressure groups, or under the constraint of the technical evolutions and of the unadapted institutional responses to the management of the conflicts they provoke. The initiative of mediation is only rarely a result of the actions of public powers, and nearly always comes from the initiatives of civil society which block the decision process or the implementation of an unconcerted decision.

In the last few decades, the attention given to ecological problems has multiplied the number of conflicts between public decisionmakers, real estate developers, industrials on one hand, and increasingly organised associations for inhabitants, users, consumers, on the other. The actions of pressure groups are presented as a social fight to impose debate, to be admitted to participate in one, and to build alliances in order to reverse the mechanisms of domination to which they are subjected.

This activism is sometimes motivated by the defence of the protection of natural areas, the presence of bears, wolves, and bearded vultures in mountainous environments, by the promotion of a participative democracy in the face of bureaucratic decision processes, the fight against corruption, with the example of the participative budgets made famous by the Brazilian Porte Alegre[4] experience. It can also be the result of phenomena such as NIMBY[5] (not in my backyard), during which individuals oppose the installation of public or private facilities that threaten their environment (disruptive noise of a motorway, the construction of a town bypass or of a railway, building of a golf course, a stadium, a prison, a centre for handicapped people; a waste disposal facility, the presence of drug addicts or homeless people in commercial zones). The effects of such mobilisation mean that none of the protagonists can attain their objectives in a unilateral way. Problematics such as NIMBY never amount to a technically satisfactory solution, the implantation of a waste site brings more nuisance to one group of people than others. The counter phenomenon PIMBY (please in my backyard), can also pose problems when the inhabitants fight for a healthcare or childcare structure to be built in their neighbourhood as opposed to another part of town. Thus, the objective is not to find a technical solution but more a socially acceptable solution. However, it seems that a decision perceived as equitable and just by the actors favours its acceptance. Its legitimacy increases when they themselves have participated in its development, as they are convinced that a decision is equitable when the level of control they have over the process is high, and same with the level of trust which exists between the parties involved.

The development of technical legislation to protect the environment has also led to a proliferation of lengthy and costly legal proceedings, which have had the effect of cancelling or delaying certain projects and increasing their cost. As court decisions often turn out to be not very satisfactory for the

4 In 1989, the elected municipality created an innovative system of formulating and following the municipal budget, called the participative budget. The technicians or rulers do not decide: the population itself defines the amount of the revenues and economic commitments, by means of debate, consultations and decisions. The population decides where to invest and which priorities to follow in this regard. This democratic and transparent management of resources has proven to be an excellent way to avoid corruption and embezzlement.

5 The 'not in my backyard' phenomenon can be explained by the unequal territorial distribution of a project's inconveniences. These inconveniences are concentrated for a specific part of the population and the project's advantages are spread out for the rest of the neighbouring population.

involved parties, more flexible, financially advantageous, quicker, and more adapted alternative solutions were proposed. These mediations spread, as we have seen, throughout the Western world and in Europe; however the presence of more centralised states hindered their exportation.

This type of process questions the distribution of a certain number of powers. Firstly, it breaks the traditional division between experts and laymen, between authorised knowledge and non-professional knowledge. Generally, technical decisions are given to experts (geologists, jurists, chemists, architects, engineers) who, without popular control, propose their projects and diagnosis. This demographic deficit is justified by the technical nature of the concerned stakes, which call for scientific skill in order to be evaluated and understood. The abolition of the gap between those elected and those they represent is similar to the abolition of the gap between experts and non-scholars. Representative democracy relies on a delegation of competence from the voters to the elected during their mandate. However, mediation, by organising the implication of civil society, substitutes representative democracy with the principle of participative democracy, which undermines this foundational principle of delegation. This double blow to the principles of power distribution explains the fact that, in many cases, mediation only constitutes a process parallel to usual procedures. Mediation is used as a tool to make decisions, as a body to formulate proposals. From then onwards, they do not constitute real mediations, since they are precisely based on the actors' decisive abilities.

2 Complex Tinkering

Implementing environmental mediation supposes a mutual wish of all the concerned parties, a common choice made by a team of mediators, a cost evaluation of the operation and the search for an adequate budget to pay the mediators but also eventually the invited experts' expenses and cover the participants' travel costs. When the mediators' fees are covered by the present institutions, one can question their independence. The existence of multiple subsidiaries coming from diverse institutions is a guarantee against subordination risks, which could affect the mediators and the suspicions that would then arise on their impartiality.

The systemic complexity which presides over the organisation of environmental mediation cannot be resolved by putting into practice easily exportable work models. The social, economic, institutional and cultural context demand constant adaptations. Thus, even if it is possible to suggest a few principles for structuring the work, in the end, it relies on the talent, the know-how and people skills, experience but also creativity of the mediators.

The process generally works as follows:

- A preparatory, organisational phase which consists in gathering the concerned actors. The mediators' work (they frequently intervene in teams or in duo) consists in making sure that all the relevant actors are present, the obvious and 'noisy' ones as well as the more discrete actors;[6] and that they all have the legitimacy to intervene. It is for example necessary to make sure that they represent the group they claim to speak for, and that they have the legitimacy to be committed in its name. Even when all these precautions are taken, it is not rare to see unexpected actors appear during the process, either because they were not identified, or because a certain number of technical or regional factors have changed the situation.
- The second phase, extremely important as it creates trust and limits areas of uncertainty, consists (once all the actors are present) in deciding on the work process, on the 'rules of the game' that shape the mediation, the elaboration of an agenda, the work rhythm, proceeding either in large committees or small groups, confidentiality, the deadlines, the funding, possibly paying people's expenses, the conditions under which the initial rules of the game can be changed, the clarification of the status, (advisory or decisive) of the committee's propositions. One does not only deliberate in one specific setting, but also on this setting, its legitimacy, the necessity to discuss and amend it. Here, it is important to cultivate the shared idea of a 'just process'.
- The third phase consists in presenting everyone's positions, exchanging point of views, and then making needs, expectations known, to share technical and scientific information but also to facilitate the expression of values. It is important to make sure that all the actors of the project, whatever their initial training is, are aware of all the technical, financial, legal, social and cultural information, and are able to understand them. This must lead to evoking all the possible strategies and the possible wording of solutions. However, all of this is only achievable if the actors are aware of their interdependence. Anything that can favour its emergence must be encouraged by the mediator.

---

6 It is necessary, if possible, to try and control the biases of an over-representation of the educated middle-class, capable of mobilising itself, and making its point of view on an acceptable mode, heard. These biases are often mentioned in the evaluation of participative processes.

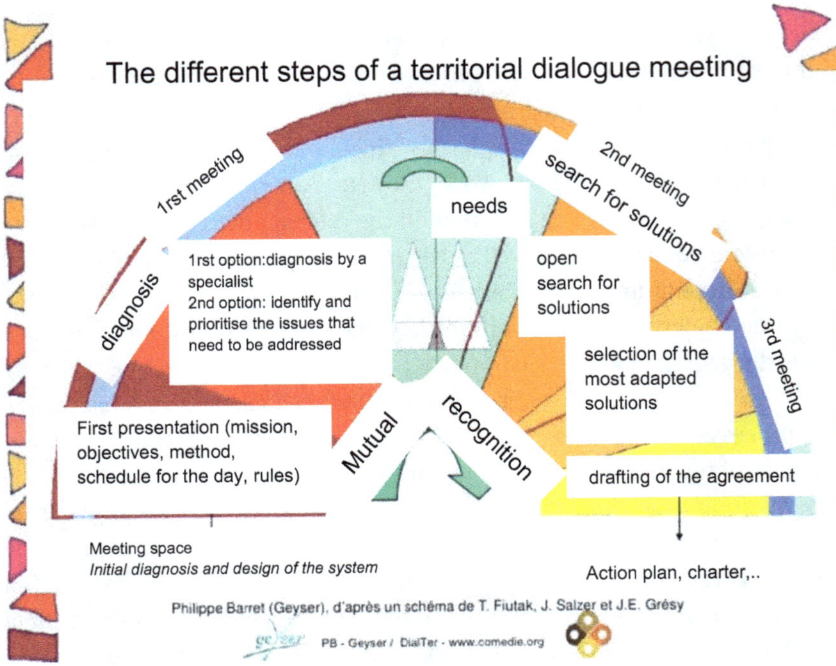

FIGURE 6.1 Example of work process in environmental mediation

- The fourth decisional phase's purpose is to challenge diverse proposition formulations, measure their advantages and inconveniences, and finally identify the one which makes a consensus emerge. A plan to implement the agreement is then created, and a process to control its execution is set up.

This diagram, inspired by Thomas Fiutak, Jacques Salzer and Jean – Edouard Grésy's work, is indicative only. It can be adapted in multiple ways. In this domain, several practice models exist, those that quickly focus on the search for a practical solution, and those which are slightly slower and privilege the creation of a cooperative climate and the processes of mutual learning. Whereas some mediations 'close the game', calibrate the communication, make sure an imparted time of speech is respected, fix an agenda for the day, impose excessively formal, abstract and rational communication styles which privilege certain cultures (notably Western cultures), others welcome a whole palette of communication styles, the expression of emotions, feelings, the occurrence of unexpected subjects, digressions, and personal stories. In that case, everyone can be interested in participating in a deliberation, as everyone knows that his/her 'arguments' will be recognised as legitimate even if they are not within the framework of a strict communicational rationality.

The necessary work is concretely illustrated by the example of the mediation organised in Austria, concerning the construction of a third runway at the airport in Vienna. The airport's management was very quickly confronted by the opposition of local residents, who blocked the progression of the construction site for nearly 5 years (from 2000 to 2005).

It was then decided to resort to the help of mediators. A call was sent out in Germany, Switzerland and in Austria, and three mediators were finally chosen by a working group composed of commune representatives, local residents' association, the environment services, the Austrian federal states and the airport society. It was decided that 60 per cent of the cost of the mediation would be covered by the airport, and 40 per cent by the federal states. The mediators formed a forum of 55 people representing all the concerned actors and institutions (environmental services, federal states, districts, nine communes, national park, airport, political parties, economic chamber, residents' association, tourist association, citizen representatives). This forum was convened 15 times. These meetings were prepared by thematic working groups (noise, ecology, financial development) which amounted to around 200 meetings, and by the examination of experts during coordination meetings. This extremely heavy and patient deliberation process lasted almost 2 years and finally led to an agreement in favour of the construction of the third runway. But this construction was only allowed under certain conditions, namely a very strict limit imposed on noise zones, the creation of a fund for the environment, the establishment of a permanent dialogue forum, the delimitation of building plots and limitations on night flights.

We can also mention mediation experiences[7] with less important financial stakes and concerning a smaller territory. For example, mediation between a bar organising concerts and local residents annoyed by noise pollution. A great number of activities that do not use the term of mediation but have both similar principles and the objective of managing custom conflicts could also be cited. This is the case in the *bassin d'Arcachon* and in the *golfe du Morbihan,* both in France, where in order for tourists, fishermen, oyster farmers, swimmers, environmental professionals and local residents to coexist peacefully, links between these populations who previously ignored each other needed to be patiently established. The construction of a 'collective intelligence' was also essential to this coexistence; it allowed the elaboration and signature of charters, which defined the principles of mutual respect between users.

---

7 Voir Guiheneuf Pierre-Yves (dir.), *40 fiches d'expérience de dialogue territorial,* Geyser/Fondation de France/Région Rhône-Alpes, 2006.

3 The Rise of a New Democratic Spirit?

The development of environmental mediation is part of a larger context of the political, scientific institutions and market's incapacity to manage the consequences of the evolution of science and techniques in domains such as GMOs, nuclear waste, mobile telephones, internet, recycling domestic waste, gene therapy, etc. Hence the suggestion of resorting to 'technical democracy' which does not only rely on specialists' knowledge but also on profane knowledge and groups that are directly concerned by this evolution. Thus, Callon, Lascoumes and Barthe suggest organising hybrid forums. Forums are open spaces where groups can mobilise to debate choices which concern groups; they are called hybrid because these groups are heterogeneous and are composed of experts, politicians, technicians, profanes, and because the questions that are tackled are part of different themes such as ethics, economy, and atomic physics.[8]

The development of science and techniques has not brought more certainty; on the contrary, it brings more and more uncertainty. The resulting controversies heighten this impression, notably in the environmental and health domains where they take on quite spectacular dimensions. Far from being harmful, they must be considered as a factor which enriches democracy as they are first and foremost a mode of expression for the concerned groups (riverside residents, or residents living close to a TGV, an airport, meat consumers, pregnant women living close to a nuclear waste reprocessing site). They also are a way of linking technical problems to a region, a story, beyond the initial and sometimes technocratic wording given by the decisionmakers. Finally, they allow for options to be listed that might not have been previously considered. All of it constitutes a collective learning process based on confrontation between expert and lay rationalities, citizens and their representatives, and on the meeting of groups which previously ignored each other and now try to create a common world.

However, this noble ambition collides with obvious instrumental limitations. There probably exist a certain number of legal levers which could help the spread of environmental mediations. In France, numerous regional procedures integrate dialogue as part of their process (Natura 2000, Environmental or landscaping charters, agenda 21). The financial support given since 1997 by the Fondation de France to develop the process of regional dialogue supports this evolution in local initiative projects relating to natural and rural

---

8 Michel Callon, Pierre Lascoumes, Yan Barthe, *Agir dans un monde incertain. Essai sur la démocratie technique*, Paris, Seuil, 2001.

spaces and whose geographical scale is limited: real estate pressure in urban or suburban zones, use of rural space for open air leisure activities, multi-functionality of productive spaces (protection of biodiversity, landscapes, of natural habitats against intensive agriculture), protection of natural spaces (ponds, rivers, pylons, high voltage lines, wind turbines), creation of social links (for example, between indigenous peoples and new inhabitants).[9]

However, in practice, environmental law only deals with public participation to ensure that the form of the debate is respected. When the mediations are put into place, the temptation that the public authorities face to instrumentalise them, to communicate politically, to perceive them as an authority to prepare decisions that are anticipated to be controversial and as a simple tool to legitimise already determined options, is great. In reality, some processes led by third parties which consist in searching for agreements are qualified as 'mediation' when they do not always have the required independence.

The evaluation of environmental mediation practices highlights that this process is moderately costly when compared to that of a long-term conflict or any legal action. We have proved that this type of mediation improves the relationships between protagonists in the long term and frequently leads to agreements (78 per cent of 161 experiences evaluated in the US).[10] It is difficult to measure certain 'collateral' effects such as the emergence of mutual learning process, establishing trust between the actors or elaborating to regulation mechanisms. If positive effects are detectable in the short term, few instruments exist to appreciate them over a longer period of time and for actor arrangements that will necessarily change. Evidently, the evaluation of environmental mediation constitutes a methodological challenge as the criteria for success or failure are difficult to define and to observe in extremely complex and permanently evolving systemic contexts.

However, we may be led to think that a 'new spirit of democracy'[11] is blowing through our postmodern societies. Pierre Rosanvallon talks of a 'diffuse democracy of interaction'[12] to qualify the way democratic power must submit to the citizens' challenges of permanent validation. Impartiality, reflexivity and proximity are from now on the foundations of an increasingly procedural

---

9 Philippe Barret, *Guide pratique du dialogue territorial. Concertation et médiation pour l'environnement et le développement local*, Fondation de France, 2012.

10 Gail Bingham, *Resolving Environmental Disputes: A Decade of Experience*, World Wildlife Fund, 1986.

11 Loïc Blondiaux, *Le nouvel esprit de la démocratie. Actualité de la démocratie participative*, Paris, Seuil, 2008.

12 Pierre Rosanvallon, *La légitimité démocratique. Impartialité, réflexivité, proximité*, Paris, Seuil, 2008.

legitimacy which demands participation, exchanging arguments and collectively constructing the final decision. It would be naive to think that the rise of this participative democracy sounds the death knell of representative democracy. In reality, mediators find themselves needing to combine and work with the two principles when they work with big groups, or when they are required to organise thematic workshops concomitantly. Large environmental conferences that gather hundreds of people together hinder the sincerity, the depth of exchanges and the discovery of otherness. The virtue of working in small groups is well established in this respect. But this hybridisation of two political models, which are antagonistic at first glance, does not from my point of view discredit a process which justifies itself by the turbulence it causes. The explicit resistances, expressed under cynical or disillusioned forms, by elected representatives or technicians against environmental mediation, are the most convincing proof that these mediations are the vector of democracy's democratisation.

CHAPTER 7

Victim-Offender or Penal Mediation and Restorative Justice

The term 'penal mediation' (in France, Belgium, Switzerland, Italy and Spain) or, more generally speaking, 'victim-offender mediation' in English-speaking countries, is used to designate a practice of mediation in criminal matters consisting in treating criminal conflicts not only in front of repressive jurisdictions, but also by the means of a mediation process organised by an independent and impartial mediator who has no decision-making power. Both expressions are influenced by ways of thinking derived from legal ideology.[1] Indeed, the expression *victim-offender mediation* assigns perpetrator and victim statuses to people, even though we are sometimes in a pretrial context. In this case, it would be more objective to use the terms 'complainant' and 'accused party', seeing how interwoven the responsibilities are in many conflicts. The phrase 'penal mediation' is not very satisfactory in this regard either. The juxtaposition of the terms mediation and penal is an oxymoron, which associates a consensual process with a notion of sanction, which is not part of its ethic.

Since the 1990s in the US, and the 2000s in Europe, the term restorative justice has been gaining ground in the world of criminology. The emergence of this new paradigm, which draws on previous experience of penal mediation, opens up new prospects for the implementation of more ambitious judicial and extra-judicial practices.

1 Victim-Offender or Penal Mediation

The development of victim-offender mediation is the product of the conjunction of three ideologically heterogeneous schools of thought.[2] The first denounces the devastating effect of the intervention of the criminal justice system on the trajectory of offenders. The second, in the face of the fracture of traditional regulation authorities, idealises the image of a lost community which must be reconstructed and empowered. The third, doubtless the

---

1 J. Faget, *La médiation. Essai de politique pénale*, Toulouse, Erès, 1997.

2 Ibid.

 | DOI:10.1163/9789004734067_012

most influential, aims to bring justice for the victim, often forgotten in criminological debates since the construction of the modern State. Crime was indeed initially conceived as a crime against the Law and the sovereign; the new necessities of public order in the social torment of the industrial revolution made the punishment of the guilty the main pillar of criminal politics. Reparation for the victims was only secondary.

The history of criminology shows that all the concerns of the judicial institutions are focused on neutralisation or the redemption of criminals. The victims only appeared timidly at the end of the 19th century in the criminal landscape, and only through the figure of the beaten, abused or abandoned child. This absence of the victim is constant until the end of the 1960s when the feminist movement attracted the attention of the public powers on the fate of beaten and raped women. The first victimology studies are contemporary of this social mobilisation which marks the start of the draft of more protective public policies concerning the victim's rights. Then, with the problematization of insecurity in the 1990s and the rise of populist public discourse, the victim became the dominant figure in the criminological debate.

Penal mediation or victim offender mediation has become widespread, quickly and intensely, in most Western democracies. This development is due to the conjunction of activist, confessional or political strategies with institutional necessity. The enthusiasm of the original Protestant movements (Mennonites, Quakers) was furthermore taken over by the activism of social workers, a few magistrates and scholars who were searching for more humanist criminal justice responses. But these different types of activism would only have had a modest effect if the legal apparatus would not have been confronted everywhere to an unprecedented instrumental crisis, as a result of the increase in its caseload. Finding itself forced to look for new ways of dealing with the considerable flow of cases generated by the increase in the number of complaints, it opened more readily than it might otherwise have done to the innovative discourse of mediation.

The institutionalisation of practices made them progressively shift from the status of being an alternative to justice system, proposing a break in the way criminal justice responses were conceived, to a tool used to diversify judicial intervention. A more reformist discourse highlighting the necessity to humanise and individualise criminal sanctions followed the initial discourse denouncing the violence of the criminal justice system. Mediation then appeared, with the necessary adaptations, as a way to treat contentious issues with more nuance and to take into account, in countries where the procedural principle of discretionary prosecution applies, situations that previously were dismissed. But it is important to emphasize that the meaning of penal or victim-offender mediation varies depending on whether the measure concerns adults (in which the management dimension is predominant) or minors (in which the educational dimension is the most important).

Certain parties see in this strategy of diversifying criminal justice responses a 'penalisation of social'.[3] It is true that mediation is very often used for offenses, which, in its absence, were not addressed in the courts. All over Europe, there is a clear prevalence of minor offences in the list of cases when mediation is used. Certain countries even determine a threshold of seriousness above which criminal mediation is excluded.

The French example perfectly illustrates the 'reappropriation of the system for internal purposes'.[4] The dependence of mediators is legally confirmed by the denomination of 'mediator of the Public Prosecutor'. The law dated 9th July 2010 on 'violence specifically against women in relationships' modifies the article 41–1 of the code of criminal procedure by replacing the phrase 'with the agreement of the parties' by the words 'at the request of or with the victim's agreement'. This modification throws the mediation off balance, makes it lean more on the victim's side and creates the idea of a forced mediation in the eyes of the presumed perpetrator. 'Very subtly the law… implicitly presupposes that criminal mediation would be a procedural disadvantage for the victim'. In such a context, the mediator clearly appears to the protagonists as the victim's ally, so much so that one can wonder if it is still possible to speak of an 'equitable procedure'.[5]

It is also true that the considerable power of judicial ideology tends to subjugate all those who contribute to judicial proceedings. The confrontation between magistrates and less professionalised, less structured and prestigious bodies, is often shaped by an imbalanced power relationship and therefore all social practices institutionalised by the legal system run the risk of being largely exploited and losing their soul.[6] A few precise examples can be given (which may fluctuate depending on the country) of how the judicial logic, and the effects of its institutionalisation, threaten the autonomy of penal and victim-offender mediation practices.

- People cannot choose to use mediation themselves but are dependent on a magistrate's suggestion.

---

3 P. Mary, *Insécurité et pénalisation du social*, Bruxelles, Labor, 2003.

4 L. Aubert, 'Appréhension systématique des phénomènes de délinquance de troisième voie: les dilemmes d'un parquet divisé', *Champ pénal/penal field*, vol VI, 2009.

5 P. Mbanzoulou, *La médiation pénale*, Paris, L'Harmattan, 2012.

6 J. Faget, *Justice et travail social. Le rhizome pénal*, Toulouse, Erès,1992.

- When the magistrate suggests a mediation, people's consent is not totally free, it is 'under legal pressure', as these actors can fear that they will have to 'pay for' their refusal, one way or another.
- The choice of the mediator of his/her association is made by a magistrate.
- The mediator is paid by the measures sent by the mandating magistrate, which places him in a financially dependent relationship.
- The reading of the legal file by the mediator is done at the detriment of the conflict's human dimensions as it transmits a reality preconstructed by the professional ideology of police officers drafting it.
- Mediation time is adapted to the needs of judicial time.
- The productivity demands that drive magistrates' work leads mediators to adopt more directive attitudes and propose solutions to increase the number of agreements, as the system tends to consider that a mediation is successful when an agreement is signed.
- The mediator is obliged to give an account to the magistrate, which goes against the principle of the confidentiality of what is said during the mediation.
- The final ratification of the agreement by a magistrate can constitute a hindrance to the consensual aspect of the agreement.

A national evaluation done in France gave a concrete image of how the courts use penal mediation.[7] The numbers collected show that penal mediation has become an important way of treating small conflicts of proximity (light physical violence or moral violence, most of these taking place within a family or between friends, neighbours or at work, non-payment of child support, obstruction by one parent of the other parent's right of access to their children). However, we cannot maintain that these are benign conflicts, as violence is often present (in 30 per cent to 40 per cent of cases), even if the consequences are not dramatic. The fact that these conflicts are present in the sphere of intimate relationships would seem to justify resorting to mediation.

When the principle of mediation is accepted by the actors, the rate of success of the mediation (number of agreements obtained) is around 70 to 80 per cent but varies depending on the offence. However, this must be put into perspective, as some agreements, sometimes signed by people wanting to stop the conflict without reflecting on its causes or considering restoring a relationship, do not have any positive effects or consequences, whereas some mediations that have not led to agreements actually reflect a better under-

7 J. Faget, *La médiation pénale. Evaluation nationale*, Fonds national de la vie associative, GERICO, nr 11, 1999.

standing of the conflict. In which case is the notion of success more present? Which are the most relevant criteria of a successful mediation?

It all depends on the model of mediation privileged by the evaluator. If the evaluator is adept at utilizing the problem-solving strategy, as mediators with a judicial background often are, he/she will focus more on treating the symptoms of the conflict and on finding an agreement. If on the contrary, the evaluator is adept at working with the transformative model, as many mediators with a background in humanities are, he/she will value working on understanding the causes of the conflict, on establishing or restoring communication, and will only grant limited value to the signature of an agreement.

Research also shows that the success rate also greatly depends on mediators. This is how the percentage of 'success' appears inversely proportional to the actors' level of competence (calculated with indicators such as the quality and the length of the training in mediation, the participation in sessions analysing practices, in modules of complementary training, in conferences, readings of specialised works). The in-situ observation helps to explain this paradox. The methods used by the less trained people are indeed often very directive whereas the respect of the ethical principles is the trademark of mediators who have the highest level of training.

A Belgian study[8] confirms that the ideal of emancipation, part of mediation's discourse, becomes eroded when in contact with the judicial system. But the consequence of the collision of these two logics does not systematically result in the feared instrumentalisation. The process is certainly influenced by different logics, by the deficit in autonomy of the actor's word and the mediator's omnipresence, but its obsession with finalising agreements is badly rewarded as the actors frequently manage to make this strategic pressure fail and the rate of signed conventions remains modest. An indeterminate space would then exist, a 'non-model' where mundane strategies of influence and power are plotted between actors, which invalidates the hypothesis of state exploitation.[9] In the end, the pernicious effects of institutionalisation would be less significant than those of a 'colonisation of the social' by criminal justice ideology.

Would penal mediation be nothing more than a wasted effort? Evaluative research on the effects of criminal mediation clash with considerable meth-

8 C. Mincke, 'La proximité dangereuse. Médiation pénale belge et proximité', *Droit et société*, nr 63–64, 2006/2–3, pp. 459–487.

9 Ibid.

odological obstacles and their results must be interpreted with caution.[10] However, all North American and European investigations take note of the high degree of satisfaction expressed by the protagonists of a mediation at the end of a measure, a satisfaction which always turns out to be more important and significant for the mediated than for those (unwillingly) following a traditional judicial treatment.

The analysis of recidivism rates also plunges us into a perplexing abyss (research shows a reduction of the percentage of people committing an offence, ranging from 10 per cent to 40 per cent comparatively to those condemned by court). On one hand, the existence of an important *dark number* prevents us from having any certainty in the matter. At most, we will only know about the recidivism of individuals who have been 'caught'. On the other hand, it is difficult to isolate the effect of mediation from a multitude of factors that interact simultaneously. These factors can be the subject's mental health, the type of habitat, the protagonists having a previous relationship or not, the degree of involvement of the actors in the process, the family support they benefit from, the mediator's charisma, the model he/she uses, the place where the mediation occurs, the number of meetings, the period of time that has elapsed since the end of the mediation.[11] It is also true that the individuals who, during the process of mediation, manifest the feeling of guilt, regret or remorse, are more apt to cooperate and participate in the search for a solution.

Despite these methodological reservations, experience shows that many actors have benefitted from mediation, notably in situations where the parties are in an ongoing relationship and will be living, working or crossing paths together in the future. It is when people know each other, are in a strong affective, social or geographical proximity that mediation is the most relevant. It allows the parties involved to envisage with greater confidence and security the inevitable future relationships that people will experience, no longer against each other, but with each other. Because, thanks to the magic of the meetings and encounters, sometimes the perpetrator takes responsibility, steps out of his/her systematic denial and recognises the victim's suffering. The most beautiful illustration is given in the words of a Basque ex-terrorist 'I do not regret participating in these meetings. On the contrary, I am very proud of it because I am convinced that one needs more courage to stand face-to-face with a victim and show him your pain for all the damage you've caused

10 J. Faget, 'Epistemological and methodological reflections on the evaluation of restorative justice practices', *British Journal of Community Justice,* vol. 6, nr 2, summer 2008, pp. 77–84.

11 P. Mac Cold, 'Evaluating restorative justice programs in a European context', *British Journal of Community Justice,* vol. 6, nr 2, 2008.

than to pick up a gun or plant bombs'.[12] With this deeply impactful testimony, we turn away from penal mediation and look more closely at the restorative paradigm.

2 Restorative Justice

Most Anglo-Saxon manuals consider Howard Zehr to be the father of restorative justice, which he introduced in his work *Changing lenses*,[13] published for the first time in 1990. However, I consider the origins of restorative justice to be older. It has its roots in works centred on indigenous justice which can be seen in the aboriginal populations of Australia, the Maoris of New-Zealand, the native tribes in the US and Canada, or in the different peoples of Africa. The adaptation of these practices to contemporary contingencies was done in the 1970s by groups of critical justice and social activists (Howard Zehr was part of one of these groups as an organiser of a victim-offender program), which developed mediation and sowed the seeds of restorative justice before Zehr's discrete Mennonite messianism was known. Their motivations were sometimes quite distant from religion, as they would participate in the political fights of the 70s in the US, fighting for the recognition of civil rights of racial, social and sexual minorities, supporting post-colonial stances in the old colonies. They led a critical criminological movement (Marxist, pacifist, feminist, abolitionist) denouncing the legal-judicial establishment, as described in the historical part of this book, and laying the foundation of alternative dispute resolution.

Thus, I consider the restorative doxa to be the result of a collective construction, gathering actors of diverse convictions and cultural backgrounds, united by the same ideals of peace, justice and fraternity. It is probably from this common concern that the slightly obscure term 'restorative justice' emerged. If there is little debate about the psychic and social restoration of individuals or of broken relationships (even though the term 'réparatrice' is preferred by some, namely in Quebec), the reference to justice is far from being clear. Are we talking about the judicial institution or, more generally, an ideal of justice? The philosophical dimension seems predominant in the discourse of restorative actors. But there is a contradiction when we observe that most of their interventions take place at the heart or on the fringes of the legal system.

---

12 E. Pascual Rodriguez et al., *Los ojos del otro. Encuentros restaurativos entre victimas y ex miembros de ETA*, Santander, Salterrae, 2013.

13 H. Zehr, *Changing lenses. Restorative justice for our times*, Herald press, 1990.

Despite this ambiguity, the concept of restorative justice spread to many Western countries. Under the aegis of the Flemish University of Leuven, which pilots the European Forum for Restorative Justice, it spread to Northern Europe before travelling to eastern and southern European countries. However, it spread unevenly in Europe and the rest of the world, and this can be explained by analysing the national and international logics of political and professional construction in the restorative field.[14] The resistance comes from diverse sources:

1. The first is linguistic. The concept was forged in Anglophone countries and there are few works specifically dedicated to it in other languages.[15]
2. The second reason is historical and political. *Restorative justice* originated in countries with a strong colonial heritage (Australia, New Zealand, the US, Canada) in which the post-colonial state was incapable of resolving the indigenous peoples' social inadaptation other than through repression. Faced with this dead end, revaluing community traditions, not always compatible with political tradition, as is the case in France, was the option chosen to satisfy the identity claims of these indigenous peoples.
3. The third reason is political and institutional. My criminological excursions and participation in the European COST group for restorative justice between 2002 and 2006 have helped me observe that certain countries with an authoritarian past have gone directly from the punitive or psychiatric model to the restorative model without having experienced the social model, characteristic of welfare states, of which France is the paragon. In these 'providential countries', social policies increased exponentially during the post-war boom, and large teams of social professionals were created. Because of their previous experiences working with either perpetrators or victims, these actors are concerned with compromising their professional identity by now fully devoting themselves to establishing or restoring communication between them.
4. The restorative doxa often neglects to mention that it is before anything else the product of values that are far from universal, as they are Christian (Protestant), Western, humanist, democratic, individualistic, liberal

14 J. Faget, 'Les dynamiques de transfert des idées restauratives', *Raisons politiques*, 2015/3, nr 59, pp. 109–119.

15 Where France is concerned, one can mention Robert Cario, *La justice restaurative, Principes et promesses*, Paris, L'Harmattan, 2005 et 2012.

and anti-state.[16] This has prompted criticism that restorative justice is a tool for a neo-liberal and neo-conservative governance[17] to assert itself, excluding entire parts of humanity that do not recognise its values.

5. The mystical Mennonite dimension of its origins hindered its spread,[18] as it did not correspond to rationalist ways of thinking as we know them in secularised countries. Thus, when Zehr began *Changing lenses* with an extract of the New Testament: 'God is merciful and gracious, slow to anger and abounding in steadfast love, God will not always accuse…',[19] it did not arouse the fervour of secular criminologists.
6. Finally, the hesitation of the restorative ideal between three conceptions leaves many practitioners perplexed.

2.1 *The Triple Conception of Restorative Justice*

- The first conception is penal and relational. The expression can only be used when a meeting is organised between protagonists of an offence and diverse members of the community (mediation, sentence circles, family or community conferences, restorative circles).
- The second is penal and restorative. Its defenders, in particular Lode Walgrave,[20] hold that the field of application of the restorative model risks being reduced if we only use it in cases where the protagonists accept to meet. It must be extended to all measures inspired by a restorative philosophy, which encompasses all sanctions ordered and put into place by the professionals of the system who have the function of making the offender repair the damage caused (reparations, community works, restitutions, compensations).
- The third conception is social and transformative. Its aim is to make our individualistic ways of living evolve via promoting community values of comprehension and respect. It stretches the concept's field of application to all transgressions that are not treated by the criminal justice system (in

---

16 Howard Zehr nuanced his position on this last point in the last edition (2015) of his founding work by restoring the role of the State, and namely European governments, to favour.

17 Barbara Hudson, *Justice in the Risk Society: Challenging and Re-affirming Justice in Late Modernity*, London, Sage, 2003.

18 J. Faget, 'The dissemination of Howard Zehr's work in France: Contribution to a sociology of (the flow of) ideas', Restorative Justice: An International Journal, 2015, vol. 3, nr 3, 1–10.

19 Zehr, op.cit.

20 L. Walgrave, 'La justice restaurative: à la recherche d'une théorie et d'un programme', *Criminologie*, vol. 32, nr 1, 1999, pp. 7–29, *Restorative Justice, Self-Interest and Responsible Citizenship*, Cullompton: Willan Publishing, 2008.

school, work, between neighbours) and fights against all the different types of oppression (economic, power related) by putting into place measures such as school, family and social mediation, community circles of conciliation, political mediation and the political processes of peace construction or consolidation.

- The relationship that these three models have with the criminal system differs. Whereas the first is derivative as the conflict regulation is delegated to an authority exterior to the system, even if the latter more or less keeps the control, the second is integrated as it is directly put into place by judicial actors, and the third is external as it escapes the criminal justice field. Despite these differences, there is a consensus that brings all restorative actors together, with the exception of a few nuances.

2.2 *The Foundational Principles of Restorative Justice*

As a reminder, the essential principles of restorative justice are the same as those of mediation. We briefly outline the objectives that guide them:

1. Giving the people ownership of their conflicts, which is traditionally 'stolen'[21] by professionals and the judiciary system.
2. Changing the perception of crime. It does not constitute an offence against the State, but above all an offence against people.
3. Changing the objectives of legal intervention. Focus on the needs of the victim, the author, and the community.
4. Changing the conception of sentencing, not sanctioning the past but preparing the future. It should not inflict a punishment to compensate for the harm caused but require a positive act to repair the prejudice suffered, and should be inclusive and not exclusive by empowering the community and the family.
5. Changing the decisional mode. The people implicated in the conflict directly participate in the search for a solution and make a decision (empowerment) that appears mutually satisfactory to them. They are not represented by professionals who decide for them. They participate in face-to-face meetings in which, thanks to an empathetic climate, they can talk confidentially about their suffering and their needs.

This school of thought is opposed to the punitive logic traditionally acknowledged by the criminal justice system and to the rehabilitative measures largely used during the 'trentes glorieuses'.

The punitive responses are only focused on symbolic effects, disinterested by the fate of the offenders, they stigmatise, exclude and precipitate into delin-

---

21 N. Christie, op.cit.

TABLE 7.1 Paradigms within criminal justice

	Punitive	Rehabilitating and therapeutical	Reparative	Restorative
Object	Guilt	Needs	Prejudice	Conflict
Focus	Perpetrator	Perpetrator	Victim	Relationship
Process	Imposed	Imposed/accepted	Imposed/accepted	Negotiated
Solution	Sanction	Help	Reparation	Agreement/pacification

quency careers, and then provide retrospective judgments without worrying about repairing or rebuilding what has been broken for the future. The judicial ritual is often only a ceremony of degradation. The institution destroys interpersonal relations instead of encouraging and building them. The adversarial procedure only aggravates conflicts. Formal justice, instead of appeasing conflicts, exacerbates antagonisms.

The rehabilitative model is equally challenged as it is too centred on the offender's needs and not enough on the reparation of their acts or empowering them. The victim is kept away from the educational processes, where instead he/she should be informed and allowed both to express his/her emotions and suffering, and to obtain material and symbolic reparation. In the same way, the offenders' community and entourage are not mobilised and empowered enough in the elaboration of educational strategies.

By comparing the different criminological paradigms that have existed one after another in modern history[22] (Table 7.1), one realises the fracture that the restorative paradigm represents compared to its predecessors, both because of its objectives and its modes of operation. Yet, by a logic of sedimentation too long to explain here, the restorative model is often combined with its predecessors, creating a new hybrid paradigm which fuses elements of all models and sometimes erodes the virtues specific to each of them.

2.3 *The Main Restorative Programmes*

Within the most restrictive penal and relational conception (and excluding penal or victim-offender mediation, which is its most widespread illustration),

22 J. Faget, *Sociologie de la délinquance* et de la justice pénale, Toulouse, Erès, 2013.

the field of restorative practices is limited to community and family conferences, sentence circles and post-sentence meetings.

The way in which these different initiatives unfold is more or less identical, though different models of practice exist. A mediator (in the broad sense of the term) meets the parties involved in the conflict separately (perpetrators, victims and possibly their supporters). He/she evaluates their cognitive ability to engage in a restorative measure and the risks that such a process can represent for their psychological equilibrium. If the diagnosis is favourable, he/she will ask for their consent to participate in a meeting. During this meeting, the mediator reminds the parties of the objectives of the mediation, then invites the actors to elaborate on the circumstances of the conflict, its origins, and its subjective dimensions. The mediator then asks them to brainstorm different ways to regulate or resolve this conflict and organises a dialogue between the parties, during which the other people present have the opportunity to intervene. Together, they construct an agreement or a project that can be oral or written.

2.3.1 Author-Victim Mediation

As I have already mentioned, everything supposedly started in 1974, in Kitchener, Ontario. In the following years, victim-offender reconciliation programs spread in the US, then in Europe, under the name of victim-offender mediation or penal mediation.

In reality, heterogeneous practices hide behind sharing the same philosophy. They are adapted, in each country, to its particular cultural, institutional or legal circumstances. Thus, the pre-eminence of the written law or of the common law systems, the adoption of the principle of legality or of discretionary prosecution, the institutional balance of power between the prosecutor, the police, and the judges, conditions the organisation of the mediation. To facilitate its comprehension, I propose to distinguish, by means of the link they have with the criminal justice system, two practice models that I qualify as 'derived' and 'integrated'. These models can be put into place cumulatively in the same country.

In the **derived model**, mediation practices constitute a parenthesis inside the justice system. They intervene at different stages of the criminal justice procedure, but before any decision is taken. The conflicts, which concern both minors and adults, are referred either by the prosecutors or the police, to a mediator whose role is to favour the communication between the opponents. If the process leads to an agreement, public action can be interrupted and the actors' decision officially approved. This model can be found in almost all Western countries, most often for minors, sometimes both for minors and adults, and in rare cases, only for adults. It is more and more defended by specific legislation. Mediators are sometimes professionals working in the public or private sector, and other times volunteers.

This model is characterised by its hybridisation, a judicialization of social logics and a socialisation of judiciary logics. The introduction of mediation into the criminal justice system was initially part of a counterculture aiming to transform repressive logics. Its implementation is sometimes the source of institutional and cultural tension among criminal justice actors who want to 'keep control of the game' and others who want to modify it. Some studies thus show the existence of a cultural conflict between the tenants of a heavily judicialized mediation practice, and those who attempt to make space for freedom and who are more respectful of its ethical principles. This conflict usually only ceases when the mediators submit to the repressive ideology or the development of reasonable compromise between the judicial and social actors.[23]

The **integrated model**: mediation practices are introduced into the judiciary process to enrich the wide range of procedural modalities that exists for dealing with conflicts. Mediation can be integrated into the sentencing and is in a way considered a probationary measure alongside the magistrate's decision. This occurrence is rare but can be seen for minors in Denmark, Poland, Slovenia and for overage people in Austria.[24] Mediation can also occur in a post-sentence context, proposed by a judge in addition to a sentence or deliberately chosen by the parties to give meaning to their conflict. This type of experiment was introduced in British Columbia in 1989, was developed in numerous Canadian provinces and can be seen nowadays in Belgium where a few programs (for example Mediante in French-speaking Belgium) have introduced mediation for more serious offenses when the convicted offender is imprisoned (crime of passion, theft or kidnapping followed by murder, parricide, rape, incest, sexual assault) but also in an increasing number of programs in Europe (United Kingdom, Netherlands)[25] or in Quebec, namely in the framework of the Equijustice organisation. The most spectacular initiative is the one initiated in 2011 and 2012 in the Spanish Basque country, between

---

23 Jacques Faget, 'les accommodements raisonnables de la médiation pénale', *Revue de science criminelle et de droit pénal comparé*, 2009, nr 4.

24 David Miers and Jolien Willemsens, *Mapping restorative justice: developments in 25 European Countries*, Leuven, European Forum for Restorative Justice, 2004.

25 Aertsen, I., 'Victim-offender mediation with serious offences', in Council of Europe, *Crime Policy in Europe, Good practices and promising examples*, Strasbourg, Council of Europe Publishing, 2004, 75–86.

direct or indirect victims of terrorist attacks and terrorist members of the ETA movement.

The main characteristic of these practices is mixing the punitive and retributive model founded on the recognition of the perpetrator's guilt, which places the opponents in an uneven power dynamic, and the restorative model which organises a horizontal process of reflection on the meaning of the conflict. The main objective of mediation is reparation, especially psychological, of the victims, and the empowerment of the actors. It exists within a homeostatic logic of complementarity with legal action. Here, no palpable tension exists, the stake is penological. The sanction is given, and only its execution modalities are influenced by the restorative philosophy. The low effectiveness of traditional criminal sanctions, their low efficiency in terms of collective dissuasion, rehabilitation of convicted offenders and reparation for victims, obliges us to search for new answers. The institution's performance can be improved by integrating mediation and reparation practices without the legal categories nor the foundational principles of the criminal trial being questioned. This simply reinforces the gap that exists within criminal proceedings, between an authority which awards legal statuses (offender-guilty) and a body which searches for the most appropriate response to the context.

This mix satisfies all those who contest the orientation of contentious issues towards penal mediation, in which the rights of the weakest deserve to be proclaimed in the public arena. This is in particular the case of feminist movements in relation to domestic violence against women, or trade unions in cases of harassment in the workplace. For them, it is preferable to pedagogically declare and assert the social prohibition on the public scene.

2.3.2 Community Conferences

The first experiences in conferencing took place in New Zealand in the beginning of the 1980s. The young Maoris were overrepresented in the courts and prisons, and their community was highly dissatisfied with the effects of the institutional treatment they received. The Maori tradition allowed the testing of another method which implicated the family in the process, making them responsible for researching solutions. This experimental model was introduced into the legislation in 1989 and then became the standard response to all the offences committed by minors, the intervention of the court becoming the exception. This model was imported in 1991 by the Wagga Wagga police in Australia, and with a few adaptations, was introduced in the Young Offenders Act of southern Australia in 1993. In this model, the parties are considered unable to resolve the problem alone. To fully address the effects of the offence and its impact, it is essential that the facilitator gathers all those affected to participate in the search for a solution to the conflict. Family members, friends, social workers and policemen can be invited. It isn't rare for the number of attendees to be more than a dozen. The meeting is prepared by separate discussions with the mediator, who organises the conference and guides the discussion, but who does not participate in its content. He/she ensures that everyone can participate and that the solution is realistic and corresponds to everyone's wishes. This program is tested with young people, but also with adults and with various issues, including theft, physical aggressions, industrial espionage, professional or sexual harassment. It can intervene either as a diversion before the legal pursuit or within the framework of the recommendations asked for by the judge before pronouncing the sentence.

An example of educative process: reintegrative shaming[26]

This concept, developed by the Australian criminologist John Braithwaite, designates all social processes that express disapproval and that have the objective of creating shame and remorse.[27] This terminology, however, can be confusing. One naturally associates shame to other adjacent notions such humiliation, infamy, disgrace, dishonour and one might fear the resurrection of mechanisms from another age. Braithwaite does not believe in the virtue of humiliation. He is aware that 'shaming is a dangerous game'. On the contrary, he believes that the humiliation practised in court is stigmatising and plays a determining role in the reproduction of delinquent conduct, which is of course the opposite of the desired effect. It has the consequence of excluding individuals, banning them and giving them no other solution than to seek refuge in groups that constitute criminal subcultures.

This disapproval that produces shame is an end in itself; otherwise it would constitute a disintegrative shame. It is only a tool to go further. Thus, it can only be conceived in a sequential process. The phase *reintegrative shaming* must succeed the phase of disapproval manifested by the community's refusal to accept certain types of behaviours, and which has the aim to provoke remorse. It has to reverse the effects of a possible stigmatisation by organising a ritual likely to 'de-labelise' individuals. In order to do this, two conditions are absolutely necessary:

26 J. Braithwaite, *Crime, shame and reintegration*, Cambridge University Press, 1989.

27 J. Faget, 'Reintegrative shaming. A propos de la théorie de John Braithwaite', *Les cahiers de la justice*, nr 1, 2006, pp. 59–70.

- The first consists in clearly distinguishing the disapproved behaviour considered as transitory from the person and his/her qualities. The blame must clearly be placed on the behaviour and not the offender's personal characteristics. Numerous acts are disapproved of, blamed informally by the parents, friends, teachers and loved ones. This disapproval is not stigmatising, as the offender is treated with respect and hears the positive comments on his/her value and potential.
- The second consists in making the reintegrative shaming the community's responsibility. The process must allow the offender to express the meaning behind the ties he/she had with their friends and supporters, and to restore them when they have been strained.

This process takes place in an informal way most of the time, without the family or limited groups of relations being fully aware. It can also be organised in a more formal way, preserving the offender's identity by showing respect and associating community with the ceremony in order for him/her to express signs of affection.

Braithwaite considers it vital to exert social control on deviant behaviour. However, this control must not be cold nor punitive, nor warm or permissive. Braithwaite defends the idea of 'firm control', based on comprehensive disapproval rather than the infliction of a sentence. The dissuasive effect of the sanction lies not in its severity but rather in the legitimacy of those who express it, not in an exogenous hierarchical legitimacy that someone such as a judge has, but an endogenous relational legitimacy that those the offender has respect, esteem or even admiration for benefit from. Its efficiency is dependent on the existence of a relationship founded on trust and security.

2.3.3 Sentencing Circles

These circles first became popular in Yukon, Canada in 1981 when the judge Barry Stuart, faced with the inadaptation of traditional responses, decided to seek help from the community of a young delinquent. The decision was made with the consent of all the people present. This type of resolution became widely developed in North America, in all the regions where indigenous populations are numerous (Saskatchewan, Manitoba, Alberta, British Columbia, Quebec, Nunavik).[28] Compared to community conferencing, this type of resolution not only associates the people closely concerned by the infraction, but

---

28 M. Jaccoud, 'Les cercles de sentence au Canada', *Les cahiers de la justice nr 1*, 2006, pp. 83–94.

also the community in its entirety. It is particularly used to treat endogenous conflicts.

An offence is considered a problem to resolve and not a transgression to punish. The behaviour is a symptom of a larger problem which questions collective values. Thus, the responsibility is not individual, even if the emphasis is put on the actor's 'recovery'; the responsibility lies with the family and the community. The circle can be organised at a police station, as a diversion but also during the process, the decision then acts like a pre-sentence report, or a post-sentence report. It can only be organised with the agreement of the community's leaders. The judges, prosecutors and lawyers can participate. There is no standard format, but it is quite common that the circle starts with a prayer or a ceremony, lasting around 3 to 4 hours and centres more around the solutions brought by the community than the behaviour itself. A circle guardian regulates the whole process and ensures that both balance and respect are maintained. As is the case for reintegrative shaming, here only the wrong behaviour is condemned, and the person themselves is never judged.

2.3.4 Meetings between Prisoners or Offenders and Victims

These meetings were initiated in England in 1983, the face-to-face approach then developed in Canada in 1987, following the initiative of the Mennonite Central committee. These meetings are named PVM (prisoner/victim meetings) or VOM (victim/offender meeting), and their objective is to allow prisoners and victims to meet either before or after the sentence is given. These two actors are not linked by the same event, but have caused or suffered a crime of the same nature. The meetings take place in a prison or under the aegis of the State's services. They are generally led by two facilitators trained in mediation and in group management, and take place in the presence of two representatives of the community. France has experimented with this model in 2010[29] and its implementation was facilitated by a 2014[30] law and popularised by the movie *I'll always see your faces*, (*Je verrai toujours vos visages*) directed by Jeanne Henry.[31]

These programmes consider harmful behaviour not in a moral way, but as an act creating consequences which cannot only be dealt with by sanctioning.

---

29 R. Cario (directed by), *Les rencontres détenus-victimes. L'humanité retrouvée*, Paris, L'Harmattan, 2012.

30 The law dated 15 August specifies in its article 10–1 of the code of criminal procedure that 'In the event of any criminal procedure and at any of its stages, even when the sentence is being carried out, the victim and the author of an offence, under the condition that the author has pleaded guilty, can be offered to take part in a restorative justice measure…'.

31 I'll always see *your faces* (directed by Jeanne Henry, 2023, Studio Canal).

The participants are not qualified by their legal status as perpetrators and victims but are perceived as human beings in suffering before anything else. Their meetings seek to find meaning in their experiences, which the judicial process has not succeeded in doing. The parties' expression through dialogue, showing their emotions provoked by their trauma, the expression of what remains unresolved, in the presence of other parties who have lived a similar or identical situation, is greatly beneficial and has the virtue of helping both the victims heal and the perpetrators to understand the impact of their actions and to feel 'rehumanised' by the victims. Inspired by Bush and Folger's transformative philosophy[32] and the Mennonite Mark Umbreit's humanist mediation,[33] these meetings initiate the process of mutual recognition within the actors, which profoundly transforms their identity.

2.4 *Conclusion and Perspectives*

Restorative ideas are starting to make their way into the judicial field and more broadly into public debate and social practices. However, despite an improvement to which all actors can attest, their development remains restrained for two major reasons. Firstly, restorative philosophy clashes with the devices of criminal populism, which becomes even easier to manage as our societies go through profound technological, socioeconomic and geopolitical upheavals (terrorism and uncontrolled flows of migration), which leave populations feeling insecure and hence create aspirations of security. Secondly, the social understanding of the restorative corpus is far from being straightforward when even the actors of these restorative practices themselves do not have a unanimous definition.

As mentioned previously, the restorative model is often combined with its predecessors, creating an institutionally hybrid entity which fuses objectives of vengeance, rehabilitation, reparation and empowerment. Thus, restorative measures appear as 'a compass pointing in a direction, but not a detailed map describing how to get there':[34] they do not appear as a coherent ensemble.

This hesitation becomes apparent in the questions its promoters have been asking themselves since the practice's inception. Is it necessary for restorative justice to be attached to criminal justice? Is restorative justice compatible with

32 J. P. Folger, R. A. B. Bush, *The promise of mediation. Responding to conflicts through empowerment and recognition*, Jossey-Bass, San Francisco, 2005.

33 M. Umbreit, 'Humanistic Mediation: a Transformative Journey of Peacemaking', *Mediation Quarterly*, 1997, 14–3, pp. 201–213.

34 H. Zehr, op.cit.

the legal institutions? Are they complementary, or will the former become a substitute for the latter?

Most restorative programmes are at present characterised by a high level of heteronomy. They represent a 'crossroads world' rather than an autonomous world.[35] Research have shown that prison life is dominated by security and punitive logic, and tributary to the objectives and constraints which weigh on the institution. As a result, their implementation demands compromise to meet the demands of both institutions and restorative principles, causing them to lose part of their potential and stray away from their initial philosophy.[36]

One way to overcome this problem is to spread restorative practices, far from courts and prisons, 'into the vast field of prevention and regulation of other types of non-penalised conflicts (in terms of deviance, notably psycho-social and psycho-cultural inadaptations)',[37] following the example of transitional justice imagined when 'criminal justice was impossible', or in order 'to meet the stabilisation needs of political order built on an unjust compromise'.[38]

It is from this perspective that I suggest their development in three different scenarios:[39]

- When a criminal response is not possible (dismissal of the case, acquittal or mental disorder of the perpetrator) or can no longer be envisaged (prescription).
- When a penal response exists but is not perceived or sufficiently visible and therefore remains misunderstood (institutional opacity).
- When the disturbances caused to social peace are harmful but cannot be precisely attributed (incivilities).

These different situations generally provoke collective emotion, worry and fears which contribute to the development of a feeling of insecurity within the population, to a collective introversion, the desertion of public spaces, and to the increase in aggressive behaviour and violence in social relations.

35 D. Griveaud et S. Lefranc, 'La justice transitionnelle, un monde-carrefour. Contribution à une sociologie des professions internationales.', *Cultures & Conflits* (119–120), 2020, pp. 71–98.

36 L. Hernandez, A. Tschanz, N. Soldadié, 'La justice restaurative à l'épreuve de l'espace-temps carcéral', in *La justice restaurative. Des frontières plurielles et mouvantes.* Les presses de l'ENAP, pp. 145–157.

37 R. Cario, op.cit.

38 S. Lefranc, 'De quoi les victimes ont-elles besoin? La justice restaurative à l'épreuve des violences de masse', in *La justice restaurative. Des frontières plurielles et mouvantes.* Les presses de l'ENAP, pp. 231–240.

39 J. Faget, 'JR or not JR? Les flottements de l'idée restaurative', *in La justice restaurative. Des frontières plurielles et mouvantes.* Les presses de l'ENAP, pp. 259–268.

Yet our societies have seldom created formal forums for the expression of these fears, anxieties and misunderstandings. They have only rarely established, outside of the ritualised and reductive forms of judicial debate, places to work on these conflicts. Restorative justice can help compensate for this deficit. It will then not only be a matter of righting wrongs between individuals, perpetrators and victims, but also of healing a wounded community.

CHAPTER 8

Civil Judicial Mediation

It was logical for mediation as a field to develop and try to address daily problems which weaken the collective well-being of our cities. Nothing opposed its emergence, especially since it was conceived to escape the logic of legal institution. As the historical part of this book demonstrates, the radical North American scholars who initiated the alternative dispute resolution (ADR) movement in the 1970s aimed to give control back to citizens over conflicts that had been stolen from them by legal professionals.

Yet mediation has gone through a spectacular and rapid expansion in the legal world,[1] which is surprising considering that the principles of mediation seem to oppose the logic of the legal system (Table 7.1). Indeed, judicial logic is founded on the principle of hierarchical power defending a collective conception of social order, referring to a general norm representing the vision and interests of the groups in power. The adversarial procedure establishes a competitive relationship, allowing the judge to discover the responsibilities of each party. In contrast, mediation offers a space for democratic debate where nothing is defined in advance, and in which the actors attempt, with the help of a third party, to construct a common relational universe in their own way, or to restore an equilibrium which has been lost.

This unlikely relationship can be explained by the fact that the legal establishment does not constitute a monolithic bloc, but it is full of fractures and

TABLE 8.1 Legal and mediation logics

Justice	Mediation
Hierarchical logic	Horizontal logic
Refers to the law	Refers to equity
Principle of competition	Principle of cooperation
Search for liability	Search for pacification
Resolution of the dispute	Regulation of the conflict

1 It is however difficult to obtain quantifiable, reliable and comparable elements between countries to measure this evolution.

 | DOI:10.1163/9789004734067_013

contradictions. The legal system always has problems adapting to the political, social and technical transformations in its environment. In an impulse of negentropy, it is obliged to regenerate itself to ensure its continued existence. One can think that the emergence of alternative dispute resolution methods is due to the necessity of a negentropic metamorphosis in an anachronistic system, asphyxiated by the plethoric social demand for law and in constant loss of legitimacy.[2] Rid of the weight of legal transcendences, of its anchor to collective values, alternative dispute resolution (ADR) represents a more pragmatic, particularistic and adaptable approach to legal regulation. Although it has long been considered by jurists as an accessory, it is in fact part of a shift in 'governmentality', from a sovereign and disciplinary conception to a managerial conception of justice in which the modes of regulation, from a neo-liberal perspective, must prove themselves to be more efficient.[3]

The European promotion of ADR has increased in intensity.[4] This promotion grew exponentially on the 23rd of April 2008 when the European Parliament gave a directive to expand civil and commercial mediation in cases of cross-border disputes.[5] This growth within a very short time period is due to the irrational increase in social demand for law which saturated the system. The stagnation of its human and material resources, the imperatives of new public management, impeded its ability to be swift and cost-effective.

For a long time now, business law has been applying this managerial rationality, avoiding legal proceedings in favour of more flexible, faster and less costly methods of regulation such as arbitration or negotiation. ADR is now

---

2 J. Faget, 'La médiation pénale, une dialectique de l'ordre et du désordre', *Déviance et société*, 1993, vol. XVII, nr 3, pp. 221–233.

3 A. Garapon, *La raison du moindre Etat. Le néo-libéralisme et la justice*, Paris, Odile Jacob, 2010.

4 See the following European legal texts:
- 98/257/EC: Commission Recommendation of 30 March 1998 on the principles applicable to the bodies responsible for out-of-court settlement of consumer disputes
- Rec (98) 1: Recommendation of the committee of ministers to member states on family mediation
- Rec (2001)9: Recommendation of the Committee of Ministers to member states on alternatives to litigation between administrative authorities and private parties.
- Recommendation Rec (2002)10 of the Committee of Ministers to member States on mediation in civil matters
- Commission of European communities: Green Paper from the Commission on ADRS concerning commercial and civilian rights, COM (2002)
- European code of conduct for mediators, 2004.

5 Directive 2008/52/EC of the European Parliament and of the Council of 21 May 2008 on certain aspects of mediation in civil and commercial matters.

spreading to all sectors of activity, concerning conflicts linked to succession, joint ownership, construction or leasing, between landlords and tenants, shopkeepers and consumers, employers and employees, members of the same family or neighbours. Their common denominator is that the parties choose to bring their conflicts into the courts. They wait for the judge to find a solution to their disputes, whereas, in many cases, they could be dealt with by conventional mediation outside of the institution. In other words, these conflicts are not intrinsically legal, and only become so because they are brought onto the judicial scene.

Is this wide implementation a sign that legal rationality is being questioned? At any rate, it has become the subject of many debates. One only has to observe the virulence of the conflict which has long pitted legal and mediation professionals against each other to see the proof. Any reflection on the function of justice represents both a questioning of the legitimacy of the actors working in that field and on the boundaries of their work.

1 A Hybridization between Imposed and Negotiated Order

The aforementioned texts do not draw a clear line between legal and non-legal regulations. No disposition, whether it be international or national, designates which disputes should come under the law and therefore under the jurisdiction of the courts, and those which should be oriented towards arbitrators, negotiators, conciliators or mediators. This relative indetermination allows for navigation of theoretical and practical obstacles. It spares itself a reflection on the nature of the social function of law, and this leads to tinkering, of which the nature varies from one country to another, to accommodate ADR in a legal manner and to control its effectiveness. The institutionalisation of practices, the standardisation of procedures, strength and power of the legal imaginary that runs through them by the omnipresent figure of the contract, lead to hybrid measures which are found neither in traditional law nor in informal regulation.

This hybridization erodes the consensual process which constitutes the cornerstone of the mediation process. In most legal systems, judges can oblige litigants to meet a mediator or to suggest a mediation. Of course, they are not able to impose a mediation, but only a pathway to mediation. However, the context in which these 'incitements' happen can make us fear a shift towards a model with more constraints. The symbolic weight of the judge's recommendation can indeed bias the actor's consent. Would they dare to refuse to invest themselves in a mediation when the judge's expectations are explicit? Would they not fear that the reticence they manifest could be prejudicial to them regarding the decision the judge will make afterwards?

We are probably going through a phase of latency which prefigures the decline of a monistic conception of law. This hybridization is one of its symptoms. The social complexity and the helplessness of the institutions to efficiently regulate the dynamics, unveils what the legal mythologies were hiding, the existence of multiple and interwoven legal galaxies. We seem to be rediscovering that there exist multiple ways to organise and make social relations safe, that the law is only one of these ways, and that there exists a dialectic relationship between the many-sided negotiated orders and the imposed order, which is not superior to them; as the 2004 European directive specifies, 'mediation should not be considered as a secondary solution compared to legal procedure'. This phrasing probably expresses the way in which it is still considered by legal professionals. But it is a safe bet that before long, priorities will be reversed, with so-called alternative methods (often referred to as amiable) will become standard, while recourse to the law and the courts will be the last resort when alternative or amiable methods have failed. This is demonstrated by the widespread introduction of contractual obligations making it compulsory to attempt mediation before going to court.

However, it will be difficult to establish a clear principle of attribution between legal cases resolved using the traditional legal system and conflicts that are resolved using ADR. The consensual characteristic of the latter likely limits its field of application to those who choose to use it or to the cases in which the judges refer the actors to mediation. The criteria of referral are not necessarily identical depending on the judicial context, the national cultures and individual sensitivities. A plethora of structural and subjective factors can influence the choices that the citizens, their lawyers or the judges make on the regulation scene.

2 The Competence of Judiciary Mediators

The European texts are surprisingly imprecise when it comes to defining the competence of judiciary mediators. They mention any person or association owning 'the qualification needed depending on the nature of the dispute' and justifying 'a training and an experience adapted to the practice of mediation'. A specific training in mediation is always required. This reluctance to create a genuine profession of mediator shows both the insufficiently defined qualities required to become a mediator and the desire to not undermine the monopoly of legal professions on the legal market.

TABLE 8.2 Choice criteria between alternative or amiable legal channels

Axis 1: Legal and judicial elements
– Demands of public order
– Appreciation of the judiciary hazard
– Representation the performances respective of mediation and the legal system
– Degree of effectiveness of judiciary decisions
– Adaptation capacity of the parties or people to the rules of the judicial game or the interactions in mediation
– Inadaptation to the rule of law
– Obvious disproportion between the cost of a legal procedure and the cost of an amicable resolution
Axis 2: Structural elements
– The conflict's degree of violence
– Problematic asymmetry in power relations
– Continual or punctual types of relation
– Urgency to resolve the conflict
– Concern for discretion or publicity
– Need to state the law on the public arena for educational purposes
Axis 3: Subjective elements
– Disputes with high emotional stakes
– Preference for a competitive or cooperative process
– Willingness to control the process
– Relational distance between the people
– Existence or non-existence of share values between the actors
– Personality of the parties involved
– Relational pathologies

In fact, when the judges suggest mediation, they tend to orient the actors towards jurist mediators, most often lawyers, under the pretext that one would need legal competences to successfully lead a mediation session. Although some of them can be excellent mediators, it is not necessary to possess legal skills to take on the role of a 'third party mediator'. This professional habit can even constitute a handicap when it comes to shifting from a high and effusive posture to the lower posture of a simple accompanying third party. The propensity to deal with disputes, to construct the legal position of one's clients can make one forget that the objective of mediation is to 'work' on the conflict, whose roots and origins are more obscure, elusive and irrational.

In so doing, the mediator does not have to know the law, give advice or judge the legal relevance of the solution envisaged by the parties. That role is reserved for their lawyers, and the judge is there, in the background, to approve or reject the agreement reached. The mediator's role is solely to act as a catalyst in establishing a dialogue, a conversation between the protagonists that cannot take place without the mediator's presence. The core of the mediator's skills therefore lies in the acquisition and application of communication techniques. Only a legal awareness will be useful in decoding the context of certain cases.

The list of accredited mediators, following the wishes of the EU Council of Ministers on the 6th of June 2014, reveals an overwhelming overrepresentation of jurists and lawyers to the detriment of 'social' mediators. This conception of competence in mediation shows an ignorance of understanding of mediation on the part of prescribers and an entrenched conceptual confusion, which is pushed to an extreme in debates on the development of e-mediation, between assisted negotiation, conciliation and mediation. Many jurists tend to consider mediation to be bargaining between diverging positions, or in other words, compromise. So much so that there is a *summa divisio* dividing the models based on the rapid search for a solution (neoliberal vision of a pragmatic, efficient and technical society which 'manages' conflict in a short-term perspective) and those based on the slower construction of communication (more reflexive and sustainable vision of society, which regulates conflict in a long-term perspective). Of course, the borders between these two models are permeable and many mediators navigate between the two depending on their culture and their competences, the type of conflict, the dominant emotional or material stakes within the conflict, the degree of implication of the actors in the process, their cognitive capacities, the nature of their relations, and the time they agree to dedicate to the mediation sessions. But these differing models are nevertheless revealing concerning the existence of two mediation cultures that struggle to communicate.

3 The 'Juridification' of Mediation Practices

The colonisation of mediation practices by legal professions is widespread. This co-optation has favoured the development of these practices in the common law countries, though its expansion is deceptive. Penny Brooker observes that the institutionalisation of mediation by the legal system in England and

TABLE 8.3 Two typical ideal conceptions of mediation

Idealist vision	**Pragmatic vision**
Works on the conflict	Works on the dispute
Conflict can have positive functions	Conflict is seen as a problem
Search for communication	Search for a solution
The mediator's stance is non-directive	The mediator's stance is directive
Psycho-social competencies	Legal competencies are dominant
Emphasis on the necessary psychological time (longer mediations)	Emphasis on institutional time (shorter mediations)
Welcoming emotions	Avoidance of emotions
Work on otherness	Work on reconciling positions
Cost base on social services provided	Cost base on that of legal services
Encouraging creativity in the search for solutions	Legal imaginary omnipresent in the search for solutions

Wales leads to a 'juridification' of mediation.[6] Its colonisation by lawyers dissolves its potential and transforms it into a conflict resolution 'technique'.

This observation is shared by Daniela Galli who argues that we are assisting in the 'capture of mediation by the law'.[7] Turning mediation into an amicable, and not just alternative, way of resolving conflicts, monitoring it in an increasingly legal framework, and giving jurists the primacy in its implementation, runs the risk of turning mediation into a procedure and depleting its humanist potential. According to her, 'each mediation taking place within a legal framework hinders, rather than encourages, the evolution of interpersonal relationships and of the actors themselves. And this is primarily because its objective is the same as the law, namely resolving a problem, whereas... mediation has the objective of restoring a relationship'. For her, 'law interrupts the exchange... and forbids a deeper reflection and understanding, and ultimately, to think'.[8]

My work has allowed me to collect many hints of this juridification:

- The legal overcoding of the terms used (parties, procedures, compromise, mutual concessions, etc.)

6 P. Brooker, *Mediation law: journey through institutionalism to juridification*, London, Routledge, 2013.

7 D. Galli 'Les effets indésirables du processus d'assimilation de la médiation par le droit', *Informations sociales*, 2012, nr 170, pp. 28–34.

8 Ibid.

- The transfer of legal routines into the field of mediation that were not previously present: advance requests and signature of a commitment contract at the start of the process, request of a professional responsibility insurance for mediators, referral to the legal nature of the agreements (whereas mediation advocates for a 'tailor-made' system of norms, a solution adapted to people's needs), incitement to written agreements.
- Jurists indexing the price of mediation practises on the hourly rate of their legal services.
- Granting legal aid[9] for lawyers based on the mediation's results. Mediators get paid for their services differently depending on whether the mediation has led to an agreement or not, and whether the latter is partial or total. This strongly inclines mediators to be pragmatic and solution – seeking.
- In France, lawyers are paid slightly more than mediators for mediation carried out under the legal aid scheme. This difference reflects the systems undervaluing of relational work compared to legal work.

This whole process of juridification is reinforced by the development of online dispute resolution (ODR). An increasing number of private platforms offer online mediation services with the objective of encouraging and increasing citizens' access to law and justice and favouring quick and cheap dispute resolution. Some observers worry about the absence of public authorities in this new market's regulation and fear that it might transform society's relationship with the law. We might wonder more precisely whether a virtual process in terms of mediation does lend itself to proper communication, dialogue, and to work on otherness, which are the foundations of mediation. One might also wonder whether two other conditions for a successful mediation – the guarantees offered by the mediator's competence, and their scrupulous respect of their ethic and deontology – will be respected and met. This retreat of human characteristics to the profit of technical normativity, fed by AI and algorithms, will reinforce the conceptual mash that alternative conflict regulation methods suffer from, namely a tenacious confusion between mediation and assisted negotiation.

9 These are procedure and lawyer fees that are completely or partially taken into charge by the State, when the financial resources of those answerable to law are insufficient.

CHAPTER 9

Family Mediation

The spectacular development of family mediation in the Western world probably makes it the most well-known type of mediation, and the type which often garners support from decisionmakers and the public. Three reasons for its social and institutional recognition are: the metamorphosis of domestic relations, the devaluing of judicial practices and the development of supportive public policies.

The rise of family mediation is correlated with the metamorphosis of family relationships. Family structures have changed, making way for precarious or new relational models. Three dynamics can explain the precariousness of the domestic model. The contemporary family is founded less on institutionalised relationship models, marked instead by a strong emotional investment which struggles to survive the increased elasticity of these new types of relationships. It is a democratic family in which marital and parental relationships are based on law and equity. Finally, it is a family where each member keeps their autonomy, as well as their psychological and legal identity as individuals.

These processes bring about a structural transformation of the very concept of family, which shifts from a stable and normalised institution to a foggy and unstable affective ensemble. Historically, we have moved from the clan family to the nuclear family, and then from the nuclear family to the rhizomatic family (unmarried, sometimes blended several times, homosexual, etc.). This evolution is correlated with the decline of the moral, legal and national conception of family to the profit of a more pragmatic and international approach. In this type of family, relationships count more than positions or blood links. These relations are polycentric, meaning it can sometimes be difficult to identify their main root.

At the same time, judicial practices are increasingly devalued. A number of legal sociologists and a few critical jurists have unveiled the way in which legal rationality enslaves human reality to its formal requirements. As Isabelle Gorchs says: 'the parties recounting the events to the judge is less the product of observing lived experience than of a psychological construction. The parties translate the conflict they're living through into 'judicial' pretensions deduced from the rules of the legal system that the judge has the task of implementing. By choosing the legal rules of the game, the party will only invoke the conclusive facts, meaning the facts to which the rules of law attach a sanction. Moreover, it interprets these conclusive facts and the evidence provided depending

 | DOI:10.1163/9789004734067_014

on the legal effects that it means to make them produce.'[1] We can thus explain why the judge has no knowledge of the 'matrix of the dispute' as only the elements of the conflict which are translatable into legal terms are submitted to him or her, all those that cannot be proven will escape him. This 'derealisation' is exacerbated by the logic of combat, the famous 'contradictory principle' which permeates the system, and during which each of the adversaries seeks to be right to the detriment of the opponent. The system will therefore provide judicial truths that are very far away from existential ones. All those that have been able, for one reason or another, to experience the legal system in the context of a domestic dispute notice that its competitive logic 'adds fuel to the fire', considerably aggravates the adults' personal, psychological and social situation and puts their relationship with their children in great peril. Judges are under the pressure of the large number of cases they have, devoting on average of 18 minutes to treat each case.[2] So, it is easy to understand the necessity to propose a process which is more respectful of the parties' sensitivity, as they are greatly affected by the problems of their private life. Since the 1970s in North America and the 1980s in Europe, these observations have opened a real avenue for the development of family mediation.

However, the structural transformations of the family and the questioning of legal practices on their own cannot explain the rise of family mediation. There were a considerable number of social professions ready to take on these changes in romantic relationship structures. The 'family police',[3] pushed to its height with the advent of the welfare state, has created multiple places where people could talk, be listened to, be welcomed and receive support. Thus, we can argue that the rise of family mediation was the product of a public policy choice. This is in particular the case in all countries which have a centralising tradition, despite a modest social demand, where the State has played a central role in its promotion. In France, the encouragement of the ministries of Social Affairs, the Family and Justice ministry, as well as the financial support of the National Fund for Family Associations allowed family mediation to emerge.

Yet it would be wrong to think that we are dealing with a top-down conception of state action. In reality, the political construction of family mediation is more a matter of governance than of stately authoritarianism. It is the result of

1 Béatrice Gorchs, 'La conciliation comme enjeu dans la transformation du système judiciaire', *Droit et société*, nr 62, 2006/1, pp. 223–256.

2 Le Collectif Onze, *Au tribunal des couples. Enquêtes sur des affaires familiales*, Paris, Odile Jacob, 2013.

3 Jacques Donzelot, *La police des familles*, Paris, Ed. de Minuit, 1977.

the convergence of a great number of actors' interests such as the significant weight of mediation organisations, the consequent role of the movement for the recognition of children's rights (child advocacy) and associations of divorced fathers. This 'bottom-up' implantation of family mediation is much more obvious in pioneer countries such as Great Britain, where the activism, large number and strong organisation of mediation services allowed this new practice to impose itself.

Because of the enthusiasm that most Western countries showed for family mediation, one could have expected a surge in practices. This was not the case in all countries, and particularly in France, where the number of mediations grew only moderately despite much promotion. The number of mediations slowly increase, representing only a small percentage of all family disputes, demonstrating a disconnect between modest social demand and robust public investment.

1 The Causes for Non-recourse to Mediation

These causes can be social, psychological or structural, such as:

- The public's and jurists' (magistrates, lawyers, notaries) lack of real knowledge of mediation, despite the frequent promotional campaigns.
- The way that couples function. Those 'who resort more easily to mediation are those who, in the relationship, were used to negotiating, making contracts, discussing each other's implication'. This capacity cannot be found in all environments.[4]
- The paradoxical injunction posed by the requirement of conversing with someone does not wish to meet again and with whom communication has been impossible or tumultuous in the past.
- The perception of mediation as a very intrusive therapeutic approach which requires speaking about oneself, listening to others, reflecting on the conflict's story; in short, which demands introspective work, which can be difficult and anxiety-inducing.
- The inadaptation of mediation's approach to 'extreme conflicts' in which the possibility of a common approach is hindered either by lethal passion of separation which feeds the desire to overpower the 'other' or by a self-centred psychological state of mind incompatible with working on otherness.

---

4 *Ibidem.*

Other causes of non-recourse to family mediation have to do with the structure of the legal field. For example:

- The consensual principle of mediation constitutes a barrier to its development.
- Citizens are forced to rely on the State to resolve their conflicts, including conflicts happening in the private sphere.
- The willingness to 'win' one's lawsuit to the detriment of the opponent leads to privileging the competitive logic of the legal system, which decides who is wrong and who is right.
- The attachment to the principle of being represented by a lawyer reassures litigants who are anxious of speaking themselves.
- Legal professionals are reluctant to favour the rise of a process over which they have no control, for which they are not trained and which threatens their monopoly over the legal market.
- Purely utilitarian reasons lead people to prefer a divorce or separation by mutual consent rather than mediation sessions that might lengthen the process.

These different reasons for not resorting to mediation mirror and sometimes intersect with institutional, ideological, identity, financial and empirical tensions that govern its implementation.

2 An Institutional Tension

The sociological, legal and political reasons for the institutionalisation of family mediation were reinforced by neoliberal rationalities concerned by cutting down budgets and reducing the stately influence. For example, a British audit showed that family mediation lasts for 100 days on average and costs 1000 euros, whereas a legal court case was settled in 450 days and costs approximately 2388 euros.[5] This argument could explain why within an extremely short period of time (around two decades), the public authorities have supported this initiative. However, this statement must also be nuanced. The promptness and firmness of this support was exclusively the prerogative of secularised societies, in which the moral opposition to the disintegration of family relationships was very quickly diluted with the irresistible reality of the explosion of the number of divorces and separations. On the other hand, the southern European countries, heavily influenced by the conservative Catholic culture, took longer than the northern countries to develop this type of initia-

5 National Audit Office, *Review of Legal Aid and Mediation*, London, 2007.

tive, which does not yet exist in regions of the world where the weight of culture and religion has hindered the recognition of equal rights between men and women.

Far from the original alternative conception, family mediation started out with a bang (and was supported by an ardent public promotional discourse) in the institutional modalities' repertoire of conflict management. Depending on the country, this institutional implementation is strengthened by legal texts which either give judges the option of orienting people towards a mediator, or of imposing an informational meeting about mediation.

However, this institutionalisation did not happen easily, especially as it became confronted by the resistance of family magistrates.[6] Their passive attitude is often overshadowed by the enthusiasm of a few 'activist judges' who are very committed to helping mediation develop. These judges can notably be found in the European magistrates' group for mediation (GEMME). Their moderation probably expresses the fear of a substantial loss of their professional identity. The feeling of being reduced to a role of orienting cases and ratifying signed agreements outside of their offices, of being deprived of the most creative and relational aspect of their mission to the profit of mediators, does not fill them with joy.

The second source of resistance came from lawyers. Their hostility to family mediation was initially massive. They perceived its development as a threat to their monopoly over the legal and judicial treatment of family conflicts. The most financially fragile part of the profession, essentially invested in individuals' rights, felt this threat the strongest. This aversion has however been wilting for a few years now. Examples such as the UK, where lawyers have been influenced by the values of mediation; Germany, where it is considered a legal service reserved to legal professionals; Catalunya and Quebec, where there is a majority of lawyers amongst mediators, are convincing. And the French legislature has largely opened doors for them these last few years by allowing them to practise family mediation without any specific training.

The jurists' increasing interest in family mediation is most probably linked to the general trend of legalising mediation practices. The resistance of the magistrates and lawyers subsides de facto as soon as family mediation practices are led within a more legal framework and they 'keep their hand over the game'. This grip is the expression of the considerable weight of their lobbies on the choices of the diverse concerned ministers. The examples given in the

---

6 J. Faget, 'La médiation familiale en tensions. Réflexions sur le cas français', *RIEJ*, 2020, pp. 179–196.

previous chapter of 'capture of mediation by the law'[7] illustrate the effects of institutionalisation on the metamorphosis of legal and judicial practices.

Mediators coming from the social field cannot stand this evolution as it makes their existence fragile. Faced with powerful and organised organisations, the world of mediation appears disarmed, influenced by a peaceful vision of social life and without any political vision or conscience. Mediators did not stand a chance, as the world of mediation lacks structure, does not fare well with uneven power dynamics, and is marked by the absence of a strong identity because of its polymorphous identity (many mediators hold other jobs, such as psychologist, social worker or lawyer for example). They are also worried about the risks that the legalisation of mediation poses to their ethical and deontological principles, notably people's consent, confidentiality of debates and even mediators' independence.

Such a context does not facilitate relations between mediators and lawyers, even though their complementarity could lead to many successful mediations. However, lawyers' complex institutional positioning, (sometimes partners when they accompany clients throughout the mediation process, sometimes competitors when they are themselves mediators), muddles and complicates their relationship.[8]

From now on, the choice is made. Family mediation is no longer considered a branch of social work of psychology but rather a technique to resolve conflicts and facilitate contractual relations. For the legal system, a successful mediation is above all else a quick mediation which leads to a written agreement whose modalities are compatible with existing legal categories.

3 An Ideological Tension

The professionals in the family mediation field cultivate a certain ideology, even if not always to the same degree. The enchanted discourse of mediation relates the idea of a 'good' way of living through the conflict, a 'good' way of being a parent, a 'good' family, an ideal of co-parenting involving the survival of the parental couple even after the failure of the conjugal couple, a 'good' separation in the name of the 'children's well-being'. The implicit model which is conveyed poses an 'obligation to listen to each other', demands that

7 D. Galli, 'Les effets indésirables du processus d'assimilation de la médiation par le droit', *Informations sociales*, 2012, nr 170, pp. 28–34.

8 S. Adijès, H. Lesser, *Médiateurs et avocats: Ennemis? Alliés?* Paris, Médias et médiations, 2014.

the relationship between children and both parents be maintained after the divorce as 'children need both parents' to blossom. I am not questioning the relevance of such a conception here. What I wish to highlight is that this model is conveyed by means of a strong moral injunction. This might seem paradoxical for an institution which sees itself as the crucible of people's empowerment. Family mediation ensures the promotion of a 'rivatised, negotiating, open, egalitarian and democratic family model'[9] which seeks to restore power in the family even though it is not accessible to everyone. It relies on the postulate of a contractual, rational family which must perpetuate obligated relations when the turmoil of passion leads to rejection and irrepressible desires of separation.

Thus, family mediation could appear as a space of control, probably soft control, but taking on by astute manipulation the function of ideological normalisation. The observation of practices, which can vary depending on the chosen model, show the implementation of a set of small obligations which added up form a relatively constraining normative framework: obligation of expressing oneself, of listening to one's opponent, of not interrupting him or her, of being respectful, cooperative and reflexive. Thus, the proclamation of the family's competence creates a strange mix with the deontological necessity of stabilising their communication. This made Irène Théry say that there is a paradox between the increasing technicality of the direction of meetings by mediators and the idea of 'giving back to the parties' the power of choosing their own destiny.[10]

Without a doubt, mediation's consensual characteristic allows it to escape these constraints. Because where motivation does not exist, 'where one is caught in fantasies of vengeance and destruction of the other, in a rigidified position, mediation will not even be considered by those who would need it the most, but who are sometimes inapt, sometimes momentarily, to take this step'.[11] But the consensual principle is more fragile than one might think. This is why most Western legal systems organise an obligatory mediation meeting before any procedure starts. In the UK, legal aid is only granted if the parties accept to attempt a mediation, and the judges can order the party (even if this party has won) to pay if it has refused the mediation process 'in an unreasonable manner'. One might think that in general, people who refuse mediation

9 Benoit Bastard, 'Mais à qui profite la médiation familiale?' *Dialogue*, nr 170, 2005/4, pp. 65–80.

10 Irène Théry, *Le démariage. Justice et vie privée*, Paris, Odile Jacob, 1993.

11 Maryvonne David Jougneau, 'La communication familiale au moment de la rupture: de la logique de la procédure à la logique de la médiation', *Dialogue*, 1999, nr 143, pp. 31–40.

during a legal procedure will, one way or another, suffer the consequences of their refusal to communicate and cooperate. And only the deliberate choice of a conventional family mediation far from the judiciary logics limits this risk. Mediation processes that escape the narrow context of the parental question also appear less normative. This is the case of succession between adults, conflicts between brothers and sisters, adult children and ascendants, cousins and allies, members of a blended or rainbow family. This is also the case when it comes to maintaining family ties for the elderly, people in hospital or in prison. Even if, then again, a certain ideal of family harmony pervades what I have qualified as 'the unthought-of' family mediation.[12]

4 Identity Tension

The practice of family mediation is now fully recognised as a job but is struggling to establish as a profession. It is indeed difficult for mediators acting within a scattered order to obtain social recognition and a professional identity. Family professions are plethoric (diverse therapists, couples counsellors, psychologist, social workers, specialised educators, specialised judges and lawyers, economic advisers) and to add another without cutting off the older ones does not facilitate a clear perception of mediation. The distinction may be especially blurred between mediators and certain therapists or couples therapists whose practices appear similar. To add to this confusion, family mediators who practise full time are rare. Most of the time, they are also therapists, psychologists, social workers, or lawyers, which considerably reduces their social visibility. This professional versatility can be understood in the still uncertain economic context of mediation, which can undermine full social recognition of the activity and cloud the general public's understanding of the mediator's role.

The construction of a professional identity presupposes a certain number of prerequisites, the existence of an initial and continuous specialised training, which needs to be demanding and with a high quality standard, a sufficiently important practice clearly perceived by the public, the existence of professional networks which structure the activity, construct its image, develop communication strategies, defend the collective interests of the profession and affirm ethical and deontological principles.

These conditions are far from being met. The fight for identity requires mediators to differentiate themselves, with on the one hand professions of

12 Jacques Faget, 'L'impensé de la médiation familiale', *Empan*, 2009, nr 72, pp. 74–80.

the soul, and on the other, legal professions. This venture is delicate as family mediation refers back to the institutional function of the law and the influence of psychoanalysis in its functioning cannot be avoided. Family mediators must be capable of both perceiving psychological conflicts and unconscious fantasies at work in the search for communication, and of implementing technical processes that are blind to the complexity of the human mind. Obtaining an agreement does not always 'simplify' things, as is frequently considered. On a psychological level for example, it can signify that the separation is definite, which can be difficult to accept in one's heart.

5 A Financial Tension

Family mediation has become a market, with its marketing strategies used on those who are hiring, the subsidiaries and the public with its aggressive competitions. It is not a goldmine (family mediation is not very lucrative compared to lawyer practices or private therapists, it is less 'flashy' than corporate, commercial and environmental mediation) but the sector is reasonably profitable. Thus, business-related tensions can be observed on both an endogenous and an exogenous level.

Endogenous tensions firstly appear at the training level where university and private structures rival. They are also the result of an unequal competition between mediators employed by big social institutions or corporations, mediators working for small associations which are not financially stable, and private mediators. The fight for funding and publicity is a blow to the ethical principle of independence, and changes the practice's values and direction. A French text written in 2018[13] highlights this rivalry by refusing to regulate access to the profession. Thus, lawyers, notaries and bailiffs are able to practise family mediation with a diploma approved by the State, which guarantees the possibility of working in a service supported by the family allowance services.

In practice, there exists a stratification of the market which opposes on the one hand family mediators (often lawyers) practising conventional mediation for free, aimed at middle or higher social classes and on the other hand, salaried 'social family mediators', who offer agreed-upon rates and who deal with the conflicts of people of lower income. Hence, the risk of a divide between mediation for the 'rich people'; more legalised as jurists are omnipresent, and mediation for 'poor people', more centred on psychology, as social workers and psychologists are in majority.

13 French ministry of justice dispatch, 8th February 2018.

6 Empirical Tensions

In the absence of explicit deontological codes, the debate rages between practitioners on when to resort to family mediation. These differences of opinion generally stem from different conceptions of family mediation and of its social function.

The first disagreement concerns family mediation's field of application. Whereas some mediators consider it quite extensive, others limit its reach to the separation of couples only. Amongst the latter, some go even further and argue that only people who are physically separated can start a mediation process, in order to avoid mediation becoming a long-term process such as couples or marriage counselling.[14]

A second controversy exists between supporters of family mediation involving children, and those who vehemently refute the relevance of their involvement by saying that the process cannot be envisaged when unequal relationships exist and one of the people is under the other's authority. For the latter, mediation between children and parents is closer to a therapeutic practice or possibly a juvenile judge's competence. The involvement of children in conflict mediation which opposes their parents is a completely different question. Whilst some mediators accept this principle under certain conditions, others limit this possibility as much as they can, because 'under no circumstances should the child have the feeling that his/her words can have an effect on the result of the mediation'.[15]

A third question divides mediations, and it concerns the abilities of the actors within mediation. The cognitive and psychological abilities are essentially the ones that pose a problem. At first glance and without any specific training, it is difficult to diagnose the deficiencies and pathologies which justify distancing people from mediation. The powerful emotional dimension of domestic conflicts plunges them into a psychological maelstrom, which makes them less clear-sighted. Identifying an unhealthy personality structure or the unhealthy dimension of a couple's relationship is complex. How practicable mediation is depends on the mediator's competence, the type of process they privilege and the objective they have in mind.

Another subject of discord divides mediators who refuse to begin a mediation process in a context involving physical violence, and those who do not reject this possibility a priori. The former argues that such acts should be punished by a legal authority to encourage the perpetrator's awareness of the

14 Jean Grechez, 'Enjeux et limites de la médiation familiale', *Dialogue*, 2005/4, nr 170.

15 *Ibidem.*

seriousness of their actions. The latter think that mediation, except in the case of grave and repeated violence, is more appropriate than an expeditious and dehumanised legal sham. Their position is justified by the fact that punctual and accidental violence does not hinder the successful development of the mediation process, and that allegations of violence sometimes disintegrate during the interaction catalysed by the mediator.

All these tensions exist in parallel with methodological quarrels about the different coexisting models, from the problem-solving model to the purest transformative model, about the use or not of the systemic approach, the use of techniques such as the genogram, and about whether or not to organize individual interviews before the mediation meeting. Without entering into these debates, the choice of model reveals different conceptions of the work and the identity of mediators.

Thus, Kruk opposes psychosocial mediations which focuses on the needs and the communication of the family and children, with legal mediations centred on the contractual and moral dimensions of the conflict.[16] This is confirmed by Bonafé-Schmitt who emphasizes that mediators coming from a professional legal background follow a more instrumental logic, whereas those who have a background in humanities tend to follow a more communicational logic.[17] It is true that many lawyers have a tendency to consider mediation as a bargaining process between diverging positions, leading to a compromise which is closer to negotiation than mediation.

Many mediators are not really aware of these methodological variants as they are sometimes ignorant, due to a lack of appropriate training, of the existence of all the available models. My observations as a trainer and analyst of group practices have led me to observe that most trainings only spread one model inspired by problem solving and Fiutak's model. The qualitative typology proposed by Morello (Table 9.1)[18] clearly shows this divide within the still homogenous group of state-qualified family mediators. We can suppose that it would be even more spectacular if it pertained to all practitioners of family mediation. Amongst those who know different models, some sacralise one, others create hybrid models depending on the type of conflict, its evolution, and people's needs. Those who have only been trained in a single model

16 Kruk, E., 'Practice issues, strategies and models', *Family and Conciliation Courts Review*, 1998, vol. 36, nr 2, pp. 195–215.

17 J.P. Bonafé-Schmitt, *L'évaluation des effets des processus de médiation familiale sur les médiés*, recherche-action, Glysi, Fenamef, 2007.

18 Th. Morello, En quoi le genre et le style éclairent-ils l'unité-diverse du métier de médiateur-e familial-e? *Tiers*, nr 21, 2018, pp. 27–42.

TABLE 9.1 The practice's frames of reference

Mediator	Aware of the existence of different models	Unaware of the existence of different models
Non hybrid	Purist	Conformist
Hybrid	Pragmatic	Empirical

either respect it scrupulously or create their own modus operandi which is more in line with the situation and the mediator's subjectivity.

7 A Communicational Effect

Even though family mediation constitutes a field of multiple tensions, all research that has attempted to evaluate its reach is generally positive and highlights its relevance. This enthusiastic undertone must be mitigated by their 'half scientific-half ideological'[19] characteristic. It is led by believers, sometimes actors of the processes they observe, and most of the research is North American or sponsored by organisations that defend the profession's interests. It is essentially descriptive and quantitative, and suffers from an ideological ambition which prevents the rigorous examination of the psychological and practical consequences on the lives of those involved.

As with all family professions, all observations point to the extreme feminisation of this activity. It is rarely a full-time occupation, but is most often combined with professional positions in law, social work or psychology, and these other professions often determine a penchant for practical mediation models. Thus, Lévesque distinguishes between the technical advisor mediator with a legal background who facilitates exchanges and stresses the agreement which needs to be reached; the mediator who is a social worker focused on communication, redefining personal relationships and reorganising common life; and the mediator therapist who centres his/her work on managing one's emotions and tries to help clients overcome their affective distress which prevents parents from fulfilling their role satisfactorily.[20] Sarrazin distinguishes

19 Pierre Noreau, Samia Amor, 'Médiation familiale: de l'expérience sociale à la pratique judiciaire', in *Famille en transformation. La vie après la séparation des parents*, Presses Universitaires de Laval, 2004, pp. 269–297.

20 Justin Lévesque, *Méthodologie de la médiation familiale*, Toulouse, Erès, 1998.

lawyers' more directive strategies from the psychologist mediators and social workers' more communicative strategies. But he also notices that the lawyers do not have more of a tendency to influence decisions than the others. Moreover, men and women do not use different techniques. Lastly, he mentions that a mediator having a lot of professional experience in his or her original professional field is not a guarantee of the mediation's success. However, a great deal of experience as a mediator ensures better performance.

Australian studies present mediation users as people tendentiously part of the educated middle class.[21] This observation echoes diverse studies showing that contractual models of conflict resolution are more the prerogative of the middle or upper class. This is confirmed by the quantitative investigation conducted by Jérome Minonzio for the Caisse d'allocations familiales.[22]

The first empirical studies highlighted the deficiencies of the legal system in terms of communication, cooperation, and people's ability to establish agreements. Kelly thus demonstrated the advantage of mediation over legal procedures in terms of communication: 76 per cent of women and 72 per cent of men who participated in a mediation process say that it has helped them to communicate better, and these figures drop to 39 per cent for women and 26 per cent for men when it comes to judicial procedures.[23] All investigations that have resorted to the method of control groups are unanimous in affirming the superiority of the results of mediation compared to those of the legal system.

The satisfaction rates recorded for those who have taken part in mediation are always quite remarkable. Kelly observed that mediation led to a satisfactory understanding or agreement in 50 per cent to 85 per cent of cases.[24] This satisfaction is always greater for the spouse who is more advantaged by the agreement (the guardian parent) and seems higher for women than for men. In particular, Minonzio notes that women are more satisfied in terms of improved communication, whereas men are especially satisfied regarding financial aspects.[25] Moreover, he noted that 68 per cent of interrogated couples consider that mediation has had a positive impact on their relationship. Jean-Pierre Bonafé-Schmitt observed that 59 per cent of people believe that starting a pro-

21 Wade, J., 'Four evaluation studies of family mediation services in Australia', *Australian Journal of Family Law*, 1997, vol. 11, nr 3, pp. 343–349.

22 Minonzio J., 'La médiation dans les CAF', *Recherches et Prévisions*, nr 89, 2007, pp. 71–80.

23 Kelly J.B., 'Mediated and adversarial divorce: respondents' perceptions of their process and outcomes', *Mediation Quarterly*, 1989, vol. 24, pp. 71–88.

24 Kelly J.B., 'A decade of divorce mediation research. Some answers and questions', *Family and Conciliation Courts Review*, 1996, vol. 34, nr 3, pp. 373–385.

25 Minonzio (2007), op.cit.

cess of mediation has been useful to them, especially when it comes to appeasing tensions, communicating about subjects that were previously taboo, and taking to account each other's needs. This feeling of usefulness is reinforced by the signature of an agreement. 62 per cent of people would be favourable to resorting to mediation for another problem, this score being higher when the participant has the feeling of being listened to, regardless of whether there was an agreement or not.[26]

In a study conducted in 1995, following 120 couples who participated in mediation sessions, Peter McCarthy and Janet Walker[27] showed that reaching an agreement was not the only end sought in mediation. Its efficiency can be evaluated by means of an improvement in communication between the spouses, a reduction of the conflict's virulence, the expression of previously unsaid opinions or emotions, or the improvement of people's negotiation skills. However, establishing an agreement allows people to envisage a more long-term impact on their improvement in communication and resolution of future problems. Bonafé-Schmitt also noticed the existence of a positive 'communication effect' as 37 per cent of people declared that their relationships improved in terms of quality of communication, especially concerning their children's needs. This improvement is noticeable even in cases of very conflictual relationships and is even stronger when the degree of freedom in the participation to the mediation process is high.[28]

For most researchers, issues relating to child custody (many emphasize the propension users have to sign agreements of shared custody) and visiting rights to the children appear more important for the mediated parties than those concerning the payment of pension or the division of property. In general, the dispositions taken in mediation appear more precise than those made in court and are more respected than court decisions. Jones and Brodtker[29] noticed that over a period of 2 years, 82 per cent of mediation agreements were respected, 12 per cent were reviewed once by the court and 6 per cent were reviewed more than once. The authors associate these results with the more equitable characteristics of the agreements obtained and with the parties having more control over the settlement of their disputes.

26 Bonafé-Schmitt (2007), op.cit.

27 Mac Carthy P., 'Walker J., A long term impact of family mediation', *Social Policy Research*, 103, 1996.

28 Bonafé-Schmitt (2007), op.cit.

29 Jones T.S., Brodtker A., 'Agreement, maintenance, satisfaction and relitigation in mediated and non-mediated custody cases: a research note', *Journal of Divorce and Remariage*, 1999, vol. 32, nr 1/2, pp. 17–30.

Generally speaking, the parties who declare to be satisfied at the end of the mediation process continue to have this feeling later on. Thus, the rate of revised agreements in mediation are around 13 per cent within two years and 35 per cent in case of court order. In the long term (10 years), the viability rates of these agreements in terms of custody and access to children are 65 per cent in mediation and 40 per cent for court proceedings.[30] Bonafé-Schmitt observes that while few actors spontaneously come back to their mediator, this is because they attempt to manage their problems directly, which substantiates the idea of them becoming more empowered.[31]

Family mediation is thus more and more institutionalised, which erodes, outside of conventional mediations, the fundamentals on which it was built. This is, however, not an argument that completely invalidates the relevance of its juridification. Even in its more 'legalised' form, it remains more subtle in its modes of action than the traditional system, which has long added distress to the already distraught minds of couples who seek to separate from each other, as well as to their children.

---

30 Pearson J., Thoennes N., 'Divorce mediation: an American picture', in Dingwall R., Eekelaar J., *Divorce mediation and the legal process*, New York, Oxford University Press, 1988, pp. 71–91.

31 Bonafé-Schmitt (2007), op.cit.

CHAPTER 10

Citizen, Intercultural and Social Mediation

Inspired by the founding model of the San Francisco Community Boards and the Community Dispute Settlement Centre of Philadelphia,[1] numerous social mediation programmes developed in the vast majority of Western countries. They have such diverse names that it is difficult to quantify them precisely. These names not only change from one country to another, they can also vary within a single country. I shall now give a few examples. The name *social mediation* is essentially used in francophone regions such as France, Quebec, Belgium and Switzerland, but it does not always refer to the same practices. In anglophone countries (US, UK, Canada, Australia) and in hispanophone countries (Spain, Argentina, Paraguay, Mexico, Colombia and Ecuador), the name *community mediation* is generally used. Citizen mediation programs are evoked in France, Quebec, but also in the Spanish Basque Country and in Argentina. Intercultural mediation is also talked about in a number of areas with high rates of immigration such as France, Belgium and Quebec. Finally, neighbourhood mediation programs exist in countries as varied as Switzerland, Italy, Germany, the Netherlands, and Sweden. The international NGO *Search for Common Ground* (SFCG) strives to implement this action model in less developed countries as is for example the case with the 'MediAction' project, which trains young mediators in underprivileged neighbourhoods of large cities in Morocco (Rabat, Salé, Fès, Meknès and Marrakech).

For the most part, the objective of these programs is to develop social links and the mediation of differences, so highly valued by Michèle Guillaume-Hofnung,[2] or to regulate conflicts. These two objectives can be pursued conjointly or invested in separately. In both cases, the argument which supports these initiatives is recurring in all countries, it is a matter of encouraging the implication of citizens in city life, empowering them in the regulation of 'problems' which affect their everyday environment, pacifying social relations, facilitating the integration of marginalised foreign populations, ensuring a larger proximity between the institutions and the public, and developing via communication a culture of tolerance and respect in a specific place, which corresponds most of the time to a commune or a neighbourhood. Resorting to

1 Shonholtz R., 'Community Mediation Centers: renewing the civic mission for the twenty-first century', Mediation Quarterly, 2000, 17 (4), 331–350.

2 Michèle Guillaume-Hofnung, *La médiation*, Paris, PUF, Que sais-je? 2020.

DOI:10.1163/9789004734067_015

social mediation can be justified by a situation considered to be difficult (high rates of crime, of immigrant populations, of unemployment, of academic failure, of dissociated families), the inhabitants having a strong feeling of insecurity as well as the powerlessness or inadequacy of the repressive and social responses that exist.

In 2000, the French ministry of the city attempted to conceptualise these mediations in the town of Créteil during the European seminar on social mediation and gave the mission to 40 European experts to formulate recommendations. The ethical principles they affirm do not go against those previously mentioned in this book; however this initiative did not have the expected effect, and the best promotion of social mediation was probably the European Forum for Urban Security. Created in Barcelona in 1987, under the aegis of the European Council and following the impulse of Mr. Gilbert Bonnemaison, former mayor of Epinay-sur-Seine and co-founder of the French prevention policy, this non-governmental organisation, which was initiated by the French magistrate Michel Marcus, brings together 250 towns and regions from 17 EU member countries. Its objective is to reinforce criminal prevention policies and to promote the role of local communities in the development of policies on both a national and European level. From its point of view, security is not a prerogative of justice and of the police, but must be co-produced by all the political, institutional and social partners along with the inhabitants' participation. Mediation, with all its different social, intercultural, family and penal forms, is one of the tools which is privileged to create these policies. It is presented as a culture and not only a technique, a prevention policy but also a policy to repair social links and empower inhabitants. This institution, which has ramifications in Africa and South America, considers that access to mediation is 'a right all citizens should have and an obligation for the public authorities'.

1 A Diversity of Organisational Modes

The different strategies of producing harmony in its different forms are generally supported by public local authorities, as is essentially the case in continental Europe, or by private charitable organisations and foundations in anglophone countries. Both public and private support can coexist.

These programmes are often dispersed, without any organisation or collective reflection, as their size and status are varied. Some notable European networks have however emerged, networks such as the *European Forum for Restorative Justice* created in 2000 at the University of Leuven in Belgium, whose objective is to promote restorative practices (penal, domestic, educational and community mediation) sometimes integrated into social programs of *restorative cities* (Bristol, Lecce, Come, Tempio Pausania, Leuven, Wroclaw, Canberra, Vancouver, Whanganui). The goal of these cities 'is to strengthen relationships, encourage active citizenship and look at conflict as an opportunity for change, rather than a threat'. On a national level, federations which enact good practice standards exist. These federations provide trainings, organise their member's reflections, and develop communication actions with the public authorities and media.

This is in particular the case with *Mediation UK*, created in 1984, which brings together 300 programmes and is primarily invested in community mediation but also in educational mediation and victim-offender mediation. This type of national organisation focused on community mediation can be found in Australia, New Zealand and in the US, where the *National Association for Community Mediation* (NAFCM) federates around 550 mediation centres and employs around 20.000 volunteers. These political entities such as *Disputacio* in Barcelona push the coordinated development of this kind of innovation in different municipalities within its reach, and even the US state of New York has implemented these programmes in its 66 counties. The most affirmed model of public policy on a national level is probably that of the Norwegian *Konfliktråd*.

The economic modalities of these programmes' functioning are extremely varied. The coexistence of public, private or hybrid models which accumulate national or local financing, with individual donations, subsidies granted by companies or foundations, and receipts which come from the work of the members of the programme (training, publishing, supervision). The access to these programmes is generally free.

Three organisational models can be distinguished depending on their mediators' status.

- The 'democratic' model relies on the commitment of volunteers, and can be found mostly in anglophone countries, in particular the UK and US, and more rarely in Quebec and in France where it is usually named 'citizen mediation'. This volunteering system is centred around favouring the involvement and empowerment of citizens in the management of conflicts concerning their territory. The mediation services are created at the initiative of municipalities or associative structures 'of the people, for the people', for the benefit of the inhabitants of a specific commune or one of the city's neighbourhoods. The mediators must be representative of the population's social and ethnic diversity and are selected by a team of mediation professionals amongst volunteering inhabitants. They then go through training, which lasts on average 30 to 40 hours, and their practice must be analysed by patented mediators. The training generally relies on an ethic of mediation which aims not to 'do things for people' but to strengthen their empowerment and autonomy.

- The professional model employs salary mediators. They can be found in Catalunya within the framework of mediation programmes launched by municipalities, but also in France, Belgium and Switzerland, following the initiatives of social mediation whose objective is as much to ensure the professional integration of young mediators coming from a working-class background or from a racial minority, as handling a social issue. This model is used especially when the programmes have the objective of managing social tensions or to work on a social link, but it can also contribute to regulating conflicts of proximity.
- The mixed model relies on volunteer citizens surrounded by mediation professionals. Its purest version can be found in Norway, where the government decided to favour the creation of mediation offices (*Konfliktråd*) following the promulgation of the 1991 *Mediation Boards Act*, in the country's 44 administrative circumscriptions. The coordinators are professionals, but the mediators are recruited within the population and their work is almost voluntary (they receive minimal remuneration so their commitment is free from financial preoccupations). In general, it is the salaried coordinator who receives mediation requests. These can be direct (by telephone or during service) or be an institutional referral (police, social landlord, municipal services, social services, administration). The coordinator then organises a meeting between the person requesting the mediation and a team of two mediators (working in pairs, known as 'co-mediators', this is more common among volunteers, whereas professionals mostly work alone.) Then, another interview is proposed to the respondent before the possible arrangement of a meeting.

In France, these mediation authorities can constitute a municipal service ad hoc. It can happen that they belong to a larger municipal structure. So they are generally articulated with an offer of access to law in cases of grouped structures within the RENADEM (National Network of Access to Law and Mediation). The people who get in contact with these structures and formulate a legal demand can be forwarded towards a legal service, a social service, or towards mediation.[3] This supposes a subtle differentiation between legal access and mediation.

3 Jacques Faget, 'Les politiques d'accès au droit. Du consumérisme à la citoyenneté', *Droit et Cultures*, 2001/3, pp. 83–96.

2 A Diversity of Objectives

The conception of social, intercultural or citizen mediation experiences varies depending on a number of cultural, political and institutional factors, but also depending on the objectives pursued. The typology which differentiates agonistic, adaptive and regulative mediations can shed light on the diversity of these initiatives. A specific type of mediator corresponds to each of the three types of mediation mentioned above, which I have named the 'accoucheur', 'facilitator', and 'peacekeeper' mediator.

2.1 *Agonistic Mediation*

This type of mediation has the objective of neutrally addressing conflicts between inhabitants of a region, of answering their need for support and to be heard, and to facilitate relations between citizens and institutions.

The conflicts most often transmitted to these authorities are linked to questions of cohabiting with neighbours (trees, hedges, noise, smells, animals), to people's uncivil behaviour (fights, insults, threats, scuffles or damages), or to disputes between landlords and tenants, shopkeepers and consumers. Generally speaking, conflicts involving grave physical violence, moral or sexual harassment, local religious conflicts, racial relations and family conflicts are not treated within the framework of agonistic mediation. Many programmes, in particular in Anglo-Saxon countries, associate the conflicts mentioned above with school or penal (victim-offender) mediation. Most of these mediations are concerned with treating an interindividual conflict but often neglect social and collective problems such as insecurity in a neighbourhood or public space (park, playground area), availability of a public piece of equipment, degradation of the quality of life, or environmental protection. In France, Cité et Mediation in Rennes and Amely in Lyon are the most committed and invested in these actions.

Most of the time, individuals and sometimes organised groups contact these organisations. They can contact them spontaneously or be referred to them by institutions such as the police, social workers, social housing organisations or town halls. In the US, most cases are referred by the court, notably for cases concerning the NJCS (Neighborhood Justice Centers). These represent 75 per cent of cases in North Carolina, 60 per cent in Michigan, and 46 per cent nationwide according to a study conducted by the NAFCM (National Association for Community Mediation).[4]

4 Hedeen T., 'The evolution and evaluation of community mediation: limited research suggests unlimited progress', *Conflict Resolution Quarterly*, 2004, vol. 22, nr 1–2, 101–133.

In France in the 1980s, these programmes were named neighbourhood mediation or social mediation, as the notion of community is not very adapted to the French political philosophy which considers the recognition of communities as contrary to the republican ideal. In the mid-1990s, I suggested the name 'citizen mediation' to highlight the idea that the process is led by a volunteering citizen mediator, to the benefit of his or her fellow citizens. The name was fairly successful and began to be used in Quebec (Canada) by Equijustice, which brings together 23 mediation services. These programmes' objective is to pacify social tensions and decrease feelings of insecurity by empowering citizens to address conflicts which in turn affect their environment. In France, citizen mediators are recruited among local volunteers who have the required abilities (open-mindedness, ability to distance oneself and listen), and who are as representative as possible of their region. They are volunteers but receive training and benefit from sessions of practice analysis. This type of action, rivalled by the existence of judicial conciliators (whose prerogatives are similar, but the latter are more focused on the dispute's solution than on the communication around the conflict), is not very developed (a dozen of cities), compared to England where the community is much more involved in public affairs.

The principles which guide the process – consent, confidentiality, impartiality and independence – do not differ from those of mediation in general. In the most widespread model, a citizen or an institution refers a conflict to a mediation body. A coordinator then solicits volunteer mediators who work in co-mediation and have diverse social, ethnic and cultural origins. The latter receive the plaintiffs, and once they have contacted and heard the respondent, they try to organise a meeting to resolve the dispute. The British model is slightly different, as it gives the mediators the possibility to go to the site of the conflict before the organisation of a meeting in a neutral space. In all cases, these mediators align with the 'accoucheur' model as they prioritise restoration or re-establishing communication and see to it that the actors come to an agreement themselves.

The performance of these programmes depends on the relationship dynamic between the diverse partners involved (town hall, local legal services, social landlords, police, social workers). Indeed, in the absence of a culture of mediation, the spontaneous referral of a case to the court by inhabitants is rare. It is thanks to the referrals of these partnering structures that the mediation authorities are plentiful, widespread and used. To facilitate the occurrence, a few organisations have associated access to law services and mediation. This is in particular the case of the legal and mediation antennas in Marseille and of the public service platform in Pessac.

These citizen mediation systems, deliberately non-professional and not very institutionalised, are however not completely independent. Their continued existence depends on the good will of the public authorities and more generally on the donations they receive, as the service they offer is always free to the public. It does happen that municipalities exert pressure on them by trying to influence their choice of mediators, or by hindering their proper functioning and not ensuring the necessary coordination. Their social usefulness was however never contradicted, seeing as their satisfaction rates are very high.

2.2 *Adaptive Mediation*

A multitude of actors, still under the guise of mediation, facilitate access to legal information or to administrations. Strictly speaking, the action of these 'facilitator' mediators is closer to the standard of social work than meditation. Their denominations vary; in quite a few countries, they are known as intercultural mediators.

These intervenors are often chosen amongst immigrant populations depending on their social competencies (commitment to local life) and their cultural proximity with the populations they support. Their mission consists of facilitating relations between the public and the institutions, as the former may not understand the logic or the language of the latter (in such cases, they act as interpreters, public writers, legal advisors). Their mission is also to orient them and help them in administrative tasks, to facilitate dialogue between generations, to support parents in the education of their children, to find solutions for problematic interactions between families and the educational system, and to help in the construction of projects and the development of associative life. This role is not properly fulfilled by traditional social workers, who do not know much about the culture and the language of these populations and cannot identify the problems they face.

These experiences are now developing in all countries that struggle to integrate new immigrants. In France, this question is not new, but the State avoids considering cultural particularities, and delegates the management of the ethnic question[5] to the private sector. Mediation allows public institutions to address these cases more adequately. Thus, a hybrid space is created, semi-public, semi-private, to treat the complexity of intercultural situations. In countries that understand the necessity of adapting to new multicultural real-

5 Stéphanie Morel, « Médiation de proximité et transformation des modes de régulation sociale: le cas de la médiation ethnoculturelle à l'école », in Faget J. (Dir.) *Médiation et action publique. La dynamique du fluide*, Presses Universitaires de Bordeaux, 2005.

ities, the problem is simplified, but in the end, the answers obey to the same logic. The increase in cultural tensions with new populations and the emergence of xenophobic attitudes which lead to the emergence of popular parties make the implementation of specific strategies an urgent task.

In this model, the mediators' principal function is to improve, by all means possible, social relations. It is not a case of managing realistic conflicts in the sense which Coser[6] understands it, where the point of discord is identifiable, but of managing non-realistic conflicts where the real object is masked by aggressive expressions rooted in socio-economic frustrations or those linked to identity.[7] These 'recognition policies' go down the wrong track when it comes to supporting the integration of immigrants. They should be more preoccupied than they are now with building truly intercultural bridges between groups that do not know each other well, and ask the concerned communities to be more empathetic and open to difference.

2.3 *Regulative Mediation*

In Western countries, the social demand for security is not exclusively addressed to the police and justice, it is increasingly addressed to local responsible people. Cities in countries such as the UK, Australia, and Italy have become increasingly mobilised around issues relating to urban crime. In France, this process started in 1983 with the creation of CCPDs (Municipal Crime Prevention Councils), and it has since intensified. Myriad municipal initiatives have emerged to fight against this feeling of insecurity:[8] prevention agents, municipal policemen, private security societies, video surveillance.

Social mediators are part of this plethora of interventions. They have different names depending on the place: 'night correspondents', 'Big Brothers', 'prevention agents for public transport', or 'local agents for social mediation'. All these 'blurry jobs'[9] fill imprecise functions: providing information, assistance to the public or clients, or ensuring the security of public places such as streets, parks, the outside of schools or public transport. The criteria used to define their mission is less the mode of action than the territory. Above all else, it is a question of occupying spaces, of putting into place a local presence

6 Lewis A. Coser, *Les fonctions du conflit social*, Paris, PUF, 1982.

7 Fathi Ben Mrad, 'La médiation sociale: entre résolution des conflits et sécurisation urbaine', RFAS, nr 3, 2004 et *Sociologie des pratiques de médiation: entre principes et compétences*, Paris, L'Harmattan, 2002.

8 See Tanguy Le Goff, (2008) op.cit., and Jérôme Ferret, Christian. Mouhanna, *Peurs sur les villes*, Paris, PUF, 2005.

9 Fabienne Barthélémy, 'Médiateur social, une profession émergente?' Revue Française de Sociologie, 2009, vol. 50, nr 2, pp. 287–314.

that the concerned professions and institutions do not provide.[10] Police intervention for the management of small disruptions to public order is considered inefficient and counter-productive, and the bureaucratisation of social work has led to the neglect of problematic spaces during night hours when the tension is high. Even though the initial idea of these programmes is sometimes that of mediation, their result is closer to security, surveillance, or conflict management, and in certain cases, possibly even sociocultural interventions.

These programmes can be found, with some exceptions, in other European countries. Overall, the functions of these 'peacekeepers' are fairly similar and can be distinguished by their place and time of intervention. Their mission is to ensure the tranquillity and security of inhabitants or users and, by their presence, dissuade disruption to public order. The locations of their intervention are often festive places at the end of the week, public spaces in working-class neighbourhoods with a high immigrant population (streets, parks, squares, playgrounds), and commercial town centres to guarantee the security of commerce, transport and school entrances/exits.

The recruitment of these actors is endogenous. Thus, they are mostly immigrants. But it is difficult to be an impartial third party when you belong to the community in which you are working. Yet certain evaluations show that they can respond to social needs not met by the traditional institutions. The cultural proximity between the mediators and the young people can, in certain cases, appease the conflicts. However, this type of territorialised intervention can create a 'normative break' between certain neighbourhoods and the rest of society, creating bubbles of security where public order is no longer ensured by state representatives enforcing general societal norms, but by members of a community with particular sociocultural norms.[11]

The characteristics of these citizen, intercultural and social mediations can be summarised in the following way:

3 Second-Class Justice?

Intercultural mediations have not been systematically evaluated. However, social mediations are less effective for neighbourhood conflict management than for other activities (dissuasive presence, relational, reminder of social rules) which participate in the maintenance of public tranquillity. Duclos

10 Jacques Donzelot, Anne Wyvekens, La magistrature sociale. Enquête sur les politiques locales de sécurité, Paris, La Documentation Française, 2004.

11 Ibid.

TABLE 10.1 Comparison of the different models

Community or citizen mediation	Intercultural mediation	Social mediation
Objective: conflict regulation or resolution	Objective: adaptation of foreign populations	Objective; security of public spaces, people and property
Volunteer mediators, mostly older, middle class	Salaried mediators, middle-aged, foreign or of foreign origin	Salaried mediators, young, foreign origin
'Accoucheur' mediator	'Facilitator' mediator	'Peacekeeper' mediator
Reference field: Mediation	Reference field: Access to law and social work	Reference field: Security and socio-cultural animation

and Grésy mention a decrease in incivilities of around 25 per cent to 30 per cent on the concerned territories during the first year of presence on site. They also observe an improvement in the relations between institutional partners (police, landlords, town halls, social organisations), as well as the fact that the inhabitants are reassured by the presence of 'mediators', which contributes to a decrease in the feeling of insecurity.[12] Despite these results, Ben Mrad fears that these modes of regulation based on community surveillance might lead to an 'ethno-rationalisation of problems'.[13]

A review of conflicts treated by all community or citizen mediation structures show that they are only marginally an alternative to institutional intervention. A limited number of conflicts reported by citizens to these authorities have been escalated to the legal system. This means that there is no subcontracting logic within the regulation of legal conflicts that are considered minor. It is most probably a process of access to law for people whose social adjustment problems are not constructed or thought of in legal terms. These programmes, far from constituting a threat to public freedom (both because of the absence of legal guarantees which characterises them and mediators' legal incompetence), could, on the contrary, provide an opportunity to treat problems that would otherwise remain unmanaged to arise. This is in particu-

12 Hélène Duclos, Jean Edouard Gresy (Dir.), *Evaluation de l'utilité sociale de cinq structures de médiation sociale*, Culture et promotion, 2008.

13 Ben Mrad (2004) op.cit.

lar the case of all the complaints which are not taken into account by police, of all small everyday conflicts, which often oppose close ones, and are aggravated because of a lack of appropriate response and an impartial authority addressing different points of view.

In the US, where community mediation has the essential function of easing overcrowding in court, the question is slightly different. Many, such as Richard Abel or Christine Harrington, believe these authorities to be second-class justice, without the law or a judge, reserved for poor people. Conversely, research shows that these programs adjust their practices to mimic the institution which constitutes their principal source of funding. Morill and MacKee speak of 'institutional isomorphism'[14] in which centres have assimilated judicial culture and insensitively shift towards routinised practices depending on efficiency objectives.[15] These mediations, far from constituting some sort of '*shadow justice*', would instead be a vector for social 'juridicization'.

However, their respect for the ethical and deontological foundations of mediation can be questioned, namely those relating to consensual nature of the process. Thus, research which attempted to evaluate the level of constraint (coercion) has concluded that the increase in constraint (for example, summonses bearing a magistrate's letterhead) leads to actors being more present at meetings. Three community mediation centres characterised by a low level of constraint had 35 per cent mediation, whereas the Florida programs sponsored by the court which have a higher level of constraint hit 56 per cent of participation, and a Minnesota project financed by a prosecutor had a participation score as high as 90 per cent.[16] When we also look at the percentage of approvals obtained, we can only be circumspect about the method used, given that the more directive the process is, the higher the 'success' rates. For example, on a sample of 426,000 cases treated over 10 years in New York State centres, 80 per cent were approved.

Be that as it may, users' satisfaction rates are always higher than 80 per cent, and so is the participants' expressed desire to resort to mediation again or to recommend it to other people. These rates are however superior when the protagonists reach an agreement. A huge majority of citizens stated that their case was treated better than it would have been by the court. Finally, all research demonstrates that the agreements obtained are sustainable, as

---

14 Morrill C., McKee C., 'Institutional isomorphism and informal social control: evidence from a community mediation center', Social Problems, 1993, 40, 445–463.

15 Hedeen (2004), op.cit.

16 McGillis D., Community dispute resolution programs and public policy, Washington D.C., National Institute of Justice, 1986.

the interviews of participants several years later show that in more than three quarters of the cases, no complication happened since the mediation.

An evaluative frenzy as such is much rarer in Europe and non-existent in France. A few rare evaluations lead to the observation that these programmes remain relatively unknown to the public, that the police and social workers do not cooperate much with them, and that town halls do not always sincerely and constantly support these initiatives. Yet, all observations show that their success is correlated with the existence of a dense and active network of partners. They also show very high rates of satisfaction expressed by citizen or intercultural mediators involved in these experiences. Because of the lack of social recognition and clear career profile, social mediators are less enthusiastic.

CHAPTER 11

School Mediation

School inhabits us, is part of our story. Everything that happens there concerns us. Each evocation brings back images, sounds, smells, satisfactions or sorrow. We are constantly aware of our fragility within an institution that is imposed on us, which defines all our behaviour, our learning. Most of the time, our first experience of socialising outside of the family happens in school. Its failure or success then conditions a great deal of our future institutional experiences. Of course, determinism is not absolute, there is space for action, but it is narrow. Everyone knows since the work of the American interactionists' that the weight of labels and stigma can shape the destiny of individuals. Just think of Rosenthal and Jakobson's famous experiment in which the classification of pupils in a primary class by intelligence level was completely 'rigged'; however it still conditioned how teachers thought of their pupils. This marking process is all the more predictive when the subject is developing, vulnerable, and often does not possess sufficient psychological and social resources to contest its weight. It is important to always bear in mind that the stereotypes we convey have the function, without our being aware of it, of dividing reality into meaningful categories, reassuring us in the face of chaos.

School has always had the function of social control, moulding behaviour, and formatting identities. Freinet, Neill, Montessori and many other specialists in education have denounced the repressive logics of schooling, without succeeding in reversing its course, so central is the mission of normalising individuals. But this mission of order takes on a particular meaning today in the face of the failure of family socialisation mechanisms. Gone are the days of docile lambs and folklorised dunces. Authority has lost its roots. It can no longer be imposed. It must be conquered daily during pedagogical interaction, exhausting games 'to gain ground' where nothing is ever granted. Without a light heart, the institution is obliged to evolve faced with the massification and heterogeneity of its publics, at risk of losing all legitimacy. What would remain of the credibility of an enterprise manufacturing failure, not that which depends on the ineluctable variation of the intellectual capacities and competencies, but that of its incapacity to domesticate children's violence, or worse still, to provoke it.

Children in school may bring with them the ways they have learned to deal with conflict outside of school, including responding with violence. The institution cannot respond in kind; everyone knows that a violent response to

 | DOI:10.1163/9789004734067_016

violence legitimises the initial violence. Now more than ever, the school needs to morph this violence, to implement strategies of participative learning, not only teach fundamental knowledge such as reading, writing and counting; but also elemental forms of knowing how to live harmoniously in society. There is no better place to instil the ideals of citizenship than in the school curriculum.

It is an opportunity to acquire democratic skills that adults often lack, knowing how to speak constructively and not aggressively, being able to listen to others, understanding or accepting one's differences, establishing a relationship, cooperating in search of a mutually acceptable modus vivendi.

The school institution fears conflict, as demonstrated by its tendency to resolve it via punishment. It rarely sees conflict as an opportunity to work profitably and implement horizontal and cooperative ways of dealing with it. From this point of view, the idea of mediation in the educational field is countercultural one. Whereas punishment is preoccupied with guaranteeing a formal order, mediation deliberately looks to the future to establish norms. While punishment imposes suffering to atone for a transgression, restorative practices calls for participants to 'do something good'. While punishment chooses scapegoats to limit the expression of blame, mediation tries to reject the reflex of immediately placing blame and to make all participants in the conflict accountable. And yet, despite still vigorous resistance, mediation is spreading slowly but surely to schools in Western countries.

The first school mediation programme started in 1972 in a public school in New York (a similar experiment also took place at the same date in Saskatchewan in Canada) to disseminate peace education. The classroom was considered the most accessible place to transmit a pacifist vision of the world in hopes that the pupils would spread this content to their families and neighbourhoods. The Children's Creative Response to Conflict Movement (CCRC) developed this educational model throughout the United-States by organising thousands of workshops not only for children, but also for their parents and teachers. It was then exported to 30 foreign countries. Recognising that 'the seeds of peace are sown in children from an early young age', its objective is to intervene as soon as the first learning processes start to model how to peacefully address conflict. However, it did not keep the monopoly on this approach, and innumerable pacifist movements, for example the Quakers, made it a primordial vector for providing non-violent education to pupils. It was in Switzerland, in the canton of Vaud, that the first European programme appeared in 1977, even before its development in the UK, in Australia and New Zealand. But it was not until the 1990s and 2000s that it spread to continental Europe and South America.

The promoters of school mediation come from extremely different cultural contexts. The Neighbourhood Justice Centres, the Community Boards (San Francisco), the National Association for Mediation in Education (NAME) in the US, *Vers le Pacifique* in Canada, and Mediation UK are generally cited. Other significant promoters are *Geus* in the Spanish Basque Country, and in France, *Génération médiateurs, Amely*[1] (Lyon), or *Alternative médiation* (Bordeaux). Some countries have developed a national policy which institutionalises the use of school mediation across their whole territory: this is the case in Belgium, Argentina and with the Finish Forum for Mediation in Finland.[2]

Such diversity of origins and organisation suggests that there exist multiple motivations linked to political and institutional contexts specific to each country. Some activists argue that mediation is used by schools to perpetuate a culture of collective control instead of prioritising individual empowerment. For others, the argument of fighting against violence, sometimes that of the institution, more often that of pupils, is put forward.

The arguments of numerous advocates present school mediation as one of the ways to spread tolerance and respect in environments that are more and more impacted by tense and aggressive behaviour. One South American school mediation office does not hesitate to highlight on its website this quote attributed to a Brazilian representative of UNESCO: 'We must place problem detectors in schools, not weapon detectors or policemen'. It refers to control strategies which are largely mediatised and implemented in a few American schools following diverse trauma provoked by the killings in Columbine and elsewhere.

In reality, the debate on violence in schools is the subject of many controversies. The definition of the concept of violence is problematic. First and foremost, violence is what is qualified as such and if a consensus easily emerges for the gravest acts, the thresholds of tolerance when it comes to less intense behaviour are extremely variable from person to person and depend on the cultural and institutional context. Some teachers consider their students' vehement way of addressing them violent, even though it is their usual mode of expression in their 'street culture', whereas others, living in the same neighbourhoods, put it into perspective. Eric Debardieux[3] holds that the question of violence at school needs to be approached with some distance and denounces a double pitfall, that of dramatisation and trivialisation. He observes that there

1 Jean Pierre Bonafé Schmitt, La médiation scolaire par les élèves, Paris, ESF, 2000.
2 Created in 2005 to develop a mediation program in all the schools of the country.
3 Eric Debarbieux, Violence à l'école: un défi mondial? Paris, Armand Colin, 2006.

is no global increase in violence. Victimisation surveys carried out in France have shown a decline since 1993. This violence is concentrated in a few schools where the populations are impacted by phenomena of social exclusion. And even in this context, there is no absolute determinism because, with an identical population, the 'school effect', the school's climate (clearly defined leadership, stable rules, a teaching staff which is tightly knit and coherent in its practices, contractually agreed principles of action, the quality of relations between teachers and students, parents associated with the school's functioning) all have an impact on the school's violence levels. However, we are witnessing changes in the ways in which traditional violence is expressed, with greater recourse to bullying and more collective forms of expression against the institution in the form of attacks on teachers, generally those who are not supported by their colleagues or the institution, and the contestation of general school order.

Even though many schools still refuse to deal with school violence in any real way other than by calling on repressive forces or behaviourist solutions, mediation is beginning to form part of the panoply of action of a growing number of them. It represents one of the aspects, even if it is minor, of a new pedagogical model that seeks to link theoretical knowledge and practical experience, to democratise the educational relationship somewhat, to develop a spirit of cooperation by implementing appropriate learning activities, and to promote an 'expressive' and creative model of education. Its object is not only oriented towards the reduction of violence but must also be seen in the broader context of a call for school citizenship, which is not without its contradictions, when the institutional reality stands in the way of the exercise of school rights and the creation of genuine democratic bodies for negotiation and regulation. Such a context leads us to fear that resorting to mediation cannot transform the institutional logics, and only constitutes a way of diversifying the pedagogical offer in an institution which is reluctant to change. Could the stake of these mediation programmes depend on the nature of the models used?

1 Different Models of School Mediation

The expression 'school mediation' designates a large diversity of practices and objectives. The model of peer mediation has had the biggest development worldwide. However, other programmes have been progressively implemented, including mediation by school staff, mediation by mediators external to the system, parent/student mediation and a range of restorative mediations.

1.1 *Peer Mediation*

This model has developed in all types of educational institutions, both private and public, concerning both young children and teenagers. According to its advocates, the school's mission should not be limited to teaching theoretical knowledge but also the ability to live harmoniously with others. Yet this type of socialisation which allows students to learn to build relationships with others and trains them in democratic debate is generally neglected by the institution. Without the pressure exerted by phenomena of violence, these practices might not have known as much success as they have today. From this point of view, independently from its real effects that I will touch on later, mediation in the educational field is first and foremost a tool to ward off fear in an institution which is going through an existential crisis.

More than any other type of mediation, peer mediation is countercultural. Schools function by promoting power struggles, rivalry, and obedience and submission to an established order; mediation prefers the principles of cooperation, discussion, negotiation and contract. While schools teach pupils to tackle challenges on their own, mediation holds that 'there exists knowledge capable of uniting them, despite their differences', in order to reach 'common ground' where they can establish 'the founding Law of refusing violence'.[4] While school values abstract intelligence, mediation favours the acquisition of emotional and social intelligence.[5] The arguments developed by peer mediation programmes can indeed be summarised as follows. It is a pedagogical approach based on students learning communication and conflict resolution techniques, to develop their sense of responsibility, of cooperation, to foster their interpersonal skills, and consequently improve the school's general climate, reduce tensions and strengthen links within the community. This education to peace and non-violence would adequately prepare young people, in the spirit of openness and tolerance, to become responsible adults.

As such, conflict is most often denied by the educational institution as it gives neither space nor time devoted to analysing it. Conflict is managed as is, in a disciplinary and vertical manner, with little ritualisation, using a range of sanctions from warning to reports to repressive authorities, including community service and even suspensions, or temporary/ definitive exclusions. Mediation, in whatever form, not only reintroduces conflict as a normal and founding element of collective life and not as a menace against the institution, but

---

4 Philippe Meirieu, Marc Guiraud, *L'école ou la guerre civile*, Paris, Plon, 1997.

5 Daniel Goleman, *Emotional intelligence: why it can matter more than IQ*. New York, Bantam Books, 1995.

also suggests a more reflexive and concerted way of taking it into consideration. It does not see it as a problem, but rather as an educational opportunity.

The conflicts treated by pupils in mediation sessions only represent a modest level on the Richter scale of institutional shocks. They only concern the conflicts between children, except for conflicts that concern problematic relations with their teachers. These can be thefts, threats, racketeering attempts, fights, insults, humiliations, racist attitudes, bullying or conflicts concerning the use and access to the school's games and recreational facilities. However it is important to keep in mind that firstly, these conflicts are 'small' seen from an adult's point of view, and secondly, they are a perfect prefiguration of the conflicts that the children will face in their future lives and which they will be less powerless to manage if they are given the opportunity to learn how to deal with them.

The objectives of the mediation programmes can be relatively diverse. Many of them are independent from the institution itself and are invited in only to deal with specific conflicts. Mediation is then considered as a practice which is relevant but meant only for pupils and is disconnected from the other activities at school. Other more ambitious programmes practise the *whole school approach*. These can be found in the US and in Scandinavia, but also sometimes in Spain or Northern Ireland. They rely on strong support from the school management and teaching staff, and train all the adults in mediation and involve parents. Their objective is to develop a democratic culture and spread mediation's philosophy throughout the institution, including relations between adults, between adults and pupils and between pupils themselves. Since 2005, the national policy led by the Finnish minister for education has made the choice to take this type of approach in all schools.

The dominant model, which can be found in more or less all countries, obeys the principles found in most specialised literature. It all starts by raising the education community's awareness about mediation, as experience shows that a programme which is not endorsed by all the staff in the school (management, teachers, social workers, nurses, cleaning and service staff, parents' association) may not last long. The people who advocate for this program may frequently confront resistance from education officials who mistrust mediation and see it as a threat to their professional identity. A systemic perspective is in this case necessary to identify the potential obstacles and to anticipate them. The students are informed about the project and made aware of mediation. Mediators with specific training and who possess the qualities required are chosen. They will need to conform to the 'classic' principles which are the foundation of the mediator's role, namely impartiality, independence, absence of decision-making power, confidentiality, and allowing the conflict's participants to be in dialogue and express their points of view in an calm manner, and possibly to reach an agreement.

Professional mediators or experienced volunteers train the school's adults before training the children. It can happen that the adults who are the most motivated participate in this training. Its duration and content can vary from one programme to another. Whereas some trainers explain the necessary basic techniques needed for manage the process, others place more emphasis on self-knowledge, the expression of feelings, emotions and needs, and the acquisition of the principles of nonviolent communication.[6]

In schools, the mediation process is almost always carried out in pairs in order to prevent inappropriate behaviour from a single mediator. These pairs are decided by an adult coordinator who uses criteria such as class, sex, age, ethnicity and the situation itself. Mediation sessions are conducted either in the playground – this practice is especially common in elementary schools – or in special rooms outside of teaching hours. Student mediators are sometimes alone, sometimes with an adult coordinator. The children involved in the conflict can spontaneously contact the mediators, whose names and photographs are pinned on an information board, or they can be referred to a mediator by a member of the management or teaching staff, or by other pupils. A high rate of direct or spontaneous referrals from the students is a good indicator of the experiment's success. A high rate of referrals from members of the institution also indicates a good integration of the experiment into the school environment.

If the mediators sometimes meet each of the actors individually before considering a joint meeting, it is in some cases required that they present themselves together. An interruption of the mediation process can be decided either by the mediators when communication proves to be impossible or by the children themselves at any moment in time, or when they have found a mutually satisfactory solution. Their agreement can be communicated orally; however, in certain programmes, a written protocol must be produced and signed by the opponents who must each receive a copy. It can consist in defining new rules of behaviour in the cafeteria or in the playground, formulating an apology, considering reparations or committing to better respect one another.

The co-mediators are not left to their own devices. They benefit from an advisor's support and periodic analysis of their practices (most often external to the institution). During this analysis, they can express the difficulties, doubts or disarray they feel, or receive additional training.

---

6 See Marshall Rosenberg's often cited work, *Les mots sont des fenêtres (ou bien ce sont des murs): Introduction à la communication non-violente*, Paris, Ed. La Découverte, 2005.

1.2 *Mediation by Adults*

The previous model is the object of criticism from those teachers or mediators who believe it is not appropriate to give the role of mediator to young children who are not yet completely mature. Embedded within the context of the school and conflicts which arise within it, students may have difficulty adopting the distant and impartial posture which is needed for mediators. It would also mean giving students responsibility which could undermine the prerogative of the adults and the school institution. Peer mediation could be seen as a sign of a lack of authority on behalf of person in charge of education. If training children to peace and nonviolence is necessary, it is the adults who must play the structuring and educational role that mediation requires.[7] The mediation board can therefore consist of either volunteers from within the school staff or those external to the school.

The field of application of these programmes is larger than that of peer mediation. Mediation concerns not only conflicts between pupils, but also the conflicts between teachers and pupils and between teachers and parents. However, the experimental protocols specify that the teacher mediators must not intervene in cases when the conflict concerns their class or when they know the pupils, to preserve their impartiality. The mediators follow a training in mediation and submit themselves to an ongoing analysis of their practices. This model has the merit of being better accepted by the educational community than peer mediation as it does not subvert the traditional asymmetry of positions between teachers and pupils. It would be more in favour of the school's educational practices, whereas peer mediation does not involve the teaching community.

Some mixed programmes also exist, which attempt to combine the advantages and avoid the inconveniences of the two previous programs. This is the case of the 'BOCES program', put into place at the beginning of the 1980s within the 'Middle County School District New-York State', which associates teacher mediators and student mediators, although the latter are only mobilised for conflicts between students or between students and their parents. Some experiments have also been set up by the Victim Service Agency (VSA) in New York City, named SMART (School Mediators' Alternative Team) which brings together pupils, parents and members of the school staff to resolve conflicts between children and parents or between teachers and pupils.

Following the example of the pioneer experiment initiated in 1977 in Vaud County in Switzerland, a second model of adult mediation can be found in

---

7 Paul Mbanzoulou, 'La médiation scolaire par les adultes de l'établissement' in B. Gaillard (ed.), *Les violences en milieu scolaire et éducatif*, 2005, pp. 429–436.

certain countries. It has developed spectacularly in Belgium where school mediators work full-time or part-time in a specific school. Their role diverges slightly from that of a traditional mediator. They help find constructive solutions to conflicts that arise between children, parents and children, pupils and teachers, managing staff and students, parents and teachers or parents and managing staff. They also provide a listening place for children and parents, give them information on study paths and existing jobs, support them in their schoolwork and intervene in situations where children are dropping out of school or truanting from school. Within the framework of their mission, these mediators must respect the principles of impartiality, neutrality and confidentiality which are essential characteristics of the mediator's stance. In a slightly different perspective, programmes endorsed by the association France Médiation try to combine educational activities (peer mediation, school-family mediation) with security measures (social mediation around schools and on the way between school and home).

1.3 *Family/School Mediation*

Many observations show that the families of pupils in difficulty lack a relationship with the educational institution. These are often families who feel they don't belong in a system whose values and logic they do not fully understand, and whose functioning they are not in control of. They are reluctant to go to institutional meetings where they leave feeling guilty because of the bad results or pranks of their children. In short, the absence of these 'fallen' families in the educational system increases the distance between two worlds with different cultural references and norms.

One could think that it is the role of parents' associations to build bridges. However, the inclusion of poor families whose students are struggling is very rare in these circumstances; their family members do not always realise the full extent of their marginalisation. This tendency is exacerbated when they behave like consumer protection movements trying to satisfy the individual interests of their members without participating in the overall construction of a genuine project.[8]

Mediation programmes aim to repair this missing link between parents and the school. Many initiatives flourished in various countries under diverse forms. Hence the French experiment of Trappes initiated in 1993. The mediators' work is sometimes focused on individual problems caused by failed communication between the family and the school, sometimes on conflict management between several parents and teachers. They also initiate new

8 Meirieu, Guiraud (1997), op. cit.

forms of meetings between the school and the parents on general issues. The creation of 'parent cafés' illustrates this dynamic. Their aim is to support parents in their parental role, favour the participation of foreign parents in school life and multiply the opportunities for sharing and communication between all parents confronted with educational difficulties. In a similar vein, the ROMED programme, launched in 2011 by the European Council in 22 countries, has the objective of training 1300 ethnically Roma mediators to facilitate the pupil's adjustment to the school community, but also to increase tolerance and ensure schools welcome these populations.[9]

1.4 *Restorative Mediations*

These programmes, imbued with the philosophy of the restorative movement, can be reactive, meaning organised to respond to a conflict between pupils or to a more general educational problem which disrupts the school life's equilibrium. They can also be proactive, developing pupil's social and emotional intelligence and creating a more 'understanding' spirit within the educational community. They are part of the previously mentioned whole school approach,[10] and spread values of 'respect, openness, empowerment, inclusion, tolerance, integrity and congruence' within the educational community. This movement transmits social skills that consist in 'staying impartial and non-judgmental, respecting others' perspective, developing active and empathetic listening, facilitating relations between the participants, strengthening their capacity to search for their own solutions rather than making suggestions or imposing them, using creative questioning, showing warmth, compassion and patience'.[11]

John Braithwaite's regulatory pyramid for schools (Figure 11.1) provides a clearer picture of the three levels of action of restorative principles in promoting responsive regulation. This 'sensitive' regulation defends the idea of a continuum of responses that must adapt flexibly to the nature and the evolution of the problems encountered. It is opposed to formal regulations which predetermine the definition of situations, respond to them with codes of conduct

9 A. Ailincai, C. Rus, 'Les défis de la médiation scolaire auprès des familles Roms', Diversités, nr 175, 1er trimestre 2014, pp. 76–82.

10 Morrison, B.E. (2006) *Restoring safe school communities: a whole school response to bullying, violence end alienation*, Sydney, Federation Press.

11 Hopkins, B. (2004) *Just Schools: a whole school approach to restorative justice*, London, and New York, NY, Jessica Kingsley.

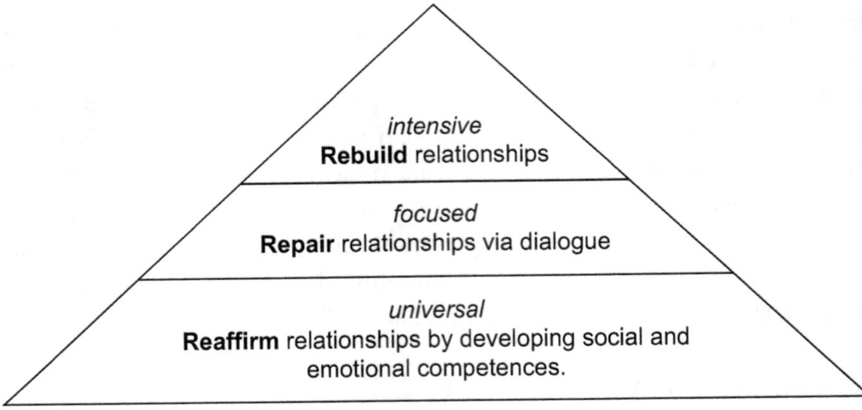

FIGURE 11.1 John Braithwaite's *regulatory pyramid for schools* (see book)

or rules, express moral judgements and offer little support to pupils often 'pathologized, placed under surveillance and increasingly criminalised'.[12]

1.1.1 Preventative Practices

The first level of the pyramid concerns all the members of the community and aims, in a strategy of prevention, to develop a strong normative climate of respect, the feeling of belonging to a community, the attachment to equitable regulation process, the development of emotional and social intelligence. All the school's staff is trained in these techniques and supported in their implementation.

An increasing number of initiatives, including the Minnesota Department of Education in the US or the Youth Justice Board for England and Wales, advocates fighting against the use of suspension and expulsion sanctions, dealing with absenteeism, improving the school's climate and contributing to the development of young people by raising their awareness of their responsibilities. To quote Braithwaite, 'it appears that a globalising approach to school is necessary not only to treat individual incidents…school must not only resolve aggressions but use them to affirm that these aggressions are not part of the school's culture'.[13] This means cultivating a concern for developing both the students' and the whole educational community's emotional and social intelligence. Emotional intelligence reinforces the capacity to perceive your own emotions, recognise their significance, manage them, recognise others' emo-

12 Fine, M and Smith, K (2001) 'Zero tolerance: reflections on a failed policy that won't die', in W. Ayers et al. (eds) *Zero tolerance: resisting the drive for punishment in our schools*. New York, NY, New Press.

13 Braithwaite (2002), op.cit.

tions, and deal with the emotional relationships that arise. Social intelligence develops a person's capacity to dialogue, listen to others, accept that they may have a different point of view, develop collective skills, to make decisions collectively, to make excuses and repair.[14] It is in this spirit, which concerns not only the pupils but also the teachers' attitude, that the system's coherence is improved. Assessments show that such a method is the basis for a calmer and more fulfilling community life.

1.1.2 Focused Practices

The second level concerns the management of all the small incidents of daily life that happen in school by implementing informal dialogue or problem resolution circles, whose objective is to avoid the development of chronic behaviours. It targets certain individuals or certain groups but can concern a large number of people. These circles can be integrated within the normal framework of classroom activities, or mobilised to respond to an incident or specific problem, whether it is individual or collective. They require the intervention of one or more mediators to facilitate dialogue between the participants. These mediators can be pupils, teachers, a member of the administration or any other representative of the educational community. The objective is to build the students' collective capacity to manage the class and school's preoccupations. This work can be based on real conflicts or take on the form of roleplay.

1.1.3 Intensive Practices

The third level concerns pupils who pose chronic and intense behavioural problems. It is characterised by the organisation of community accountability conferences (Queensland, Australia), school community forums (New South Wales, Australia), community group conferencing (Colorado, US), community conferencing (Calgary, Canada), restorative conferencing (Home Office, England) family group conferencing (New Zealand), and peacemaking circles (Canada). To make things simpler, I will only distinguish between community and family conferences.

The community conferences were initiated in Australia, in the Queensland province, in 1994, following similar experiences in the criminal field. They were then exported to Canada, the US and England. Instead of considering conflict regulation as a problem between two people or between a person and the institution, they advocate for a systemic approach which mobilises the whole community. The participants are gathered in a support circle composed

14 Goleman (1995), op.cit.

of their parents, siblings, professors, friends, social workers, and people for whom the young show respect. From then on, an open, honest and respectful dialogue develops under the conduct of a mediator or a coordinator. During this dialogue, the individuals can reconstruct their shared history, take responsibility by determining what the best way of repairing the damage caused is and bring safety to the community. These conferences are organised especially for violent assaults, some of these which could be the subject of criminal proceedings, but also for disciplinary issues such as recurring disruptions in class, truancy, bullying, degradations, theft or racist behaviour. Most assessments show extremely high satisfaction results from the participants. Family conferences function on the same model but only bring together pupils, members of the school community and families. Their objective is to engage the family in the child's problems, for him or her to feel better supported, and to develop better relationships between the family and the school.

2 School Mediation: A Placebo Effect?

These programmes have been assessed many times, especially peer mediation. One of them, carried out by two Israeli researchers, refers to the educational theories of Vygotsky's[15] zone of proximal development (ZPD) and Feuerstein's[16] cognitive modifiability. By using data collected from a large sample of children who followed a complex protocol of tests, compared to a control group who was not trained to mediation, they claim that 'peer mediation is a powerful strategy to facilitate one's own cognitive processes'.[17] Learning mediation would help children change their cognitive performances by themselves, especially because they do not practise the processes of interactive communication much with their family or in their classroom. This type of experiment benefits the students trained in mediation, and especially those who are mediators.

15 Children are capable of being aware and in control of difficult problems when they are guided and helped by a competent person, usually an adult, during a collaborative process.

16 Children's intellectual functioning is sometimes hindered by cognitive rigidities which stops them from gaining knowledge. These resistances are even stronger when children are confronted to new situations. In such cases, they need to be guided, accompanied by a mediator who helps them to decode and interpret the context. The mediator's role is not to act in place of the child but to develop his/her autonomy.

17 Tzuriel, D et Shamir, A, 'The effects of Peer Mediation with Young Children (PMYC) on children's cognitive modifiability', *British Journal of Educational Psychology*, vol. 77, 2007, No. 1, March 2007, Page 143 – 165.

Less systematised sociological observations nuance the previous diagnoses and condition these good results to factors such as the school climate. Indeed, it is not possible to intrinsically evaluate the effect of a conference or a mediation programme without taking into account the quality of the institutional context. The results will notably be correlated with the educational project. Interactive, respectful and empowering educational practices, for example the participation of children in the creation of school rules, the institution's respect for equitable legal and contradictory principles, favour the mediation programme. On the other hand, in case of a dissonance, the mediation experiment will only be considered as a gadget, and the experiment will wilt in the long term. This 'disharmony' can be illustrated by the institution maintaining a model of conflict management based on arbitrary and punitive sanctions, humiliating measures or the choice of legalising internal conflicts. It would be futile to wait for the positive effects of mediation without following up on the experiment by acting on the school environment's[18] cooperative context. However, a systematic review of the work on peer mediation programmes demonstrates that, even in favourable institutional conditions, their effects will not be spectacular when it comes to transforming the attitudes of the most disruptive students or transforming the institution's normative climate.[19] Diaz and Liatard-Dulac argue that the training of student mediators 'cannot be aimed, without an important adaptation work, at students already swept into a spiral of violence: it requires a minimum of vocabulary, of trust in adults, and project planning'.[20]

Lastly, there is the risk that adult mediators in schools are introduced to act as the declining institution's spare wheel[21] rather than transforming students or educational practices. Their emergence would not be justified by the need to treat new problems, but rather by the need to fill a void. They could be charged with communicating with families and maintaining relationships in which no one else is really committed, or with the management of violence problems that the institution is very reluctant to do. All in all, mediators could take on the workload that the institutional actors do not want to take care of.

18 Johnson D.W., Johnson R.T., 'Conflict resolution and peer mediation programs in elementary and secondary schools: a review of the research', *Review of Educational Research*, vol. 66, nr 4, 1996, pp. 459–506.

19 Gottfredson, D., 'School based crime prevention' in L. Sherman et *al.* (eds) *Preventing crimes: what works, what doesn't, what's promising*. A report to the United States Congress, Washington D.C.: National Institute of Justice, 1997.

20 Diaz, Liatard-Dulac, (1998), op.cit.

21 François Dubet, *Le déclin de l'institution*, Paris, Seuil, 2002.

The ambiguity of the school system's position towards the parents does not help the relationships with the family. The system is in search of their support to its projects and choices, but never consults with them in the development of its educational policy, over which the teachers have the monopoly.[22] This means that the mediators' mission is to exert a soft form of social control over families to adapt them to the institution's demands and thus maintain a form of status quo.[23]

As we can see, the diagnosis varies depending on the point of view that one adopts, that of the institution or the actors. It also fluctuates depending on the type of mediation. Peer mediation's social function must not be confused with that of adult mediation, or with community mediation's social function. The counterculture that mediation represents naturally creates resistance and defensive withdrawals which limit its efficiency. This is how the metaphor of the placebo effect can be justified. Resorting to programmes of innovative actors would before anything else bring legitimacy to an institution crippled with ideological and institutional weaknesses, not very inclined to change, as shown by the battering of the last century's educational utopias. If it is however necessary to nuance the enchanted visions that some advocates of mediation have; a pessimistic perspective would also be distant from the reality of mediation practices. Experience shows that the introduction of mediation in the educational institution instils a little bit of otherness and democratic values in the disciplinary logics which subjugate pupils.

---

22 Bouveau, P., Cousin, O., Favre-Perroton, J., *L'École face aux parents. Analyse d'une pratique de médiation.* Paris, ESF, 1999.

23 Ibid.

CHAPTER 12

Company and Commercial Mediation

The business worlds have always been reluctant to bring their conflicts to court. They always prefer endogenous modes of treating their conflicts, such as negotiation or refereeing. It is true that the corporate world is full of questions about power, characterised by its hierarchical structures, subordination links between employers and salaried employees, which do not align with the horizontal nature of the mediation process. It is also rare that conflicts born in the business world are interindividual. They often pose organisational questions which engage the whole system and weaken the structure of responsibilities. Behind the slightest disagreement, systemic stakes concerning a large number of actors may appear.

As can be deduced, this world is not very favourable to the emergence of mediation, yet mediation has appeared in business contexts. The reasons for this can be found in the dynamics that have recently impacted this world. The emergence of mediation can be correlated with the decrease in influence and representativeness of trade-union organisations, the consequence of this being a decrease in the collective treatment of conflict. This can also be interpreted as a sign of the management styles becoming harsher, more autocratic, less participative, therefore favouring conflicts. The collapse of corporate culture also plays a role in this. It has long been impacted by strong patriotism, a relative intensity of professional relations which built a collective identity, which makes way for competition (each partner has an instrumental vision of the other, the employee uses the company by putting his or her career first, and the company prioritizes productivity, leaving aside human considerations) which are expressed by the development of individualistic and consumerist strategies which are very different from traditional processes of affiliation. This competitive context characterised by limited professional paths and the increased pressure on workers' productivity leads to new types of conflict, whose nature is highlighted by problems such as stress and harassment at work.

For the sake of clarity, I shall distinguish three types of mediation in the business world. Inter-company mediation concerns the company's relations with their suppliers, clients and political, administrative and financial contacts. Intra-company mediation, also known as mediation at work, emerges within the framework of work conflicts between employers and different categories of personnel, or between employees. Lastly, consumer mediation

 | DOI:10.1163/9789004734067_017

takes place within the framework of relations between companies and consumers.

1 Inter-company Mediations

Developed in the US alongside the development of alternative dispute resolution (ADR), these mediations progressively spread to all Western countries where they have been legally recognised multiple times. Since 2001, many charters, such as the International Chamber of Commerce, recommend the inclusion of clauses in all contracts making mediation obligatory before any litigation proceedings. Texts such as the 2008/52/CE directive of the European Parliament for the development of civil and commercial mediation ensure its promotion. As a result, charters or codes of conduct, signed by chambers of commerce, large companies quoted on the stock exchange and leading business law firms, now require recourse to mediation before any legal action.

The nature of this support shows that we are far from the romantic conceptions of mediation's origins and closer to a liberal vision which aims to avoid the legal and judicial systems, because of their decisional hazards, their rigidity and absence of confidentiality, their slowness and cost. A study of the Paris Chamber of Commerce and Industry (CMAP) shows that its members consider the law a constraint.[1] The pragmatic character of entrepreneurial values is opposed to a frame of action which is too rigid, and the desire for flexibility is constantly expressed by the search for informal and negotiated modes of conflict regulation.

However, behind the facade of international texts and the declarations of the American Bar Association which claim that thousands of mediations are treating several hundreds of thousands of files each year, commercial and inter-company mediation is in reality not very developed. Their number, which is impossible to properly quantify, stays modest according to the mediators. This gap between official discourse and real-life practices comes from the fact that North Americans have a 'flexible' conception of mediation, integrated in the 'package' of alternative dispute resolution in which it occupies only a marginal place compared with negotiation or arbitration.

When a mediation is put into place, it is often based on hybrid modalities such as the 'Med'Arb' model in which the mediator becomes an arbitrator when the protagonists fail to reach an agreement, or even the 'Arb'Med'

1 Corinne Delmas, « La Chambre de commerce et d'industrie de Paris: un ordre négocié », *Droit et société*, 67/2007, 600–613.

model in which the third party gives an opinion that the parties have the right to renegotiate between themselves with their help, or which they can impose in case of persistent disagreement. So, in this type of mediation, the third party is most often in an advisory role, rarely a facilitating third party and never a 'midwife' third party, whether in a pre-litigation or litigation phase. Their background and training (these mediators are often business lawyers, former magistrates, heads of companies, consultants or coaches) predispose them to implement a problem-solving type of process, focused on the search for a solution to the dispute.

Mediation is generally sought when the actors want to guarantee the continuity of their business relations beyond the relational or financial conflict that divides them. This is also the case when knowledge of the conflict risks, if it is placed on the judiciary scene, spreading in the professional circles and tarnishing the parties' image.

In any case, as already mentioned, the aim is to find a quick, efficient and discrete solution to the conflict, a less uncertain and more economical solution than resorting to the courts.

Although 'agonistic mediation', aiming to resolve a problem, is struggling to develop, preventive mediation (also known as project mediation) is on the rise. Its objective is to prevent conflicts. The efforts of facilitators, whether or not they are called mediators, focus on training managers to adopt non-violent modes of communication and management. It can also entail transforming corporate governance or restructuring an organisation in a more horizontal and empowering way. These interventions require a deep knowledge of the organisation and its power plays and must rely on solid competences in social psychology and mastery of group communication techniques.

2 Mediation at Work

Like company mediation, mediation in the workplace is rare. This is the case everywhere in Europe and particularly in France where the existence of a 'Conseil des Prud'hommes' [a labour court] blocks its emergence, even though this jurisdiction has a marginal role to play, since only 10 per cent of obligatory conciliation attempts planned by labour legislation reach an agreement. The decisions of this council take an average of 14 months and are subject to a 63 per cent appeal rate, revealing that they are very poorly accepted.[2] These

2 Key justice figures, minister for justice, 2022.

appeals induce long procedures, which are materially and psychologically harmful to the employees and employers.

A part of specialised research sees the introduction of mediation in employment law as a way to intelligently treat conflicts by giving meaning to them, sometimes unveiling their hidden side, because 'one conflict can hide another', by taking into account the situation's psychological and personal stakes[3] (for example, the dismissal of an employee who contacts a mediator not only to obtain a larger compensation to those proposed to him or her, but also to have his or her dignity, honour, competences and investment in the company recognised by the employer).

Other specialists see the emergence of mediation as a neoliberal strategy to avoid the current legal norms that jeopardise workers' rights. These authors worry that this process might favour a psychoanalysing and individualising approach to labour relations to the detriment of an analysis of the company's management methods and the collective expression of tensions. Mediation would constitute for many of them a psychological coating to the legal dispute and both a 'chance for patronage and a trap for employees'[4] in the sense that it leads to compromises that are likely to favour employers who violate their workers' rights. In a context of individualisation of labour relations, trade-unions fear a decrease of the legal guarantees offered to employees but also a transformation of their role within companies.

Mediations at work concern collective conflicts between management and trade-unions, hierarchical power conflicts between diverse categories of personnel, conflicts between management and employees with an employee over dismissal, refusal of a promotion or transfer, or a wage increase, interpersonal conflicts such as moral or sexual harassment between a superior and his or her subordinate, or even horizontal conflicts between employees at the workplace.[5] The dispute can concern the relational atmosphere or contractual relations when the authority's arguments or the regulatory and organisational resources (for example a human resources department) do not find a mutually satisfactory way out to the conflict.

Amongst these conflicts, those regarding harassment, as shown by the works of Marie France Hirigoyen,[6] which build on the work of Swedish psych-

---

3 See in France, J.E. Gresy, F. Duret-Salzer, C. Kuri, *La médiation au travail*, Deboeck Supérieur, Louvain, ainsi que les travaux de Lise Casaux-Labrunée.

4 Augier B., « La médiation dans les conflits du travail, une chance pour le patronat, un piège pour les salariés », *Droit ouvrier*, 1999, 610, p. 225.

5 A. Stimec, S. Adijès, *La médiation en entreprise*, Paris, Dunod, 2015.

6 Marie France Hirigoyen, *Le harcèlement moral: la violence perverse au quotidien*, Paris, Syros, 1998.

ologist's Heinz Leymann,[7] are becoming more frequent. Hirigoyen defines bullying as 'any abusive conduct which is manifested by behaviours, acts, gestures or written material, which can undermine the personality, dignity, physical or psychological integrity of a person, endangering that person's employment or degrading the social climate.' She describes psychological harassment as a continuous dynamic process. Every act in itself can be considered benign, but their repetition creates a feeling which can quickly become destructive. Even though this constitutes a specific offence in most legislatures, the judicial responses regarding these cases seem insufficient (the number of convictions remains low compared to the number of allegations) to repair the turmoil caused, often due to the absence of sufficient evidence.

In many Western laws, mediation can be required by one of the parties in cases of harassment, either before any procedures, or during the procedure. The judge is also able to make a referral to mediation, but this has been met with resistance. Increasingly, people may consider harassment to be a form of victimisation, and, in a highly competitive context, see the managerial pressures for productivity and for a sustained work rhythm as abuse. The company's environments (company directors, managers, human resources directors) fear that the political measures meant to combat bullying could constitute an interference in their functioning, namely hindering their management of incompetent or unproductive staff.

Research carried out on the mediation mechanism implemented in 2002 to 2006 by the SFR Cetegel group to manage daily conflicts at work shows that the representations of mediation fluctuate depending on the place of the individuals in the company's power structure and their strategies.[8] 83 per cent of collaborators see this as an opportunity to present their point of view themselves and welcome the 'right to be the protagonist in one's own professional career path, and to question the soundness of the management's decision'. 72 per cent of managers are happy to resort to mediation. Most perceive it as a way to avoid possible media repercussions of ill-managed conflicts which could tarnish the company's reputation and image, but some fear that it could look as if their management is being questioned. Lastly, 58 per cent of staff representatives are favourable to mediation. This lower score must be interpreted as the sign of defiance regarding a method which calls into question the role of the trade-unions.

7 Heinz Leymann, *Mobbing. La persécution au travail*, Paris, Seuil, 1996.

8 Alice le Flanchec, 'Médiation, autonomie et justice procédurale. Le cas SFR Cegetel', *Négociations*, 2006/2, nr 6, 113–126.

In such an organisational context, mediation asks the more general question of its relevance in cases of asymmetrical relationships. If mediation between employees is not met with much opposition, some studies show that the people who have the most power in the company are in general less fond of mediation than those who have less power. The only way for a mediator to temper their concerns is to properly differentiate what concerns the non-negotiable power structure and what concerns the relational and evolving dimension of the conflict.[9]

For all these reasons, work mediation remains still relatively underdeveloped even if there are no reliable statistics concerning the matter. It is possible to know the number of mediations referred by the courts. In France, it remains extremely modest and linked to the practice of certain pioneer magistrates.[10] For the rest, only the mediators' testimony allows us to measure its impact and many express that it is impossible for them to make a living out of this job, and must diversify their services (as a consultant, coach, trainer). Even when they only practise mediation, it is rarely strictly limited to the work and corporate domains. It can be commercial, environmental or even family mediation, because the number of family conflicts which appear in industrial, agricultural and service companies is considerable. The mediator must then integrate the affective, cultural, intergenerational, succession, economical and professional aspects of reality[11] in his or her approach. This is namely the case when the spouses but also their children are involved in the running of the business. The private sphere then becomes intertwined with the professional sphere. These conflicts are complex as they concern not only the emotional and economic interests of the persons but also their entire social identity. This context makes accepting a third party's intervention difficult, whether this party is a mediator or not. And this 'protectionism' explains the fact that mediation has not known much success in this domain.

The mediators implicated in labour disputes have varied profiles. Amongst these are business lawyers, consultants trained in economy, psychosociology, neurolinguistic programming and transactional analysis, and former company executives with experience in human resources management. Some have not been trained in mediation specifically. Their statuses are diverse. They can be a part of the company, be paid by it and attached to the human resources

---

9 Jean Poitras, Vivian Wiseman, 'Comment réussir une médiation dans le contexte d'une structure hiérarchique?' *Négociations*, nr 3, 2005.

10 Béatrice Blonhorn-Brenneur, *Justice et médiation. Un juge du travail témoigne*, Paris, le Cherche Midi, 2006.

11 Manel Canyameres Sanahuja, *La mediacion en la empresa familiar, Reus, Madrid, 2022.*

department. It is then very difficult for them to maintain their independence from the company's hierarchy and its objectives. They can also be external to the company, intervening to regulate a particular conflict.

3 Consumer Mediation and Online Mediation

These forms of mediation have received a lot of support from the European Union thanks to the 2013/11/EU directive of 21 May 2013, relative to the extra-judicial settlement of consumer disputes. They were already implemented before this reform with the European Parliament and the Council's 2008/52/CE directive on certain aspects of mediation, namely in the civil and commercial domains. However, the 2013 text sets them apart from other conventional forms of mediation, opening their scope to new economic sectors such as crafts, shops and supermarkets which were not previously included.

Consumers can have free recourse to mediation if they have a dispute with a professional over the performance of a sales or service contract. Mediation is imposed on the business owner, whereas it was previously optional, and the owner must pay for it in full. Consumer mediators are generally authorised by national organisations which ensures the certification of consumer dispute mediators depending on independence and competence criteria.[12]

The European directive participated in the creation of a new conflict management market.[13] In addition to traditional face-to-face or telephone mediation services, there are now consumer mediation platforms offering online mediation and adopting competitive pricing policies. This online alternative dispute resolution market now constitutes a global phenomenon generally designated by the acronym ODR, or online dispute resolution. It would represent a new 'Wild West', or if one wishes to confirm to digital terminology, a new Wild Www.est.[14] These new services have a number of different names, such as *cybersettle.com*, *settletoday.com*, *resolvedisputes.online* or even *rapidrulings.com* in Canada and in the US, *mediacaonline.com*, in Brazil or *fastarbitre.com*, *justice.cool*, and *madecision.com* in Europe.

---

12 See S. Bernheim-Desvaux, G.Raymond, *Droit de la consommation*, LexisNexis, 2022.

13 S. Bernheim-Desvaux, 'Le marché français de la médiation de la consommation', *Revue Internationale du Droit Economique*, 2017/4, pp. 35–44.

14 N. Ebner et J. Zelevnikow, 'No Sheriff in Town: Governance for Online Dispute Resolution', *Negotiation Journal*, octobre 2016, pp. 297–323.

These online platforms can be put into different categories.[15] The first category groups together the platforms that offer various services in which technology plays an auxiliary role of putting physical people in contact: online mediation or conciliation (without or with recommendations), arbitration, med'arb process, mediation followed by arbitration in case of failure. In the second category, technology participates in the dispute's resolution by means of automated programmes based on AI.

These services undeniably offer a few advantages, flexibility, tailor-made proposed solutions, a relatively speedy process compared to a judicial treatment; and they are free of spatial (when people are geographically distant) and time (documents can be instantaneously transmitted) constraints.

They are however inconvenient for several reasons, starting with the inequality between users in terms of access to the Internet and computer equipment. They also threaten the mediation process confidentiality principle and the safety of exchanges (screen captures, presence of a secret third party in the mediation space, recording of confidential information). This non-controlled risk leaves for doubt regarding the sincerity and the profoundness of the words exchanged, as the relationship between the people involved, including the third party, plays a considerable role in the success of the process. Another handicap is the fact that these services are essentially focalised on positions, on the search for a solution to the explicit dispute, ignoring research into the real roots of the conflict. Finally, the structure and the functioning of algorithms and the consequences of resorting to AI, due to a lack of information and training, deprive users of control over the nature and the quality of the services offered. As Antoine Garapon and Jean Lassègue point out, 'the new way of writing information technology … transforms the majority of us into ignorant users'.[16]

Hence the question of regulating these *legaltechs*. Do they have to be entrusted to business actors themselves, to ethical committees, soft law initiatives (codes of good conduct, recommendations), as is the case in the US and Australia? Or would it be best for them to be organised by state legislations, like in Europe? To guarantee the quality of these services, is it a good idea to create certification processes relying on certain criteria? Would this requirement be enough without intensive control and assiduous monitoring of how

15 A. Biard, 'Justice en ligne: un nouveau Far Www.Est? La difficile régulation des plateformes en ligne de règlement extra-judiciaire des litiges', *Revue Internationale du Droit Economique*, 2019/2, pp. 165–191.

16 A. Garapon et J. Lassègue, *Justice digitale*, Paris, PUF, 2018, p. 196.

the platforms operate? Who would certify the independence and the competence of the members of this certification authority?

Article 22.1 of the General Data Protection Regulation (GDPR)[17] requires the explicit consent of users, ensuring they are sufficiently informed about the functioning of the algorithm and the decision process. It opposes resolutions founded exclusively on an algorithm and argues that human intervention in the process is imperative, without however precisely detailing its nature. This disposition echoes the consumer's fear, which is attested by numerous studies, of being confronted with dematerialised and entirely automated services which abolish face-to-face relations.

To sum things up, while intercompany mediations have become an obligatory exercise, even while using hybrid processes, labour mediation still meets a great deal of resistance. However, commercial mediations, namely because of the rise of online mediations that use AI, have the wind in their sails. One might wonder whether the new operators, the businessmen and mathematicians of these services, have the competencies required to plan mediation processes on a human scale, allowing the users to remain the subjects of their conflict and not the objects of technical procedures on which they exert no control.

---

17 Regulation (EU) 2016/679 of the European Parliament and of the Council of 27 April 2016 on the protection of natural persons with regard to the processing of personal data and on the free movement of such data.

CHAPTER 13

Sanitary and Hospital Mediation

The healthcare field is probably the one which has recently opened itself most to mediation. It concerns both conflicts within the hospital environment (public hospitals, regional or university hospitals, clinics, or social-medical establishments), as well as conflicts surrounding any other medical relationship. But there also exists a type of mediation in the healthcare field which isn't centred on resolving medical disputes, but which aims to reduce inequalities in access to the healthcare system. It informs, educates, advises and gives support to vulnerable people to reinforce their capacity to make their own choices to preserve or improve their health. However, in this chapter, I will not focus on this second type of mediation which deals with access to rights at the intersection of social work and health.

1 Towards a Health Democracy?

The emergence of mediation in the medical[1] and hospital environments is correlated with the rise, albeit timid, of a health democracy.[2] This rise is part of a set of global patients' rights which took off with the publication of the European Charter for Patients' Rights, on 15th of November 2002, whose influence can be seen in diverse legislation. It gives the 'consumers' rights of representation and participation (approval of associations, users representation in hospitals, creation of a user relations committee), reinforces individual rights (information, access to medical files) and creates a procedure to help and give compensation to victims. The traditional image of the 'good patient', adopting a submissive posture, progressively gives way to that of the sick person as a consumer and strategist.

The will to restore balance between the different actors of the healthcare field, to make the choice and performance of medical acts more transparent and cooperative, to organise information, dialogue and means of appeal, constitutes a counter-culture within a 'total' institution, in the sense that Erving

1 Michèle Guillaume-Hofnung (Dir.), *Hôpital et médiation*, Paris, L'Harmattan, 2001.

2 Marie Boender Lecoeur, L'impact de la loi et de la démocratie sanitaire sur le fonctionnement hospitalier, *Droit et société*, 67/2007, 631–647.

 | DOI:10.1163/9789004734067_018

Goffman gives it,[3] in which people have been reified and robbed of their identity for a long time. This evolution represents a real shift from the authoritarian practices that had long prevailed in this environment, as it integrates the experience of the suffering patient, the way he or she experiences illness, feels pain and evaluates the institutional trajectory. It was made possible, or at least accelerated, by the emergence of pathologies such as the AIDS pandemic, Alzheimer's disease, diabetes, osteoporosis, heart disease, among others, and the modes of social mobilisation which resulted, and which placed a number of users' claims in the public eye. The scandals surrounding haemophilia and iatrogenic illnesses, the mediatisation of medical errors damaged the trust given to medical staff, when individuals became not only victims of their illness, but potentially also of those responsible with their medical care. Another factor which is sometimes forgotten is the increasing technicality of medicine and the growing specialisation it creates. The fragmentation of treatment favours a technical and organic approach to the detriment of patients, whose treatment is then not taken into account wholly. The hyperspecialisation of medicine leads to a fragmentation of medical care, altering the regular follow-up of patients who might, during their journey, meet dozens of different intervenors whose therapeutic options turn out to be not very coherent when the exchange of information concerning a patient is done synthetically and digitally. Hence a sense of dehumanisation which is felt by both patients and doctors.

These different mutations must, on top of all of this, be placed in the general context of the evolution of public policies which are constructed around the figures of the user or the victim. The transformation of the hospital institution and more generally of medical practices can then be understood in a more global perspective, which imposes the omnipresent principle of precaution to face the increasing legalisation of social hazards. The medical profession is particularly haunted by the North American spectre of an explosive increase in legal proceedings for malpractice. This is particularly the case for surgeons, anaesthetists and other specialists in invasive disciplines, but also obstetricians and psychiatrists (in case of suicide or crime). This incentivises doctors to try to prevent such incidents. Hospitals, for their part, are engaged in an increasingly competitive healthcare market, seeking to maintain or improve their public image or their ranking printed periodically in different magazines. An increase in complaints could only be harmful to their reputation and their profits. But these functional rationalities should not obscure the

3 Erving Goffman, *Asiles, Études sur la condition sociale des malades mentaux*, Paris, Ed. de Minuit, 1968.

work carried out within institutions since the 1970s, by an activist minority of care staff, attached to the principle of equal access to care, to the defence of humane and high-quality medicine respectful as possible of all users, faced with the increasing weight of management logics.

As can be seen, the reasons for the development of a health democracy are complex and are not as virtuous as one might think. Observation shows that the democratic principles aren't integrated by all medical professionals. It is not possible to transform, within a few years, old institutional ways of functioning or professional cultures by the sole magic of a law. The charter of patients' rights, even though it is scrupulously displayed in every establishment, is not equally respected by all contributors. Distributing a welcome brochure before any operation or a questionnaire afterwards to all patients does not suffice to make them subjects of law. The organisations that support patients play a more and more visible role in terms of information and can even exert powerful influence in certain specialised domains (autism, patterning for example). But they are not involved when it comes to important decisions concerning hospital policy and are often reduced to the role of the messenger. However, signs of evolution are visible.

2 A Delicate Promotion of Dialogue

Health mediation has developed in several European countries such as Norway, the UK, Belgium, Italy and Switzerland. But most of the time, the functioning modalities of the mediation authorities place great emphasis on specialist commissions, doctors or officials who are not very independent and not always well trained in mediation. However, the National Health Service in the UK allows complaint managers (whose role is to receive complaints in every institution, to resolve problems, to investigate, make information available, guide people) and to the person making the complaint to both agree to use an external certified mediator.

In Belgium, all hospitals must have a mediator at their disposal, a mediator who isn't a doctor but who is paid by the institution. He or she is competent in the rights of patients involved in his institution, while a federal mediator is dedicated to the rights of patients involved outside a hospital institution (dispute with a doctor, a dentist, a physiotherapist, a recovery home, a prison, a medical specialist, a private nurse, and so on). In the francophone part of Switzerland, most counties have integrated hospital mediation in their legislation. In 2004, the canton of Vaud (Lausanne) created a regional bureau of health and social mediation, concerning hospitals and social educational establishments. In 2007, a mediation space opened in the teaching hospitals in Geneva, and one opened in 2012 in the Vaudois teaching hospital where mediation between patients, close relatives and professionals (EMP) could take place, devoted to the treatment of grievances between patients, close relatives and the medical staff. In France, the rise of mediation is less dramatic, and practices rely on doctors and health executives who are members of the institution, which makes their independence and impartiality questionable.

In general, medical mediators intervene in cases where there is harm done to medical practice or functioning, whereas non-medical mediators are employed to deal with other complaints. A few mediation initiatives focusing on health conflicts in care and retirement homes have recently emerged.

These different initiatives question the fragility of the hospitality characteristic of the hospital as a place of care,[4] dedicated to treatment of physical and moral pain, and which paradoxically reveals itself as a place of abuse, dissatisfaction and frustration. The patients' grievances are diverse but almost all of them come from a need for recognition, a demand for dignity after all the contempt they have felt. They express their revolt, anger, the need to be listened to, to be better informed or understand what has happened, the desire to hear the healthcare provider admit his or her share of responsibility, to improve the quality of future healthcare services, to modify the behaviour of some members of staff, or even to find personal appeasement and closure allowing them to 'move on'.

From the doctors and healthcare staff's perspective, motives to use mediation can be the incivility of patients or relatives, their physical or verbal violence, questioning therapeutic options, or even their consultations being filmed without their knowledge and posted on social networks. Finally, there are internal conflicts between staff and their superiors or between staff members themselves. Generally speaking, mediation does not cover labour disputes that fall within the remit of trade unions or disputes that are the subject of disciplinary proceedings.

The work of health mediators is multifaceted and does not always boil down to organising meetings between the parties. It always involves listening to the complainants. Often, a meeting with the mediator is enough to bring comfort and a feeling of having been heard and understood. The need to testify so that the situation does not recur is very frequently expressed. The mediator can also act as a guide, redirecting the complainant to the appropriate

4 B. Schaad (Dir.) *(in)hospitalités hospitalières. Conflit, Médiation, Réconciliation*, RMS Editions, Médecine et Hygiène, 2023.

department if he or she has not knocked on the right door. Finally, the mediator can organise a mediation meeting between the parties.

The first objective that healthcare-related mediation has is not to find a solution to the conflict, but to create a dialogue between the mediation participants. The mediator's work varies, however, and depends on how the mediation space is organised, the mediator's competence, to what degree they are independent, and how accepted mediation is by the administrative and medical staff. It also depends on the public's knowledge of the mediation offer. Thus, the mediation initiative for patients, relatives and professionals in Lausanne hospital remains, despite its long history and its members' dynamism, relatively unknown by the 13000 workers across their 180 positions at the university hospital. The mediation rate is around 10 per cent for all expressed complaints.[5]

Resistance towards mediation is still strong. Non-medical mediators in hospitals must interfere in functioning systems they do not fully understand, and clarify their position so as to not encroach on other people's roles. Whereas the patients may suspect the mediator is defending the interests of the institution, the practitioners fear that the mediation space might feed the users' complaints, that a horizontal process might erode their hierarchical positions and their professional image. This fear also affects medical staff outside of the hospital environment.

However, the rare assessments regarding the effects of mediation show that the participants are largely satisfied. As Thierry Currat says in his previously mentioned work, 'the parties that stay focused on reconstructing the facts have a tendency to become opposed, whereas the narration of the subjective experience of the conflict and various emotions… allows people to build trust'. He highlights that the exercise of finding words to describe the actor's emotional experience is the very foundation of mediation. This is however difficult for some health professionals who have received the order to 'leave their emotions in the changing room'. The mediators in Lausanne university hospital encourage these professionals to 'tell their patients and their close ones what they are going through, the anxiety they might feel when entering a room of an aggressive patient, the shame of having given the wrong medicine… the bitterness of not having time for people in an overloaded department… the suffering of not being able to calm a patient's suffering.'

---

5 Ibid.

The patients predominantly express positive thoughts about mediation:[6] 'I was able to express myself, it was a moral relief, I had such a weight on my chest', 'I was able to talk, to explain, he didn't know all the pain, all the suffering that I had experienced', 'I shared my feelings, my sense of injustice, he heard and listened to me', 'he learned a lot about the general chaos of this institution and the consequences it can have on the patients'. However, sometimes the complainants are not fooled by the stakes of the situation – 'he tried to minimise the facts, his excuses were made backwards' – and may still have a negative opinion of their doctors, others have been able to develop trust with them, after having cleared some misunderstandings: 'the doctor was very touched', 'I do not resent them, they were humble and showed compassion.' The meeting can also be cathartic: 'I cried a lot during the mediation, I also cried a lot afterwards for a few days, and then stopped crying completely, I was able to look forward'.

The heavy emotional load that is expressed in these mediations shows how relevant and necessary a space for patients and the healthcare staff to meet and talk is. Despite the difficulties inherent to the unbalance of power and knowledge between the parties, communication between them is possible and desirable. Such initiatives, as long as they do not harm the patients' rights, could temper the excesses of making victims sacrosanct and the judicialization of medical practices, in order to establish more understanding, empathy and trust in therapeutic relations.

---

6 Isabelle Jeanneret, *La médiation sanitaire: une réponse à l'insatisfaction du patient*, mémoire master européen de médiation, IUKB Sion, 2009.

Conclusion

Free societies where individuals' autonomy is pushed to its paroxysm are a source of conflict. Everyone fiercely defends their identity, their interests, with an ardour that subjective rights have reinforced. When citizens are only hindered by the chains they decide to wear themselves, their mutual coexistence is difficult to ensure. The free, consumerist and solitary members of contemporary society find it difficult to perceive their interdependence and to build a shared meaning within their collectivity. The difficulties of safeguarding the meaning of general interest within this tangle of identity can be seen at many levels, from family quarrels, trouble in the neighbourhood, to shopkeeper squabbles which stop political elites from thinking about common interests in the face of ecological disturbances which threaten the planet's survival.

One of the big challenges of the future is to make these blurred social ensembles composed of fragmented identities work, to help them keep a common conscience. The big metaphorical or ideological narratives that recounted collective perspectives have gone downhill, the institutions on which social order was built on are losing their legitimacy, traditional conflict regulation authorities have been blown to pieces. It is now necessary to invent new ways of cultivating team spirit. Mediation workshops described in this book are on way of doing this. Here, more peaceful ways of coexisting are patiently created. They are not talked about much, and are only visible to attentive eyes because their success depends on the delicacy and the confidentiality which they must demonstrate in order to succeed. The construction of social links is a task too subtle for it to get on well with the entertainment society. It is with discretion that mediators and peacemakers try hard to convince the torn, disunited, egocentric, and quarrellers to 'sit down at the same table', put words on their conflicts, their disagreements, their resentments or aversions, and to construct scenarios of peaceful coexistence. Without this 'haute couture' work, community life would be even more unstable and tormented than it is.

Of course, mediation cannot bring a solution to all misunderstandings, to all chicanes and quarrels. Their first and main limit lies in the fact that they cannot be imposed and they only concern groups or individuals that are willing to renounce the fighting and confrontation. They cannot be used immoderately, as the explosion of alternative (or amiable) modes of conflict resolution is the expression of a form of risky liberalism, a perilous deregulation. The contractualisation of society, correlated with the State's retreat, opens the

 | DOI:10.1163/9789004734067_019

uncertain road for the re-feudalisation of social links.[1] It exalts the belief of an equal distribution of gifts and clear-sightedness between equal and responsible individuals. Nancy Fraser[2] argues that the liberal model tends to drown social inequalities in the deliberation process it organises, thus favouring dominant groups to the detriment of those who are subordinated to it. The use of mediation to manage violence against women could be considered a specialised domination space obscuring public debate on causes of female alienation, without ensuring gender parity in the participation because 'certain actors lack the necessary resources to interact with others as peers.' The desertion of public ritual forms of conflict management to the profit of their increasing procedural privatisation hinders the perception of their political dimension and is ultimately a way of obscuring its existence. This 'buissonnier' treatment of social conflicts is detrimental to the interests of the most disadvantaged.

As a former lawyer with an unshakeable attachment to the humanist defence of the weakest, I am naturally very receptive to these arguments and many others that stigmatise the practical dangers of mediation when the institutions instrumentalise it to pursue undemocratic internal objectives, and when mediators themselves are not very respectful of the foundational principles of their art. This is the reason I have always asserted the necessity to be extremely vigilant about the ethical conditions of mediation practices and the requirement for an in-depth and selective training of future mediators.

However, this wind of contractualisation is not always negative. A democrat must celebrate that the proportion of imposed social relations is declining in favour of chosen relations, that heteronomy is supplanted by autonomy, and that constraint is progressively leaving space for will. He or she can also rejoice that the heavy and blinding state apparatus is being lightened, enlightened and humanised by the promotion of flexible and adaptable authorities for adjusting interests. He or she must celebrate the progress of democracy when citizens can speak their own words, acquire the foundation of a dialogue culture, develop their otherness, become their own legislator by imagining the conditions of their future lives themselves. He or she must celebrate all the initiatives that construct social relations based on plurality and diversity and not the totalitarian levelling strategies that erase the latter. Because mediation

1 Alain Supiot, 'La contractualisation de la société', in Y. Michaud (dir.), *Qu'est-ce que l'humain?* Paris, Odile Jacob, 2000.

2 Nancy Fraser, *Qu'est ce que la justice sociale? Reconnaissance et redistribution*, Paris, La Découverte, 2005.

is close Hannah Arendt's definition of politics, a space that 'is about community and the reciprocity of different human beings'.[3]

Despite those who are nostalgic of long-triumphant legal rationality, the choice between state regulations and alternative modes is largely constraining in practice. The institutional world that found its apogee in the flourishing of the welfare state is now seriously fissured. The bureaucratic rationality which organised it no longer has sufficient capacity to manage hypercomplex realities where the speed and instantaneousness of communications have transformed our ways of thinking, where our relation to time and space has become dematerialised, and where personal relations, work and commitment are now volatile. These new immaterial universes seem to escape our control. The nation-states, institutions, laws and principles that guaranteed a certain social order are still useful. One needs overhang, verticality, transcendence, centre, mapped paths to ensure collective order and to set goals. However, these are obsolete when it comes to proposing a permanent framework for the small tyrannies of perpetual movement. In such cases, the prevention of social chaos, the regulation of new communication universes requires the conception of new forms of social control based on contingence, horizontality, periphery, nomadism; and paths that are made by walking. Collective order demands its necessary part of disorder in a permanent dialectic relationship. It demands firm yet flexible, structuring yet understanding regulations, relatively channelled configurations that are sufficiently fluid. Too many constraints would bring us back to the rigidity of past bureaucracies, and too much flexibility would restore the law of the jungle.

We are going through a period of uncertainty. Mediation is an orthopaedic way to help the allegedly sovereign individuals of postmodernity learn more about the autonomy they claim but which they do not have the capacity to fully assume. This pedagogical role of transition and support is difficult, as it is affected by antagonistic forces that oblige people to conform to institutional expectations of order or push for the exaltation of democratic ferments of disorder. This tension between two opposite forces can be represented using two different axes. The first one, which I shall name 'system axis', distributes mediation practices on a continuum which ranges from the power of institution to the power of inspiration. The second, which I will call the 'actor axis' spreads these practices on a continuum which ranges from the emancipation of individuals to their normalisation.

These dialectical tensions are without hope of rest, are ceaselessly evolving depending on the weight of institutional, professional or economic logics or of

3 Hannah Arendt, *Qu'est-ce que la politique?* Paris, Seuil, 2001.

the activism of political and social movements. For one same industry, they are expressed differently from one period or country to another, based on the cultural characteristics of their implementation. Because of this, every reader will be able to interpret the following drawing as they want, moving the different professional fields a little higher or lower, a bit more to the right or to the left, depending on their knowledge or empirical realities. This figure is thus only a suggestion, a way of assessing and measuring how torn mediation is as a result of these tensions.

1 System Axis: Institutional Forces/Inspirational Forces

Institutional forces are 'interested' in the regulatory potential of mediation. Its negative entropic functions are appreciated to better manage the flux that asphyxiates the exhausted public and private institutions. Mediation is said to be cheaper, quicker, more efficient, and hence more apt to bring legitimacy to authorities in search of recognition. In countries where the culture is centralised and bureaucratic, mediation is more a mode of legitimation than a mode of construction for public decision-making. The institutionalisation of mediation, far from changing these logics internal to the system, are a way to disguise vertical power mechanisms in a democratic veil.

The forces of inspiration searches for greater amenity, non-violence and more harmony between human beings and strives to invent new ways to live together in society. These are expressive forms of counter power faced with the power of bureaucratic rationality. They are also a way of introducing cooperation into competitive universes, humanity into impersonal mechanisms, deliberative democracy in abstract schemes of representative democracy and reflexivity into institutional mimicry. They represent the vector of an experimental democracy embodying the preservation of a social ideal of conviviality, the necessity of linking disjointed narratives, fragmented universes, and divided affiliations.

Mediation practices can be considered countercultural if they scrupulously respect the ethical principles that give them meaning. They can conversely be analysed as a soft power, a gentle and concealed way to hide the hold of institutional logics that want to subject them to their rationalities. From this point of view, the institutionalisation of mediation produces paradoxical effects. It allows the recognition of practices, facilitates the conditions for their long-term survival. At the same time, it also weakens the critical weight of their ethics.

2 Actor Axis: Emancipation/Normalisation

Supporters of a transformative mediation model define it as a relational and communicational space. They adopt a non-directive attitude, let emotions be expressed, encourage exchange and mutual understanding. The objective is to transform conflict by changing the way the actors perceive it, leading them to greater tolerance, comprehension, and self-esteem. The search for the most horizontal relation possible (nature and disposition of the place, speech time, adequate modes of expression) between the parties aims to avoid the institutional formats of communication. The action plan which is the most often advocated for is there to reinforce the symmetrical and contractual character of the exchanges, to edify a specific relational space which abolishes the representation principle. 'Good mediation' is one that encourages speech, the expression of feelings and the actors' needs, which establishes mutual active listening and debate, which empowers and reinforces the capacities of people and groups, which emancipates them and truly makes them the masters of their own destiny.

Conversely, those who have a regulative conception of mediation consider it chiefly a technique to fluidify institutional functioning or to facilitate contractual relations. They adopt communication models which are more closed. Their attitude is more directive, the debate is more focused on the relevant legal or economic elements. This model does not have the objective of transforming individuals, how they see and experience the world; rather, it seeks to transform the conflictual context that divide them. Of course, the actors play a privileged role that previous institutional practices denied them. They have an essential part in searching for solutions, but the mediator remains the game master. The process of normalising behaviour is all the more subtle in that its participants consent to it.

Naturally, the location of these different activity areas is not very precise. It does not take into account the dynamics that flow through them; it only suggests a global diagnosis of the dominances that affect them. The aim of this diagram is not to discredit certain mediation types compared to others, but to highlight that they do not have a similar nature and are not exposed to the tensions presented here in the same way.

Even though the normative dimension of social mediation does exist, asserting that civil, sanitary and company mediation lean more towards the institutional side cannot erase the fact that they give people a safe space to express themselves and speak. It might seem exaggerated to argue penal mediation as the type of mediation that does not leave much space to empower actors, and that gives more importance to institutional matters because there exists an

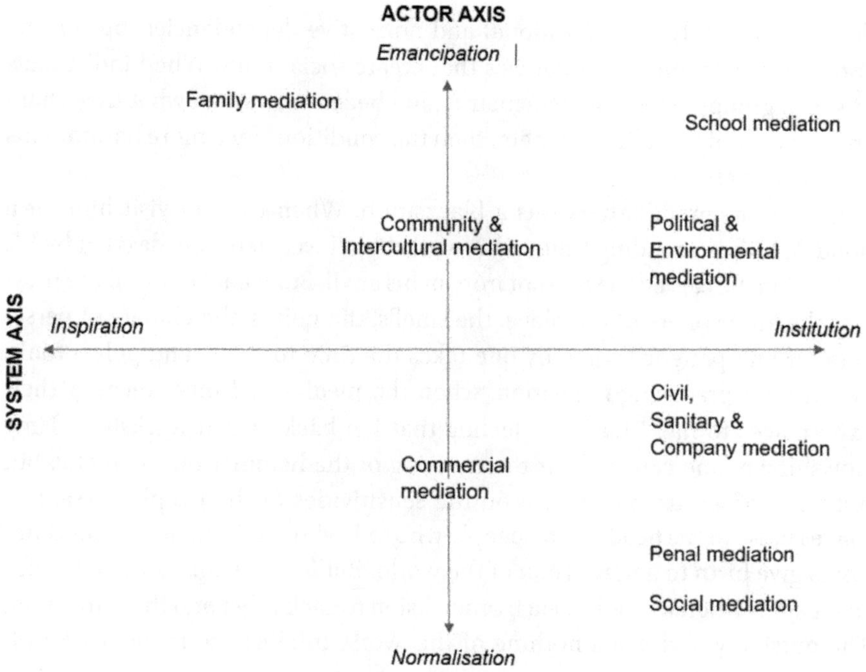

FIGURE 14.1 Dialectical tensions by sphere of activity

alternative model supported by the international rise of the restorative justice movement, whose influence might grow in the next few years. The degree of emancipation of individuals by family mediation varies depending on whether it is conventional or takes place in the legal field, and on the type of model (legal or transformative) applied by the mediator. Despite its strong benefits of emancipation and education, school mediation is more conceived in the interests of the institutions than those of the students, except in cases where it is embedded within a whole school approach. Community and intercultural mediation do emancipate people and can escape the hold the institutions have, except when they are driven by logics of political display or social control. Political and environmental mediation tend to lean more on the soft power side of things, except when they are organised from the bottom-up; then they become really participative. Even though the principal motivation of commercial mediation is to escape state regulations, it remains however unplaceable on the system axis, as it lacks the power of inspiration.

But whatever the ethical power that drives them or the institutional erosion that affects them, all the mediation workshops I've mentioned sow the seeds of a new form of interactive democracy throughout society. A democracy that opens up spaces for subjectivity. A reflexive democracy where social control does not only rely on institutional and normative dependencies, but on the construction of interdependencies that create social links. When individuals or social groups assert their singularity and become aware of what they share and not only of what divides them, then the conditions for a more harmonious coexistence are met.

One of my grandfathers was a blacksmith. When I would visit him for a holiday, I liked spending time in his workshop. I was naturally dazzled by his skills when he carved the red-hot iron on his anvil. But what I enjoyed the most was the atmosphere of the place, the smells, the noises, the climate of perseverance and patience whereby one takes the time to shape and polish tools. When I am practising mediation, when the mediators I meet recount their experiences to me, I have the feeling that I'm back in that workshop. Time slows down, one cannot hear the clanging of the hammer on the metal, but only that of words and silence on the sensitivities of the people present. It makes noise in the heads of the people who toil, who think and who sometimes cry to give birth to a new vision of the world. But it is the noise of intelligence that begins when we look at each other, listen to each other and think together. The outside world hears nothing of this work. Intelligence is silent when it searches for unity.

Bibliography

Abel R. (1982), *The politics of informal justice*, New York, Academic Press.

Adijès S., Lesser H., (2014), *Médiateurs et avocats : Ennemis? Alliés?* Paris, Médias et médiations.

Aertsen, I., (2004), "Victim-Offender Mediation with Serious Offences", in Council of Europe, *Crime Policy in Europe, Good practices and promising examples*, Strasbourg, Council of Europe Publishing, p. 75–86.

Ailincai A., Rus C.(2014), « Les défis de la médiation scolaire auprès des familles Roms », *Diversités*, n 175, p. 76–82.

Alinsky S., (1976), *Manuel de l'animateur social. Une action directe non violente*, Paris, Seuil.

Allain S., (2005) « La Médiation Environnementale Comme Système Politique de Régulation. Application Au Gouvernement de L'Eau », *Médiation et action publique. La dynamique du fluide*, Presses universitaires de Bordeaux, 135–150.

Allan P., Keller A. (2006), *What is a just peace?* Oxford University Press.

Arendt H., *Qu'est-ce que la politique?* Paris, Seuil, 2001.

Arnaud A.J., (Dir.) (1993), *Dictionnaire encyclopédique de théorie et de sociologie du droit*, Paris, LGDJ, 2ème éd.

Assefa H., (1987), *Mediation of civil wars.: approaches and strategies- the soudan conflict*, Boulder, CO, Westview.

Aubert L., (2009) "Appréhension systématique des phénomènes de délinquance de troisième voie: les dilemmes d'un parquet divisé", *Champ pénal/penal field*, vol. VI.

Augier B. (1999), « La médiation dans les conflits du travail, une chance pour le patronat, un piège pour les salariés », *Droit ouvrier*, 610, p. 225.

Badie B. (1999), *Un monde sans souverainetés*, Paris, Fayard.

Barret P., (2003), *Guide pratique du dialogue territorial*, Fondation de France.

Barthélémy F. (2009), « Médiateur social, une profession émergente? » *Revue Française de Sociologie*, vol. 50, n 2, p. 287–314.

Barthes, R. (2002), *Le Neutre. Notes de cours au collège de France, 1977–1980*, Paris, Seuil.

Bastard B. (2005), « Mais à qui profite la médiation familiale? », *Dialogue*, n 170, 4, p. 65–80.

Bauman Z. (2000), *Liquid modernity*, Cambridge, Polity Press.

Beardsley K., Quinn D., Biswas B., Wilkenfeld J., (2006), "Mediation styles and crisis outcomes", *Journal of Conflict Resolution*, vol. 50, n 1, p. 58–86.

Beck U. (2001), *La société du risque. Sur la voie d'une autre modernité*, Paris, Aubier.

Ben Mrad F. (2002), *Sociologie des pratiques de médiation: entre principes et compétences*, Paris, L'Harmattan, 2002.

Ben Mrad F. (2004), « La médiation sociale: entre résolution des conflits et sécurisation urbaine », *RFAS*, n 3.

Bercovitch J., Anagnoson T., Wille D. (1991), "Some conceptual issues and empirical trends in the study of successful mediation in international relations", *Journal of Peace Research*, vol. 28, p. 7–17.

Bercovich J., Houston A. (1996), "Influence of mediator characteristics and behavior on the success of mediation in international relations", *International Journal of Conflict Management*, n 4.

Bercovitch J., Derouen K. (2004), "Mediation in international ethnic conflicts: assessing the determinants of a successful process", *Armed Forces and Society*, 30 (2), 147–170.

Bernheim-Desvaux S., G. Raymond, (2022); *Droit de la consommation*, LexisNexis, 2022.

Bernheim-Desvaux S., « Le marché français de la médiation de la consommation », *Revue Internationale du Droit Economique*, 2017/4, p. 35–44.

Biard A., « Justice en ligne : un nouveau Far Www.Est? La difficile régulation des plateformes en ligne de règlement extra-judiciaire des litiges », *Revue Internationale du Droit Economique*, 2019/2, p. 165–191.

Bingham G. (1986), *Resolving Environmental Disputes: A Decade of Experience*, World Wildlife Fund.

Blankenburg E. (1990), « Cultures juridiques comparées », *Droit et société*, n 16, p. 321–333.

Boltanski L., Thévenot J.P. (1991), *De la justification. Les économies de la grandeur*, Paris, Gallimard.

Blondiaux L. (2008), *Le Nouvel Esprit de La Démocratie. Actualité de la démocratie participative*, Paris, Seuil.

Blonhorn-Brenneur B. (2006), *Justice et médiation. Un juge du travail témoigne*, Paris, Le Cherche Midi.

Boender Lecoeur M. (2007), « L'impact de la loi et de la démocratie sanitaire sur le fonctionnement hospitalier », *Droit et société*, 67, 631–647.

L. Boltanski, L. Thévenot, *De la justification. Les économies de la grandeur*, Paris, Gallimard, 1991.

Bonafé-Schmitt J.P. (1992), *La médiation. Une justice douce*, Paris, Syros, 1992.

Bonafé-Schmitt J.P. (2000), *La médiation scolaire par les élèves*, Paris, ESF.

Bonafé-Schmitt J.P. (2007), *L'évaluation des effets des processus de médiation familiale sur les médiés*, recherche-action, Glysi, Fenamef.

Bonny Y., (2004), *Sociologie du temps présent. Modernité avancée ou post-modernité?* Paris, La Découverte.

Bourdieu P. (1986), « La force du droit. Eléments pour une sociologie du champ juridique », *Actes de la recherche en sciences sociales*, n 64, p. 40–44.

Bouveau, P., Cousin, O., Favre-Perroton, J. (1999), *L'École face aux parents. Analyse d'une pratique de médiation.* Paris, ESF.

Boy D., Donnet-Kamel D., Roqueplo P. (2000), « Un exemple de démocratie délibérative: la conférence française de citoyens sur l'usage des organismes génétiquement modifiés en agriculture et dans l'alimentation », *Revue française de science politique*, vol. 50, n 4–5, p. 779–809.

Braithwaite J. (1989), *Crime, shame and reintegration*, Cambridge University Press.

Briand (de) V. et Palau Y. (2000), *La médiation. Définition, pratiques et perspectives*, Paris, Nathan.

Brooker P. (2013), *Mediation law : journey through institutionalism to juridification*, London, Routledge.

Burton J. (1972), *World society*, Cambridge University Press.

Burton J. (1990), *Conflict. Human needs theory*, London Macmillan.

Bush R.B, Folger J. (1994), *The promise of mediation. Responding to conflicts through empowerment and recognition*, Jossey-Bass, San Francisco.

Callières (de) F. (1716), *De la manière de négocier avec les souverains* (Pour la Compagnie, Amsterdam).

Callon M., Lascoumes P., Barthe Y. (2001), *Agir Dans Un Monde Incertain. Essai sur la démocratie technique*, Paris, Seuil.

Cana J. (1998), « La privatisation de la diplomatie. Une expérience caucasienne", *Critique Internationale*, n 1, p. 169–178.

Canyameres Sanahuja M.,(2022), *La mediacion en la empresa familiar*, Reus, Madrid.

Cario R. (2005), *La justice restaurative, Principes et promesses*, Paris, L'Harmattan.

Cario R. (2006), « Changing lense. Autour de l'œuvre d'Howard Zehr », p. 45–58, *Les Cahiers de la Justice*, n 1.

Cario R. (directed by) (2012), *Les rencontres détenus-victimes. L'humanité retrouvée*, Paris, L'Harmattan.

Chevallier J. (2003), *L'Etat post-moderne*, Paris, LGDJ, coll. Droit et société.

Christie N. (1977), "Conflicts as property", *British Journal of Criminology*, 17, p. 1–15.

Colson A., Pekar Lempereur A. (2008), Un pont vers une paix durable. Reconciliation et médiation post-conflit au Burundi et en république Démocratique du Congo, *Négociations*, n 9, p. 13–28.

Commaille J., Jobert B. (1998), *Les métamorphoses de la régulation politique*, Droit et société, Paris, LGDJ, coll. Droit et société.

Coser L. (1982), *Les fonctions du conflit social*, Paris, PUF.

Crawford A., « La justice de proximité: appels à la « communauté » et stratégies de responsabilisation dans une idéologie managériale », in Wyvekens, Faget (Dir.) (2001), *La justice de proximité en Europe*, Toulouse, Erès, p. 37–64.

Crocker C., Hampson F., Aall P., (eds.) (1999), *Herding Cats: Multiparty mediation in a complex world*, Washington D.C., United States Institute of Peace Press.

Cunneen C., "Reviving Restorative Justice Traditions?" in Johnstone G. and Van Ness D.W. (Eds.) (2007), *Handbook of restorative justice*, Tavistok, Willan Publishing, p. 113–131.

Curle. A. *In the middle*, Oxford, Berg, 1986.

Cusset F. (2003), *French Theory. Foucault, Derrida, Deleuze et Cie et les mutations de la vie intellectuelle aux Etats-Unis*, Paris, La Découverte.

David Jougneau M. (1999), « La communication familiale au moment de la rupture: de la logique de la procédure à la logique de la médiation », *Dialogue*, n 143, p. 31–40.

Debarbieux E. (2006), *Violence à l'école: un défi mondial?* Paris, Armand Colin.

Deleuze G., Guattari F. (1980), *Mille plateaux. Capitalisme et schizophrénie*, Paris, Editions de Minuit.

Delmas C. (2007), « La Chambre de commerce et d'industrie de Paris: un ordre négocié », *Droit et société*, 67, 600–613.

Diamond, L., McDonald, J.W. (1996), *Multi track diplomacy: a systems approach to Peace*, Kumarian Press.

Diaz B., Liatard-Dulac B. (1998), *Contre violence et mal-être. La médiation par les élèves*, Nathan.

Dixon W. (1996), "Third-Party techniques for preventing conflict escalation and promoting peaceful settlement", *International Organization*, 50, p. 653–681.

Donzelot J. (1977), *La police des familles*, Paris, Ed. de Minuit.

Donzelot J., Wyvekens A. (2004), *La magistrature sociale. Enquête sur les politiques locales de sécurité*, Paris, La Documentation Française.

Dubet F., Danilo Martucelli (1998), *Dans quelle société vivons-nous?* Paris, Le Seuil.

Dubet F. (2002), *Le déclin de l'institution*, Paris, Seuil.

Dubois V. (1999), *La vie au guichet. Relations administratives et traitement de la misère*, Paris, Economica.

Duclos N., « Pacification sans réconciliation. Les apories de la politique de réconciliation conduite par les Nations Unies au Kosovo » in Sandrine Lefranc (Dir.) (2006), *Après le conflit, la réconciliation?* Michel Houdiard Editeur.

Duclos H., Gresy J.E (Dir.) (2008), *Evaluation de l'utilité sociale de cinq structures de médiation sociale*, Culture et promotion.

Ducousso Lacaze, A. (2006), « La médiation familiale. Le mythe de l'individu et les liens familiaux », *Dialogue*, n 170, p. 17–30.

Duss-von Werdt J. (2005), *Homo Mediator. Geschichte und Menschenbild der Mediation*, Stuttgart, Klett-Cotta.

Ebner N., Zelevnikow J.,, « No Sheriff in Town: Governance for Online Dispute Resolution », *Negotiation Journal*, octobre 2016, p. 297–323.

Ehrenberg A. (1998), *La fatigue d'être soi. Dépression et société*, Paris, Odile Jacob.

Faget J. (1992), *Justice et travail social. Le rhizome pénal*, Toulouse, Erès.

Faget J. (1993), « La médiation pénale, une dialectique de l'ordre et du désordre », *Déviance et société*, vol. XVII, n 3, p. 221–233.

Faget J. (1997), *La médiation. Essai de politique pénale*, Toulouse, Erès.

Faget, J. (2001), « Les politiques d'accès au droit. Du consumérisme à la citoyenneté », *Droit et Cultures*, 3, p. 83–96.

Faget J., De Maillard J. (2002), « Les Agents locaux de médiation sociale (ALMS) en quête de légitimité. Déficits de reconnaissance et oppositions professionnelles », *Les Cahiers de la sécurité intérieure*, n 48, p. 127–147.

Faget J. (2003), « La juridicisation de la médiation », *Les modes alternatifs de règlement des litiges: les voies nouvelles d'une autre justice*, La Documentation française, Mission de recherche Droit et Justice, p. 75–88.

Faget J., « L'institutionnalisation de la médiation: réflexions à partir de l'exemple français », in Mylène Jaccoud (Dir.) (2003), *Justice réparatrice et médiation pénale. Convergences ou divergences?* Paris, L'Harmattan, p. 227–242.

Faget J., De Maillard J. (2003), *Les Agents Locaux de Médiation Sociale En Quête D'Identité*, Etudes et documents, IHESI, Ministère de l'Intérieur.

Faget J. (2004), « Médiation et violences conjugales », *Champ pénal / penal field*, Revue électronique, vol. I.

Faget J. (Dir.) (2005), *Médiation et action publique. La dynamique du fluide*, Presses Universitaires de Bordeaux.

Faget J. (2006), « Reintegrative shaming. A propos de la théorie de John Braithwaite », *Les Cahiers de la Justice*, n 1, p. 59–70.

Faget J. (2006), « Médiation et post-modernité. Légitimation ou transformation de l'action publique? », *Négociations*, n 2, 51–63.

Faget J. (2007), Ombudsman, Mark Bevir (Ed.), *Encyclopedia of Governance*, vol. II, Thousand Oaks (Ca), Sage Publications Ink, p. 633–634.

Faget J. (2007), Street-Level Bureaucrat, Mark Bevir (Ed.), *Encyclopedia of Governance*, vol. II, Thousand Oaks (Ca), Sage Publications Ink, p. 935–936.

Faget J., « Gouverner Par La Médiation » in Berthet T., Costa O., Gouin R., Itçaina X., Smith A. (dir.), (2007), *Les nouveaux espaces de la régulation politique*, Paris, L'Harmattan, coll. « logiques politiques », p. 231–255.

Faget J. (2008), "Epistemological and methodological reflections on the evaluation of restorative justice practices", *British Journal of Community Justice*, vol. 6, n 2, p. 77–84.

Faget J. (2008) « Les métamorphoses du travail de paix. Etat des travaux sur la médiation dans les conflits politiques violents », *Revue française de science politique*, vol. 58, n 2, avril, 309–333.

Faget J. (2009), « L'impensé de la médiation familiale », *Empan*, n 72, p. 74–80.

Faget J. (2009), « les accommodements raisonnables de la médiation pénale », *Revue de science criminelle et de droit pénal comparé*, n 4.

Faget J. (sous la direction de) (2011), *Mediation in political conflicts. Soft power or counter-culture?* Oxford, Hart Publishing.

Faget J., (2013), *Sociologie de la délinquance et de la justice pénale*, Toulouse, Erès.

Faget J., (2015) « Les dynamiques de transfert des idées restauratives », *Raisons politiques*, 3, n 59, p. 109–119.

Faget J., (2015), « The dissemination of Howard Zehr's work in France : Contribution to a sociology of (the flow of) ideas", *Restorative Justice: An International Journal*, vol. 3, n 3, 1–10.

Faget J. (2020), « La médiation familiale en tensions. Réflexions sur le cas français », *RIEJ*, p. 179–196.

Faget J. (2021), « Jr or Not Jr? Les Flottements de L'Idée Restaurative », *in La justice restaurative. Des frontières plurielles et mouvantes.* Les presses de l'ENAP, p. 259–268.

Fine M., Smith K., "Zero tolerance: reflections on a failed policy that won't die", in W. Ayers et al. (eds.) (2001), *Zero tolerance: resisting the drive for punishment in our schools*, New York, NY, New Press.

J.P. Folger, R.A.B. Bush, D.J. Della noce (Ed.) (2010),, *Transformative mediation: a source book, Resources for conflict intervention, practitioners and programs*, Association for conflict transformation, institute for the study of conflict transformation Inc., USA.

Fraser, N. (2005), *Qu'est ce que la justice sociale? Reconnaissance et redistribution*, Paris, La Découverte.

Faure G.O, « La négociation internationale: un transfert de technologie en Chine », in G.O Faure, L. Mermet, H. Touzard, C. Dupont (1998), *La négociation. Situations et problématiques*, Paris, Nathan, p. 59–103.

Féron E. (2002), « Irlande du Nord: la paix en haut, la guerre en bas? » *Critique Internationale*, n 18, 3, p. 24–30.

Féron E. (2008), « Restaurer la confiance en Irlande du Nord? La négociation aux interfaces urbaines », *Négociations*, n 9, 1, p. 41–54.

Fisher R., Ury W., *Getting to yes*, Houghton Mifflin Company, Boston,1981,

Fisher Ronald J. (2001), "Cyprus; the failure of mediation and the escalation of an identity-based conflict to an adversarial impasse", *Journal of Peace Research*, p. 307–326.

Fisher Ronald J. (2006), « Coordination entre les diplomaties de type 1 (officielle) et de type 2 (parallèle) dans des cas réussis de pré-négociation », *Négociations*, 1, p. 5–33.

Fiutak, T. (2009), *Le médiateur dans l'arène. Réflexion sur l'art de la médiation*, Toulouse, Erès.

Fretter J., "The united nations and the mediation in international conflicts", in Jacob Bercovitch (ed) (2002), *Studies in International mediation*, Basingstoke, Macmillan.

Galli D. (2012), « Les effets indésirables du processus d'assimilation de la médiation par le droit », *Informations sociales*, n 170, p. 28–34.

Galtung J. (1971), "A structural theory of imperialism", *Journal of Peace Research*, 8 (2), 81–117.

Galtung J. (1975), *Essays on peace research*, Copenhague, Ejlers.

Galtung, J., Jacobsen, C.G. and Brand-Jacobsen, K.F. (2000) *Searching for Peace; The Road to TRANSCEND*, Pluto Press.

Garapon A. (1996), *Le gardien des promesses. Justice et démocratie*, Paris, Odile Jacob.

GaraponA., Lassègue J., (2018), *Justice digitale*, Paris, PUF.

Gauchet M. (1985), Le désenchantement du monde: une histoire politique de la religion, Paris, Gallimard.

Gaudin J.P. (1999), *Gouverner par contrat*, Paris, Presses de Sciences Po.

Giddens A. (1994) *Les conséquences de la modernité*, Paris, L'Harmattan.

Gil Tébar P. (1997), "Entre la médiation politique et la recomposition sociale: l'Eglise catholique dans le conflit du Chiapas », *Archives de Sciences Sociales des Religions*, n 97, p. 63–72.

Gottfredson D., "School Based Crime Prevention" in L. Sherman et al. (eds.) (1997), *Preventing crimes: what works, what doesn't, what's promising*. A report to the United States Congress, Washington D.C: National Institute of Justice.

Goffman E. (1968) *Asiles, Etudes sur la condition sociale des malades mentaux*, Paris, Editions de Minuit.

Goffman E. (1973), La présentation de soi (1). La mise en scène de la vie quotidienne, Paris, Editions de Minuit.

Goleman D. (1995), *Emotional intelligence: why it can matter more than IQ*. New York, Bantam Books.

Gorchs B. (2003), « La médiation dans le procès civil: sens et contresens. Essai de mise en perspective du conflit et du litige », *Revue trimestrielle de droit civil*, n 3, 409–425.

Gorchs B. (2006), « La conciliation comme enjeu dans la transformation du système judiciaire », *Droit et société*, n 62, 1, p. 223–256.

Grechez J. (2005), « Enjeux et limites de la médiation familiale », *Dialogue*, 4, n 170.

Greig J.M., Diehl P. (2005), "The peacekeeping-Peacemaking dilemma", *International Studies Quarterly*, 49, 621–645.

Gresy J.E., Duret-Salzer D., Kuri C., (2019), *La médiation au travail*, Deboeck Supérieur, Louvain,

Griveaud D. Lefranc S. (2020), « La justice transitionnelle, un monde-carrefour. Contribution à une sociologie des professions internationales. », *Cultures & Conflits* (119–120), p. 71–98.

Guiheneuf P.Y. (Dir.) (2006), *40 expériences de dialogue territorial, Geyser/Fondation de France*, Région Rhöne-Alpes.

Guillaume-Hofnung M., (Dir) (2001), *Hôpital et médiation*, Paris, L'Harmattan.

Guillaume Hofnung M., (2020) *La médiation*, Paris, PUF.

Habermas, J. (1987), *Théorie de l'agir communicationnel*, Paris, Fayard.

Hareide D., "Peace mediator: the new norvegian missionary?" http://www.nordiskforumformediationandconflictmanagement,peacemediation, Norway, 26/07/2003.

Harrington, C. (1985) *Shadow Justice. The ideology and institutionalization of alternatives to court*, Westpoint, CT, Greenwood Press.

Hedeen T. (2004), "The evolution and evaluation of community mediation: limited research suggests unlimited progress", *Conflict Resolution Quarterly*, vol. 22, n 1–2, 101–133.

L. Hernandez, A. Tschanz, N. Soldadié, (2021), « La justice restaurative à l'épreuve de l'espace-temps carcéral », in *La justice restaurative. Des frontières plurielles et mouvantes*. Les presses de l'ENAP, p. 145–157.

Hibou B. (1998), « Retrait ou redéploiement de l'Etat », *Critique Internationale*, n 1, p. 151–168.

Hirigoyen M.F. (1998), *Le harcèlement moral: la violence perverse au quotidien*, Paris, Syros.

Honneth A. (2000), *Politiques de reconnaissance*, Paris, Editions du Cerf.

Hopkins B. (2004) *Just Schools: a whole school approach to restorative justice*, London, and New York, NY, Jessica Kingsley.

Horming G. (1999), "Citizen's panels as a form of deliberative technology assessment", *Science and public policy*, vol. 26, n 5, p. 351–359.

Hudson B.(2003), *Justice in the Risk Society : Challenging and Re-affirming Justice in Late Modernity*, London, Sage, 2003.

Itcaina X. (2007), *Les virtuoses de l'identité. Religion et politique en Pays Basque*, Rennes, Presses Universitaires de Rennes.

Jaccoud M. (2006), « Les cercles de sentence au Canada », *Les Cahiers de la Justice*, n 1, p. 83–94.

Jeanneret I. (2009), *La médiation sanitaire: une réponse à l'insatisfaction du patient*, mémoire master européen de médiation, IUKB Sion.

Johnson D.W., Johnson R.T. (1996), "Conflict resolution and peer mediation programs in elementary and secondary schools: a review of the research", *Review of Educational Research*, vol. 66, n 4, p. 459–506.

Jones T.S., Brodtker A. (1999), "Agreement, maintenance, satisfaction and relitigation in mediated and non mediated custody cases: a research note", *Journal of Divorce and Remariage*, vol. 32, n 1/2, p. 17–30.

Jouve B., Lefevre C. (1999), « De la gouvernance urbaine au gouvernement des villes en Europe? Permanence ou recompositions des formes d'action publique », *Revue française de sciences politiques*, vol. 49, n 6, p. 835–853.

Jues I. (2009), « Ethique et déontologie du médiateur familial », *Empan*, n 72, p. 40–44.

Juston M. (2006), La médiation dans le contentieux familial: un changement de culture judiciaire, *Gaz.pal.*, p. 12.

Kaufman E., Sosnowski S, « The Peru-Ecuador peace process: the contribution of track two diplomacy » in Ronald J. Fisher, (Dir) (2005), *Paving the way: contributions of interactive conflict resolution in peacemaking*, Lanham, MD, Lexington Books, p. 175–201.

Keller A. (2004), *L'accord de Genève: un pari réaliste*, Paris, Seuil, Labor et Fides.

Kelly J.B. (1989), "Mediated and adversarial divorce: respondents' perceptions of their process and outcomes", *Mediation Quarterly*, vol. 24, p. 71–88.

Kelly J.B. (1996), "A decade of divorce mediation research. Some answers and questions", *Family and Conciliation Courts Review*, vol. 34, n 3, p. 373–385.

Kelman H., « Interactive Problem Solving in the Israelian–Palestinian Case: past Contributions and Present Challenges » in Ronald J. Fisher (2005), *Paving the way: contributions of interactive conflict resolution in peacemaking*, Lanham, MD, Lexington Books, p. 41–63.

Kelman M. (1987), *A guide critical legal studies*, Harvard University Press.

Kleiboer M. (1996), "Understanding success and failure in international mediation", *Journal of Conflict Resolution*, 40, 360–389.

Kruk, E. (1998), "Practice issues, strategies and models", *Family and Conciliation Courts Review*, vol. 36, n 2, p. 195–215.

Kydd A. (2003), "Which side are you on? Bias, credibility and mediation", *American Journal of Political Science*, vol. 47, n 4, 597–611.

Lascoumes P., (1978), « Consultations juridiques et boutiques de droit. Une critique en acte du droit et de la justice », *Déviance et société*, vol. 2, n 3, p. 233–259.

Lederach J.P. (1995), *Preparing for Peace: Conflict Transformation Across Cultures*, Syracuse University Press.

Lederach J.P. (1997), *Building peace. Sustainable reconciliation in divided societies*, Washington, United State Institute of Peace.

Lederach J.P., (2005), *The moral imagination: the art and soul of building peace*, Oxford University Press.

Le Flanchec A. (2006), « Médiation, autonomie et justice procédurale. Le cas SFR Cegetel », *Négociations*, 2, n 6, 113–126.

Lefranc S. (2007), « Convertir le grand nombre à la paix. Une ingénierie internationale de pacification », *Politix*, 80, 7–29.

Lefranc S. (2008), « Du droit à la paix. La circulation des techniques internationales de pacification par le bas », *Actes de la recherche en sciences sociales*, n 174, 48–67.

Lefranc S. (2021), « De quoi les victimes ont-elles besoin? La justice restaurative à l'épreuve des violences de masse », in *La justice restaurative. Des frontières plurielles et mouvantes*. Les presses de l'ENAP, p. 231–240.

Le Goff J.P. (2008), *La France morcelée*, Paris, Gallimard.

Leng R., Regan P. (2003), "Social and political cultural effects on the outcomes of mediation in militarized interstate disputes", *International Studies Quarterly*, 47, 431–4

Le Roy Etienne (1999), *Le jeu des lois. Une anthropologie dynamique du droit*, Paris, collection Droit et Société, LGDJ.

Lévesque J. (1998), *Méthodologie de la médiation familiale*, Toulouse, Erès.

Lewis.A. Coser (1982), *les fonctions du conflit social*, Paris, PUF.

Leymann H. (1996), *Mobbing. La persécution au travail*, Paris, Seuil.

Lipsky M. (1980), *Street level bureaucracy. Dilemmas of the individual in public services*, Russel Sage foundation.

Luhmann N.(1999), *Politique et complexité. Les contributions de la théorie générale des systèmes*, Paris, Cerf.

Lyotard J.F. (1978), *La condition postmoderne*, Paris, Éditions de Minuit, 1978.

Mac Carthy P., Walker J. (1996), "A long term impact of family mediation", *Social Policy Research*, 103.

Mac Cold P. (2008), "Evaluating restorative justice programs in a European context", *British Journal of Community Justice*, vol. 6, n 2.

McGillis D. (1986), *Community dispute resolution programs and public policy*, Washington D.C., National Institute of Justice.

Mack A. (Dir.) (2005), *Guerres et paix au XXIème siècle*, Presses Universitaires d'Oxford, University of British Columbia.

Magnette P. (2001) « Entre contrôle parlementaire et « Etat de Droit »: le rôle politique du médiateur dans l'union européenne », *Revue française de science politique*, vol. 51, n 6, décembre, p. 933–948.

Mangabeira Unger R.(1983), *The critical legal studies movement*, Harvard University Press.

Mansvelt-Beck J., (2005), *Territory and terror: Conflicting nationalisms in the Basque Country*, London, Routledge.

Marc E., Picard D.(2000), *L'école de Palo Alto. Un nouveau regard sur les relations humaines*, Paris, Retz.

Marret J.L. (2000), « Les ONG et la médiation de la paix: l'exemple de la communauté Sant'Egidio », *Annuaire Français de Relations Internationales*, vol. I, 1–11.

Marret J.L. (2001), *La fabrication de la paix, nouveaux conflits, nouveaux acteurs, nouvelles méthodes*, Paris, Ellipses.

Mars P. (2001), "Ethnic politics, mediation and conflict resolution: the Guyana experience", *Journal of Peace Research*, p. 353–372.

Martucelli D. (2002) *Grammaires de l'individu*, Paris, Gallimard.

Mary P. (2003), *Insécurité et pénalisation du social*, Bruxelles, Labor.

Mbanzoulou P. (2005), « La Médiation Scolaire Par Les Adultes de L'Établissement » in B. Gaillard (ed.), *Les violences en milieu scolaire et éducatif*, p. 429–436.

Meirieu P., Guiraud M. (1997), *L'école ou la guerre civile*, Paris, Plon.

Milburn P. (2002), *La médiation: expériences et compétences*, Paris, La Découverte.

Miers D., Willemsens J. (2004), *Mapping restorative justice: developments in 25 european Countries*, Leuven, European Forum for Restorative Justice.

Mincke C. (2006), « La proximité dangereuse. Médiation pénale belge et proximité », *Droit et société*, n 63–64, n 2–3, p. 459–487.

Minonzio J. (2007), La médiation dans les CAF, *Recherches et Prévisions*, n 89, p. 71–80.

G. Monk, J. Winsdale, *Narrative mediation: a new approach to transformative resolution*, San Francisco, Jossey Bank, 2001.

Monroy M., Fournier A. (1997), *Figures du conflit. Une analyse systémique des situations conflictuelles*, Paris, PUF.

Mooradian M., Druckman D. (1999), "Hurting stalemate or mediation? The conflict over Nagorno-Karabakh, 1990–1995", *Journal of Peace Research*, vol. 36, n 6, p. 709–727.

Morel S., Médiation de Proximité Et Transformation Des Modes de Régulation Sociale: Le Cas de La Médiation Ethnoculturelle À L'École, in Faget J. (Dir.) (2005), *Médiation et action publique. La dynamique du fluide*, Presses Universitaires de Bordeaux.

Morello T. (2018), En quoi le genre et le style éclairent-ils l'unité-diverse du métier de médiateur-e familial-e *Tiers*, n 21, p. 27–42.

Morrill C., McKee C (1993). "Institutional isomorphism and informal social control: evidence from a community mediation center", *Social Problems*, 40, 445–463.

Morrison B.E. (2006), *Restoring safe school communities: a whole school response to bullying, violence end alienation*, Sydney, Federation Press.

Muller P. (1994), *Les politiques publiques*, Paris, PUF.

Munck (De) J., « de La Loi À La Médiation », in *France: les révolutions invisibles* (collectif) (1998), Paris, Calmann Levy, 1998, p. 315.

Nay O., Smith A. (Dir.) (2002), *Le gouvernement du compromis*, Paris, Economica.

Noreau P. (1998), « La superposition des conflits: limites de l'institution judiciaire comme espace de résolution des conflits », *Droit et société*, n 40, p. 585–612.

Noreau P., Amor S., « Médiation Familiale: de L'Expérience Sociale À La Pratique Judiciaire », in *Famille en transformation. La vie après la séparation des parents*, (2004), Presses Universitaires de Laval, p. 269–297.

Nye J. (1990), « Soft power », *Foreign policy*, 80, p. 153–171.

Ost F., Jupiter, Hercule Ou Hermès, Trois Modèles Du Juge in Pierre Bouretz (Dir.) (1991), *La force du droit. Panorama des débats contemporains*, Paris, Esprit, p. 241–272.

Ost F., Michel Van de Kerchove (Dir.) (1992), *Le jeu: un paradigme pour le droit*, Paris, LGDJ, coll. Droit et société.

Palard J. (2006), « Médiation et institution catholique », *Archives de sciences sociales des religions*, 133, janvier-mars, p. 9–26.

Parkinson J. (2006), *Deliberating in the Real World. Problems of Legitimacy in Deliberative Democracy*, Oxford University Press, Oxford.

Pascual Rodriguez et al. (2013), *Los ojos del otro. Encuentros restaurativos entre victimas y ex miembros de ETA*, Santander, Salterrae.

Pearson J., Thoennes N., "Divorce Mediation: an American Picture", in Dingwall R., Eekelaar J. (1988), *Divorce mediation and the legal process*, New York, Oxford University Press, p. 71–91.

Pekar Lempereur A., Jacques Salzer, Aurélien Colson (2008) *Méthode de médiation*, Paris, Dunod.

Politis N. (1910), « L'avenir de la médiation », *Revue Générale de Droit International Public.*

Poitras J., Wiseman V. (2005), « Comment réussir une médiation dans le contexte d'une structure hiérarchique? » *Négociations*, n 3.

Princen T. (1992), *Intermediaries in international conflict*, Princeton, NJ, Princeton University Press.

Princen T. (1994), "Joseph Elder. Quiet Peacemaking in a Civil War", in *When talks Works*, Deborah Keble ed. San Francisco Jossey-Bass, p. 428–445.

Rapport du Conseil d'Etat, "Le développement de la mediation dans le cadre de l'U.E", 39 juillet 2010, La Documentation Française.

Regan P., Stam A. (2000), "In the nick of time: conflict management, mediation timing and the duration of interstate disputes", *International Studies Quarterly*, 239–260.

Revon C. (Dir.) (1979), *Boutiques de droit*, Paris, Solin.

Richmond O. (1998), "Devious objectives and the disputants view of international mediation. A theoretical framework", *Journal of Peace Research*, p. 707–722.

Richmond O. (2001), "A genealogy of peacemaking: the creation and re-creation of order", *Alternatives*, vol. 26, Issue 3.

Ricoeur, P. (1990), *Soi-même comme un autre*, Paris, Seuil.

Rogers C. 1968 (1961), *Le développement de la personne*, Paris, Dunod.

Rosanvallon P. (2008), *La légitimité démocratique. Impartialité, réflexivité, proximité*, Paris, Seuil.

Rosenberg, M.B. (2005), *Les mots sont des fenêtres et parfois des murs. Introduction à la communication non violente*, Paris, La Découverte.

Rouland N. (1991), *Aux confins du droit. Anthropologie juridique de la modernité*, Paris, Odile Jacob.

Rubin J. (1992), "International Mediation in Context", in J. Bercovitz, J. Rubin (eds) *Mediation in International relations: approaches to conflict management*, New York, St Martin's Press, 249–272.

Santiso J. (1998), « Circulation Des Idées Et Relations Internationales », dans Marie Claude Smouts, *Les nouvelles relations internationales*, Paris, Presses de Science Po, p. 227–251.

Saunders H. (2001), "Prenegociation and Circum-Negociation: Arenas of the Multilevel Peace Process" in Chester Crocker, Fen Hampson and Pamela Aall (eds.) *Turbulent peace: the challenges of managing international conflict*, Washington D.C., United Institute of Peace Press, p. 483–496.

Schaad B., (Dir), (2023),.) *(in)hospitalités hospitalières. Conflit, Médiation, Réconciliation*, RMS Editions, Médecine et Hygiène..

Schnapper D. (2002), *La démocratie providentielle. Essai sur l'égalité contemporaine*, Paris, Gallimard.

Shonholtz R. (2000), Community Mediation Centers: renewing the civic mission for the twenty-first century, *Mediation Quarterly*, 17 (4), 331–350.

Simmel G. (1992), *Le conflit*, Editions Circé.

Singly (De) F. (2005), *L'individualisme est un humanisme*, Paris, Editions de l'Aube.

Siniver A. (2006), "Power, impartiality and timing: three hypotheses on third party mediation in the middle east", *Political Studies*, vol. 54, 806–826.

Six J.F. (1995), *Dynamique de la médiation*, Paris, Desclée de Brouwer.

Six J.F. (1990), *Le temps des médiateurs*, Paris, Seuil.

Smith A., Stam A. (2003), "Mediation and peacekeeping in a random walk model of civil and interstate war", *International Review Studies*, 115–135.

Stimec A., Adijès S., (2015), *La médiation en entreprise*, Paris, Dunod.

Supiot, A. (2000), « La contractualisation de la société », in Y. Michaud (dir.), *Qu'est-ce que l'humain?* Paris, Odile Jacob.

Taylor, C. (1994), Multiculturalisme. Différence et démocratie, Paris, Flammarion.

Théry I. (1993), *Le démariage. Justice et vie privée*, Paris, Odile Jacob.

Touval S., Zartman W. (1985), *International Mediation in theory and practice*, Boulder, Westview Point.

Tzuriel D., et Shamir A. (2007) "The effects of Peer Mediation with Young Children (PMYC) on children's cognitive modifiability", *British Journal of Educational Psychology*, vol. 77, No. 1, March 2007, Page 143 –165.

Umbreit M. (1997), "Humanistic Mediation: a Transformative Journey of Peacemaking", *Mediation Quaterly*, 14–3, p. 201–213

Urry J. (2005), *Sociologie des mobilités*, Paris, Armand Colin.

C. Vigour et A. Hastings-Marchadier, « L'Économie Budgétaire de La Justice Pénale », J. Danet, *La réponse pénale. Approche empirique et pluridisciplinaire du traitement des délits*, Rennes, Presses Universitaires de Rennes, 2013, p. 422–494.

Volkrick, E. (2007), « Intervenir en tiers aujourd'hui ». *Négociations*, 1, p. 75–88.

Wade, J. (1997), Four evaluation studies of family mediation services in Australia, *Australian Journal of Family Law*, vol. 11, n 3, p. 343–349.

Walgrave, L. (1999), « La justice restaurative: à la recherche d'une théorie et d'un programme », *Criminologie*, vol. 32, n 1, p. 7–29.

Walgrave L., (2008), *Restorative Justice, Sel-Interest and Responsible Citizenship*, Cullompton, Willan Publishing.

Weber M. (1971 (1921)), *Economie et société*, Paris, Plon.

Wehr P., Lederach J.P. (1991), "Mediating conflict in Central America", *Journal of Peace Research*, 98, p. 85–98.

Wicquefort (De) A. (1681), *L'Ambassadeur et ses fonctions*, La Haye, J et D. Stencher.

Williams A. (1999), « Conflict resolution after the cold war: the case of Moldovia », *Review of International Studies*, n 25.

Wyvekens A., Jacques Faget (Dir.) (2001), La justice de proximité en Europe, Toulouse, Erès.

Yarrow C.H. (1978), *Quaker experiences in International Conciliation*, New Haven, Yale University Press.

Zartman W., Touval S. (1996), "International Mediation: Conflict Resolution and Power Politics" in Crockett C., Hampson F., Aall P., (Eds.), *Managing global chaos*, Washington D.C., United States Institute of Peace Press, 445–461.

Zartman W. (2000), "Ripeness: the Hurting Stalemate and beyond" in *International conflict resolution after the cold war*, P.C Sternand, Daniel.Druckman, Washington D.C., National Academy Press, p. 225–250.

Zehr H. (1990), *Changing lenses, a new focus for crime and justice*, Herald press.

www.ingramcontent.com/pod-product-compliance
Lightning Source LLC
Chambersburg PA
CBHW071247230926
51849CB00001B/260
* 9 7 8 9 0 0 4 7 3 4 0 5 0 *